It Takes Two

The Family in Law and Finance

Douglas W. Allen
and
John Richards,
editors

Policy Study 33

C.D. Howe Institute

C.D. Howe Institute publications are available from:
Renouf Publishing Company Limited, 5369 Canotek Road, Unit 1,
Ottawa, Ontario K1J 9J3; phone (613) 745-2665; fax (613) 745-7660

and from Renouf's stores at:
71 Sparks Street, Ottawa (613) 238-8985
12 Adelaide Street West, Toronto (416) 363-3171

For college book orders, please contact:
Prentice-Hall Canada Inc., 1870 Birchmount Road,
Scarborough, Ontario M1P 2J7; phone (416) 293-3621

Institute publications are also available in microform from:
Micromedia Limited, 20 Victoria Street,
Toronto, Ontario M5C 2N8

This book is printed on recycled, acid-free paper.

Canadian Cataloguing in Publication Data

Main entry under title:

It takes two : the family in law and finance

(Policy study, ISSN 0832-7912 ; 33)
includes bibliographical references.
ISBN 0-88806-445-4

1. Family policy – Canada. 2. Divorce – Canada. I. Allen, Douglas W.
(Douglas Ward), 1960–   . II. Richards, John. III. C.D. Howe Institute.
IV. Series: Policy study (C.D. Howe Institute) ; 33.

HV700.C3182 1999   362.82'0971   C99-930317-1

Contents

Foreword

Readers who are familiar with the C.D. Howe Institute and its areas of research interest may wonder why a volume bearing its imprimatur contains essays on the implications of changing divorce rules, same-sex marriages, and the impact of the tax and welfare systems on family structure. Yet, as editors Doug Allen and John Richards remind us in their Introduction to this volume, "[w]e are all born into families, and most of us spend most of our years living in families."

More to the point, the sea change in family-related law and social programs that has taken place since the 1960s has had profound effects on our economy in the form of greatly increased taxation, welfare rates, and public spending. It has also led, arguably, to an undue weakening of the institution of the family, the ramifications of which are still unfolding but which may not be entirely positive.

The Institute presents these essays, not to pass judgment on questions of morality or on how people choose to conduct their lives, but out of a belief in the healthiness of an open, vigorous debate on how our society is structured and on the role of government and the law in shaping that structure.

The book was copy edited by Elizabeth d'Anjou, Lenore d'Anjou, and Sheila Protti, and prepared for publication by Wendy Longsworth and Barry A. Norris.

As with all C.D. Howe Institute publications, the analysis and opinions presented here are the responsibility of the authors and do not necessarily reflect the views of the Institute's members or Board of Directors.

Thomas E. Kierans
President and
Chief Executive Officer

Introduction

Douglas W. Allen
and
John Richards

We live in an era of social policy frustration. There was a time in the 1960s when hope sprang eternal: when low government debt levels combined with new theories of social engineering and baby-boom effervescence promised greener pastures. The Americans undertook a war on poverty and Canadians introduced an abundance of new social programs, such as universal health insurance and the Canada Assistance Plan. There was the *Canada Divorce Act* to free those trapped in dead relationships. Thirty years later, Canadians cannot avoid admitting to major failures. Some of these programs have succeeded, but in matters of family policy Canada is encumbered with federal and provincial programs that somehow failed to deliver.

Arguably, the world is now a worse place. The percentage of children who live in poverty is as high now as it was in the 1970s. The number of single-parent families and the number of children living in such families has roughly doubled over the past two decades. The divorce rate in Canada is approximately three times higher now than in 1967.

We all are born into families, and most of us spend most of our years living in families. Accordingly, families are a subject about which everyone has an opinion. Families are also immensely varied and complex: it may require the skill of a novelist ever to grasp the nuances of family life. Thus, the two of us approach this book with a certain modesty: we are not novelists, we neither agree on all aspects of family policy nor do we pretend that the book is definitive. Nonetheless, we claim that a common denominator of the *increase* in many of the social ills that plague our society is the weakening of marriage as the primary institution for raising and educating children. The attacks on marriage are many, but here we focus on four:

- the effect of the *Divorce Act* on the rate of divorce and on the welfare of wives and children;
- the tax treatment of single-earner relative to dual-earner families, and of families with children relative to families without;
- the consequences of long-term welfare transfers on family structure and children's outcomes; and
- the potential weakening of the symbolic importance of marriage by extending the marriage contract to include homosexual and other relationships.

The essays in this book fall into two broad categories. The first group deals with aspects of law and the family, the second with a variety of tax and fiscal incentives that bear on families.

Law and the Family

Marriage is an efficient institution. Were there a more efficient means to raise children, marriage would not have lasted over the millennia as the primary form of organization for procreation and social structure. Raising children — not just providing for them physically but embodying them with what is good and productive — is a complicated business. Historically, the family has been a type of "firm" that has provided parents with proper incentives to see the job through. Marriage is not for everyone, and it is not a formula for personal bliss. But relative to other arrangements (such as communes or intentional single parenthood), marriage minimizes cheating problems that are common to all forms of organization and maximizes the probability that biological parents will undertake long-term investment in the success of their children.

Traditionally, marriage has been viewed as a relationship in which there are many stakeholders: children, parents, the church, and the state. Ours may be a more secular and individualist age, but that does not absolve us from collectively caring about the success of marriage as an institution. At a minimum, we all have a stake in successfully rearing the next generation.

Over the past 30 years, there has been a revolution in family law in Western society. Douglas Allen argues in his essay that the introduction of "no-fault" divorce inadvertently went a long way toward promoting the unsustainable doctrine that marriage should be no more than a private contract between two equal partners, and has contributed to negative consequences that few anticipated. Perhaps the most dramatic effect has been the great increase in the number of children growing up poor and with only one parent.

In this decade, academics, legislators, and policy think tanks have started to take seriously the consequences arising from no-fault divorce. A fundamental re-evaluation is now taking form: current law is flawed and band-aid remedies (such as regulations to enforce financial support by noncustodial parents) have failed.

As with all crossroads, this one offers multiple routes to follow. Marching along one path are the children of the 1960s' reformers, who argue that we have not gone far enough in destroying historical notions of the family. The definition of marriage is being pushed to include all intimate relationships with some claim to permanence, such as homosexual and common-law unions, and even relationships between individuals with no sexual intent. Some legal scholars even argue that the entire body of family law should be abandoned in favor of a simple rule of contract. Moving along another path is a collection of strange bedfellows who argue that the way of the future requires rehabilitation of some traditional notions of marriage and the family. These traditionalists claim that marriage is efficient in dealing with the particular problems of raising children and that efforts to abandon this arrangement will lead to further social ills. This volume joins those travelers on the second path.

Canadians often think of their country as distinct from the United States in its provision of more generous social programs, but this distinction has been valid only since the mid-1960s. In the 1930s, the United States was more generous than Canada in terms of social spending and, until the 1960s, had more liberal divorce law. Canada's 1968 *Divorce Act* was one of the significant legislative reforms that helped to create Canadians' self-image of being a more liberal society than elsewhere. Canada was the first country to launch into the era of no-fault divorce, although with a law that was almost modest compared with divorce acts that were being contemplated in other jurisdictions at the time. It was, however, a radical change for a country in which two provinces had previously required an act of the federal Senate to grant a divorce and in which the others essentially allowed only one ground, adultery, for divorce. For the first time, Canadian law now allowed individuals merely separated from their spouse for a minimum of five years to file for divorce.

The new *Divorce Act* seemed innocuous at the time. Social scientists claimed that an end to unhealthy marriages would be better for the parents and, implicitly, for the children. Legal scholars suggested that the new law would eliminate the guilt that often arose when couples perjured themselves to fulfill the adultery condition of the old law, and that henceforth there would be less animosity among divorcing couples since no one would be "at fault" for the divorce. Religious leaders gave their blessing to the new law in the belief that courts and social workers would be able to determine those marriages that had truly broken down and restrict divorce to those cases. Taking their cue from all this, politicians enacted the new legislation with little debate and absolutely no opposition.

The new law's effect has not, however, been innocuous. Within five years of its passing, the divorce rate soared to a level almost three times higher than before and has essentially remained there ever since. The dynamic effects of increasing the flow of divorces from something rare to something common are only now being realized. In his essay, Donald Moir, a retired family lawyer in Vancouver, surveys the literature on the effect of divorce on children (complicated understandings of statistics are often not necessary here because the results are so obvious): divorce, to be blunt, is a disaster for them. Children of divorce face higher probabilities of virtually every social ill one can think of relative to children from intact marriages, even when such marriages are "bad." Having a dad at home is important. Divorce is creating a large cohort of children with low human capital. What will happen to their children when they become adults?

The effect of divorce on children is but one of the unanticipated negative consequences of the *Divorce Act*; the consequences for wives and husbands have been more complicated. For wives, divorce is, on average, a financial hardship. Most wives suffer a fall in their personal consumption after divorce that often lasts until they remarry or their children leave home. Yet wives usually receive either full custody of their children or, where they receive joint custody, retain most of the control over them. This is a source of stress for mothers, but separation from their children becomes a major emotional hardship for fathers. Although husbands often increase their personal consumption after divorce, the simple fact is that many divorced families cannot financially support two households at the former standard of living. Often, divorce is a unilateral act of independence by one partner rather than a mutual parting of the ways. In her paper, Margaret Brinig, an expert in family law, outlines the effect divorce has on both wives and husbands.

When the family fails as the primary institution in which to raise children, people seek substitutes. The lobby for publicly funded child care programs, full-time kindergarten, and preschool programs is driven in part by the needs of single parents who are looking for assistance. When the family fails, lobbies invite government intervention into family affairs. School programs now contain "life-skill" training that was unheard of a generation ago. Virtually every school has a significant budget devoted to the "resource room," where the ever-growing number of problem children wind up. Teachers are now required not only to teach core academic subjects, but also to deal with career and personal planning, ethics, and basic health education — areas that are normally the purview of parents of functioning families. When this instruction is inconsistent with parents' wishes or values, the result is tension and migration to private schooling. As two-parent families move their children into private schools, adverse selection problems arise in the public schools, which begin to devolve into low-quality education centers. To the extent that marriage is the efficient place for the formation of "social capital," substitution via schools and other government institutions serves only to damage the ability of the public schools to perform their basic task: teaching the skills and knowledge on which there is broad social consensus.

Back to the Crossroads

To mitigate the unintended negative consequences of liberal divorce laws, different jurisdictions are now pursuing divergent paths. The state of Louisiana, for example, recently became the first North American jurisdiction to recognize two types of marriage simultaneously: an ordinary no-fault marriage, and a covenant marriage that stresses the permanence of the union and that is both harder to enter into and to dissolve. In practice, there is not a great difference between the two types of marriage in Louisiana, but it is a revolution in precedent and symbol.

If two types of marriage can exist at the same time, why not three, four, or more? The French government is currently debating a proposal to create a third category (joining religious and civil marriage), a *pacte civil de solidarité*, or PACS. Access to a PACS would be open to a wide range of partners in (presumably) stable relationships: heterosexual and homosexual couples, and those (for example, priests and their housekeepers) who may have no sexual bond. Restrictions would, however, apply to couples linking siblings, first cousins, and parent/uncle to child/nephew. A PACS would afford many of the fiscal benefits of religious and civil marriages, such as the tax reductions implicit in joint filing and joint property ownership, but not all. PACS couples could not, for example, adopt children.

In Canada, British Columbia has begun to recognize homosexual unions as legitimate marriages. In summary, along this path the traditional notion of a marriage as a union of one man and one woman is being abandoned for the more nebulous concept of a loving and committed couple.

Aside from the fiscal implications of expanding the definition of marriage — it is estimated that PACS marriages would cost France the equivalent of C$1.1 billion to C$1.6 billion annually (Lanez et al. 1998, 107) — there may be other hard-to-measure costs of further diluting the cornerstone institution of the family. This is the subject of Frank Buckley's essay. Buckley tackles a number of arguments in favor of homosexual marriage and concludes that they ultimately are not convincing:

> The efficiency gains that homosexuals might exploit through marriage would be small since they have far less incentive to marry than child-rearing heterosexuals. What remains is the symbol of state approval that the recognition of homosexual marriage would accord them. (P. 126.)

The legitimate reasons for which homosexuals may want to marry can be accommodated under existing contract law, Buckley argues, so there is little reason to provide for homosexual marriage. Buckley also opposes the *symbolic* sanction of marriage for homosexuals, arguing that this would further lower the respect afforded heterosexual marriages, which need more, not less, support. Refusing homosexuals the symbolism of marriage, Buckley insists, is not tantamount to "a constable standing before Oscar Wilde at the Cadogan Hotel but a restriction not even recognized as a disability until very recently" (p. 122).

Taxing and Rewarding Families

Just as rewriting divorce laws has, over time, wreaked major change on families, so too has apparently minor tinkering with tax policy and transfer programs. With the growth in the size of government over the past half-century, such tinkering has often become sizable wedges between pre-tax, pre-transfer income and post-tax, post-transfer income.

In his essay, Ken Boessenkool traces the tax treatment of marriage and children in Canada since World War II. At that time, Ottawa maintained a universal per child social policy transfer (the family allowance) and a deduction from taxable income for each child. The tax system treated single- and dual-earner families at various income levels the same. In the decades since, this universal transfer has been transformed into a targeted program (most recently, the Canada Child Tax Benefit — CCTB) that is clawed back aggressively once family income reaches a threshold level. Income tax deductions for children have been eliminated, but families receive a per child deduction for child care expenses — a deduction that is primarily of benefit to dual-earner families. In sum, low-income families now receive higher transfers, and families with child care expenses receive a large deduction to taxable income, but middle- and upper-income single-earner families receive negligible tax recognition of the costs of child rearing.

Boessenkool argues that this development arose because social policy mechanisms confounded sound tax policy. He emphasizes

> three difficulties that arise from this confusion of social and tax policy objectives. First, the tax system no longer recognizes the cost of raising children in all families. Second, to the extent that the tax system has relieved the burden for middle- and upper-income families with children, it has done so disproportionately for dual-earner families through generous child care exemptions. Finally, the combination of clawed-back social policy transfers plus income and other taxes has created unacceptably high effective marginal tax rates for families earning between $20,000 and $30,000. (P. 130.)

After carefully discussing the evidence on these matters, Boessenkool assesses four options for reform:

- Universalize targeted low-income programs, such as the CCTB and the refundable goods and services tax (GST) credit, thereby transforming them into demogrants (refundable credits) for all families with children. The advantage of this approach would be to eliminate very high effective marginal tax rates over the income ranges at which these programs are aggressively clawed back. The cost in terms of forgone federal income tax would, however, be high: about $6 billion annually for the CCTB alone, and up to $10 billion if other programs were included.

- Increase the generosity of personal, spousal, and child deductions sufficiently to provide tax-free "room" over the income ranges at which targeted programs are aggressively clawed back. This implies that a family with two children would pay no income tax until family income exceeded roughly $25,000. In principle, Boessenkool favors deductions over credits, and this option would recognize explicitly the costs associated with child raising. Like the first option, however, this would be costly to the federal treasury.

- Introduce a tax deduction of $2,000 per child. This more modest option would cost Ottawa about $3 billion annually. The cost could be reduced and equity between dual- and single-earner families enhanced, however, if the amount of the per child deduction were subtracted from the eligible claim under the Child Care Expense Deduction (CCED).

- Integrate the CCTB, GST tax credit, CCED, and personal income tax among low-income families. This option, which Boessenkool prefers over the others, would also cost the federal treasury about $3 billion a year. It would smooth the effective marginal tax rate over the $15,000 to $35,000 range and would offer a modest tax cut to families earning above $25,000.

A brute fact to keep in mind is that families with children comprise slightly over half of all Canadians deemed poor by conventional poverty measures. The increasing prevalence of single parent- hood means that the proportion of the poor living in single-parent families has also been rising. For example, in 1980, Canadians in such families comprised 16 percent of all those deemed poor. By 1996, they were 22 percent of the poor, and 93 percent of poor, single-parent families were headed by a mother.

The overall incidence of poverty among elderly families has been declining (from 19 percent in 1980 to 9 percent in 1996). Among non-elderly families, however, the incidence of poverty has been rising (from 12 percent in 1980 to 16 percent in 1996). Several factors are at work to explain these trends. One is the generous government transfers that go to the elderly. For the non-elderly, the state of the business cycle matters: between 1980 and 1996, the lowest incidence of poverty was in the boom year 1989. Another important reason for the increase is a rising share of families that are headed by a single parent: throughout the 1980–96 period, the incidence of poverty among families with children was roughly five times higher among single-parent than among two-parent families.[1]

In his contribution to the volume, John Richards argues that, among low-income families, public policy has erected not one but two "poverty traps."

The first is well known: beyond a modest earnings exemption, provinces typically claw back welfare benefits dollar-for-dollar as earnings increase. The result is that, if parents with limited market skills forgo welfare for work, they may do little to increase family income and, taking into account loss of noncash welfare benefits (such as extended medical coverage), they may well lower it. Over the last generation, this first trap has become more acute because, across provinces, welfare benefits for families with children have either risen or remained constant and earnings of men with low or narrow skills has fallen. Increases in transfers targeted to low-income families have offset the effect of a decline in male earnings at the bottom so that, to date, while there has been little change in the distribution of family income, an increasing share of income among families at the bottom derives from transfers as opposed to earnings.[2]

---

1 All figures cited in this and the previous paragraph are derived from Statistics Canada (1997).

2 In Ontario, for example, welfare benefit levels in 1995 were 20 percent higher in real terms than in 1975. After the cuts imposed by the newly elected Progressive Conservative government, 1996 benefits returned to 1975 levels. A comprehensive nationwide survey reported an 18 percent increase in the real value of single-parent welfare benefits between 1981 and 1993. By contrast, earnings from low- or narrow-skilled work have declined. A typical result is that published in a recent study by Statistics Canada: between 1973 and 1989, real annual earnings among men in the bottom fifth of wage earners declined by 16 percent; roughly half of this decline occurred because of a reduction in hours worked, but even among men who worked full time full year, real annual earnings fell by 7 percent over the period (Brown 1995, table 3; Canada 1997, table 5; Lefebvre et al. 1998, table 5; Morissette et al. 1995, 28).

In addressing this first poverty trap, Richards argues that the provinces should experiment with ambitious earnings supplement programs that subsidize work among low-income families. Such programs provide ongoing subsidies to any and all earnings by family members, and are accessible to all low-income families with children — as opposed to a host of discretionary programs that subsidize employment among designated groups for a limited time. The intention is to increase work among families that currently have no earnings, by increasing dramatically the wage-to-welfare ratio. Earnings supplement programs are not intended for single individuals or childless families.

The case for earnings supplement programs rests on two propositions: that financial incentives matter in determining the extent of employment, among both the poor and the rich, and that the role model of working parents matters a great deal in predicting whether the children of poor families avoid repeating the cycle of poverty.

Earnings supplement programs have become significant in a number of countries. The United States, for example, has an Earned Income Tax Credit. In Britain, the newly elected Labour government gave a high priority in its first budget to enhancing an equivalent, the Working Families Tax Credit. In Canada, Quebec's APPORT is the pioneer program, while in the 1990s Ottawa has undertaken a pilot earnings supplement project in regions of both New Brunswick and British Columbia. Saskatchewan introduced its version of a universal earning supplement program in 1998. Crucial to the success of such programs is close attention to their design and administration: they must "feel" like wages as opposed to welfare or an income tax rebate.

A second poverty trap has arisen in recent years because of the aggressive clawback of targeted benefits other than welfare. These other benefits include the recently expanded CCTB, the GST tax credit, and numerous provincial add-ons. Aggressive clawback of these benefits begins when families earn roughly $20,000. By design, targeted programs claw back benefits as earnings rise, and they generate work disincentives similar to those of explicit income taxes. The stacking effect of income taxes plus targeted program clawbacks has meant that modest-income families face marginal effective tax rates on incremental earnings well in excess of 50 percent at very low earnings. In British Columbia, for example, a family with two children faces a marginal effective tax on incremental earnings approaching 70 percent in the range of $21,000 to $26,000.

The appropriate policy to address this second poverty trap, Richards argues, is to restore universality to the CCTB. To extend the present CCTB (of roughly $1,500 per child) into a universal tax credit would lower personal income tax revenues by nearly $6 billion annually — a sizable tax reduction. While this proposal must compete with other tax-reduction strategies — such as lowering employment insurance premiums or raising the income thresholds at which higher marginal tax rates take effect — it deserves a serious hearing. This disarmingly simple reform could achieve two important social policy goals:

- It would appreciably lower the marginal effective tax rate faced by modest-income families, particularly those in the $21,000 to $26,000 range over which the CCTB is presently clawed back aggressively. At present, the CCTB is clawed back at a rate between 12 and 27 percent in that range (the rate varies by number of children).
- Poor families are not the only ones that have children; middle- and upper-income families do too. Currently, Canada's tax regime takes inadequate account of the costs of good child rearing among those who are not poor. By construction, universalizing the CCTB would provide no additional benefit for single individuals, families without children, or families already receiving the maximum CCTB. But, to repeat Boessenkool's argument, a sound income tax policy should use as its base some measure of income after deducting costs — including costs attendant on good child rearing.

In a scene from the film *Jurassic Park*, a character explains how mathematical chaos theory works: a butterfly flapping its wings on a leaf in a rain forest on the equator may generate air flows that, several months later, culminate in a tidal wave on the other side of the world. In the same way, small changes in social policy ultimately may have large impacts on people's lives. These impacts may not be felt immediately, nor are they easy to trace. "What's to be done?" is a question to which the authors in this volume bring divergent answers, but all share an intuition: the cumulative effect of many seemingly small changes in social policy has been to weaken unduly the family as an institution.

References

Brown, D. 1995. "Welfare Caseload Trends in Canada." in J. Richards et al., *Helping the Poor: A Qualified Case for "Workfare"*. The Social Policy Challenge 5. Toronto: C.D. Howe Institute.

Canada. 1997. *Welfare Incomes 1996*. Ottawa: National Council of Welfare.

Lanez, E., et al. 1998. "PACS: Polémique autour d'un mariage du troisième type." *Le Point*, October 3, pp. 102–111.

Lefebvre P., P. Merrigan, and M. Dooley. 1998. "Lone Female Headship and Welfare Policy in Canada." Department of Economics working paper 98-02. Hamilton, Ont: McMaster University.

Morissette R., J. Myles, and G. Picot. 1995. "Earnings Polarization in Canada, 1969-1991." In K. Banting and C. Beach, eds., *Labour Market Polarization and Social Policy Reform*. Kingston, Ont.: Queen's University, School of Policy Studies.

Statistics Canada. 1997. *Income Distributions by Size in Canada, 1996*. Cat. 13-207. Ottawa.

No-Fault Divorce
and the Divorce Rate:
Its History, Effect, and Implications

Douglas W. Allen

The history of the no-fault divorce debate is fascinating for several reasons. First, it has gone on for such a long time. After all, the question is simple: did the change from fault-based to no-fault divorce cause the divorce rate to go up, fall, or remain the same? Yet, although the divorce rate is measurable and the change in law observable, demographers, sociologists, lawyers, and economists have struggled for an answer for 25 years. Second, in looking back over the initial debate, one is struck by the marked absence of anticipation about the actual outcomes of the legal changes. Of course, no one can see into the future, but the complete failure even to consider what no-fault divorce might mean for the divorce rate — let alone what effect it would have on poverty, education, and family structure — mostly reflected a misguided view of the family and human behavior. Third, the assessment of data, outcomes, and the suggested solutions has often been driven by similarly inappropriate models of the family and a resistance to honestly confront beliefs with solid evidence.

The divorce rate debate is now over, however. Canada's *Divorce Act* and other no-fault laws around the world have unquestionably contributed to increased divorce rates over the past 25 years. These significant increases in divorce have, by the best US estimates, raised annual divorce rates permanently by about 6 percent. Nor were the increased divorces simply the welcome outcome of unhappy indi-

Thanks to John Richards and Ken Boessenkool for their comments.

viduals' being freed from dead marriages. Rather, these laws have permanently altered the incentives and bargaining strengths of husbands and wives, and allowed some viable marriages to terminate at the will of a single party. As a result, the no-fault divorce revolution affects the lives of most of us beyond the divorce rate. This paper discusses some of these effects and implications.

Such a discussion requires a model of marriage that is consistent with the empirical record because inappropriate models lead to misguided policy implications. This paper rests on the dominant law and economics view that marriages and marriage law are designed to police opportunistic behavior in the production of children. In this light, the introduction of no-fault divorce has offered *some* individuals an unparalleled opportunity to abandon their marital responsibilities and, in the process, abscond with large fractions of marital assets.

My survey of the evidence of the effects of no-fault divorce laws on the divorce rate concludes that there has been a significant increase in divorces that, from a social standpoint, should not have happened.[1]

The policy implication is quite clear. If two parents are better than one and if no-fault divorce laws have created incentives for individuals in these functional marriages to divorce, then the laws are perverse and should be changed. In the last section of this paper, I argue that the appropriate change is to move to a mutual divorce law. Very seldom in the complicated world of social policy does an opportunity arise in which the solution is so simple, achievable, and effective.

No-Fault Divorce: History

No-fault divorce laws quietly swept over most of the western world between 1968 and 1975.[2] These changes were unquestionably radi-

---

1 These divorces are called inefficient. I define and elaborate on the concept below.

2 Canada was one of the first nations to change, with its 1968 *Divorce Act*. The then justice minister, Pierre Trudeau, ushered in the law with his well-known remark:...

cal and affected a massive fraction of the population.[3] A proper historical perspective is important here. Some popular writers (for example, Whitehead 1997) lend the impression that divorce is something discovered in the 1960s, while others (for example, Talbot 1997) almost suggest that divorce was commonplace in the past and there is nothing different about the current situation. Neither position is true. Divorce did exist in the past, and there is nothing intellectually new about no-fault divorce. However, the laws written in the late 1960s and the 1970s were a watershed both legally and in terms of the divorce rate.

Centuries of Background

Conceptually and occasionally in practice, no-fault divorce has had a long history. The pre-Christian Romans, for example, viewed marriage as a civil contract that each party was entitled to dissolve at will.[4] Although the Christian notion of marriage as indissoluble eventually took hold, divorce by mutual consent was legal as late as

---

Note 2 - cont'd.

..."the government of Canada has no business in the bedrooms of Canadians" (an ironic sentiment given that, since the passage of the law, the government of Canada and its courts have never been more involved in the marital affairs of its citizens). As in most countries, the law passed in Canada virtually without opposition. There was little debate in the House of Commons, and all parties of the day voted for it (Allen, forthcoming).

Britain quickly followed in 1969, the Netherlands in 1971, Sweden in 1973, Australia in 1974, and France in 1975. In the United States, where divorce is a jurisdiction of the states and divorce law varies widely across them, California became the first no-fault state in 1970 and South Dakota the last in 1985; the bulk had changed by 1975.

3 The legal changes affected large numbers because, although a small fraction of couples divorce in any year and most marriages survive a lifetime, divorce has large indirect effects on the whole population, as other papers in this volume show. Furthermore, as discussed below, no-fault divorce laws altered the bargaining power in *all* marriages.

4 In his famous treatise on European morals, Lecky reports that marriage "[b]eing looked upon simply as a civil contract, entered into for the happiness of the contracting parties,...Either party might dissolve it at will....There can be no question that under this system the obligations of marriage were treated with extreme levity" (1869, 324).

the sixth century (Rheinstein 1972, 16). Then, for almost a thousand years, legal divorce was essentially impossible throughout Europe.

The notion of divorce resurfaced during the Reformation and the Enlightenment. For the first time in a Christian society, some writers began to consider "unhappiness" a critical ground for divorce. John Milton, though more commonly thought of as a religious puritan, argues in his famous pamphlet *Doctrine and Discipline of Divorce* that the sole grounds for divorce should be incompatibility:

> that divorce be based on "that indisposition, unfitness, or contrariety of mind, arising from a cause in nature *unchangeable*, hindering and ever likely to hinder the main benefits of conjugal society, which are solace and peace. ([1643] 1959, 242; emphasis added.)[5]

Notice that Milton hits on an idea ubiquitous among modern divorce reformers: that individuals are fundamentally either compatible or incompatible and that the couple or the state can do little about this harmony or lack of it.

In 1751, King Frederick II of Prussia became the first modern leader to enact a no-fault divorce edict.[6] Although difficult to obtain, a unilateral divorce could be granted if "through relevant facts the existence of so violent and deeply rooted an aversion that no hope remains for a reconciliation and the achievement of the ends of the marital state" (quoted in Rheinstein 1972, 26). However, the great no-fault experiment of the eighteenth century immediately followed the French Revolution. It seemed self-evident to the intellectual leaders of the time that the pursuit of happiness was an inalienable natural right, and what could be more miserable than an unhappy marriage? And so, declared the likes of Voltaire and Rousseau, what right did the church or state have to prevent such a pursuit and restrict the ability to enter and exit contracts? Thus, the French consti-

---

5 It is interesting to note that Milton had hastily married a younger woman who quickly abandoned him for over one year. Though she later returned to him and they remained married, the experience probably forged his opinion on divorce.
6 This edict became law in 1794 and was repealed in 1896.

tution of 1791 recognized marriage as a civil contract, and the Law of 1792 allowed divorce on the grounds of "incompatibility of temper."

Parisians moved rapidly toward divorce, despite the bureaucratic safeguards that had been put in place. In the first quarter of 1793, the number of divorces almost matched the number of marriages, and the divorce rate was between 20 and 30 percent, according Rheinstein. But it is difficult to draw much from this example, says the historian, because

> the overwhelming number of marriages terminated by divorce shortly after 1792 had been concluded in prerevolutionary days. Many of these marriages must have been "dead" before their parties were at last restored to the freedom of legitimate remarriage. In addition...there were the marriages whose viability was destroyed by the physical and emotional upheavals of a tumultuous era, war, and general reordering of values. (1972, 207.)[7]

The no-fault experiment in France was short-lived. The new constitution of 1795 repealed the Law of 1792, and the Divorce Code of 1803 essentially gave the country a fault-based law that limited the grounds mostly to adultery, notorious living, criminality, and maltreatment.

Although some Scandinavian countries traditionally played down the role of guilt in terminating marriages, in all instances roadblocks were put in place that, in principle, prevented frivolous or inefficient divorces from occurring. In this regard, the historical examples of no-fault divorce were unlike their modern counterparts, which often have no such impediments.

By the turn of this century, certainly in the English-speaking parts of the world, no-fault divorce was nonexistent and would remain so until the late 1960s.

Fault-Based and No-Fault Divorce

Comprehension of the sea change in divorce law is aided by an understanding of the fault-based laws in place earlier in this century

---

7 Essentially the same arguments were made in the early evaluations of the California experience with no-fault divorce.

and of the behavior they encouraged. The essence of a fault-based divorce law is that one party must breach the marriage contract by committing a specific act in order for a divorce to occur.

At the turn of the century, these faults were mostly adultery, desertion, and cruelty. Some jurisdictions had more, others fewer, and the tendency throughout the century in all jurisdictions was to add to the list.[8] In Canada, the 1968 *Divorce Act*, for example, included 15 faults for divorce. Before that time, divorce in Canada was a provincial responsibility; eight provinces essentially legislated adultery as the only ground, while Quebec and Newfoundland required a private act of the federal Senate to dissolve a marriage (for more details, see Allen 1998). In the United States, the addition of "insanity" to the faults for divorce was a turning point because it was the first instance in which legislatures recognized that a marriage could be over without one partner's being culpable.

Essentially, fault-based laws assigned the property right or power to divorce to the spouse *who least* wanted to divorce.[9] In addition, fault often played a role in determining the property settlement; for example, a spouse who committed a fault might be punished in terms of loss of child custody or of marital property.

One of the major consequences of fault-based divorce was the incentive it provided for privately negotiated divorce settlements. Since many marriages died for reasons other than those listed by legislation and since a legal fault could be difficult to prove, in actual practice the husband and wife often negotiated a private divorce settlement and simply agreed to a fault. (Throughout this century, before the introduction of no-fault divorce, the preferred fault to agree on was cruelty.) When the couple proceeded with an uncon-

---

8 The list of faults can become quite colorful. In Lebanon, if one belongs to the Greek Orthodox Community, fault includes, among other things, "willful destruction by the wife of the husband's seed; if wife...attends banquets or bathes with men in mixed baths, all against the husband's order; if she goes to the races, theaters, or gambling halls surreptitiously or against the husband's orders" (*Martingale-Hubbell Law Digest* 1991, LEB-5).

9 Historically, this person was most often the wife. In modern times, however, when women often have options outside of marriage equal to that of men, many wives instigated divorces.

tested divorce and had an agreed property settlement, the agreement would supersede the state or provincial laws on marital property. This practice described the vast majority of divorce cases,[10] and it *de facto* created a mutual-consent divorce law.

As early as the 1930s, reformers argued that the fault-based law should be changed. Many felt that, by focusing on moral faults and guilt, the process encouraged couples to become spiteful and more antagonistic toward one another.[11] Others, saying that law should reflect the world and not be opposed to it, argued that the law should be changed to recognize the rising demand for divorce. As Zuckman and Fox put it, "[the entire fault divorce system creates strains on our legal system. But perhaps more important, fault divorce fails to reflect sociological and psychological realities" (1972/73, 528). And an extremely influential book by a group appointed by the Archbishop of Canterbury stated:

> When [reformers] call for reform of the law, they are not asking for "easy divorce", but that the law should have regard to the empirical state of affairs, and that the court should be empowered to declare defunct *de jure* what in their view is already defunct *de facto*. (Archbishop of Canterbury's Group on the Divorce Law 1966, 38.)

---

10 According to Fain: "Well over 90 percent of American divorces were uncontested. Marital fault usually was significant only as it affected the negotiation process and provided leverage for financial or property terms eventually agreed upon" (1977, 34). Freed and Foster say the same: "Under the traditional nineteenth and early twentieth century grounds for divorce, over 90 percent of divorces were uncontested and hence there was divorce by mutual agreement" (1979, 107).

11 Indeed, one of the goals of the no-fault laws, according to Weitzman, was to "recognize the inevitability of divorce for some couples and to try to make the legal process less destructive for them and their children" (1985, 17). In fact, in the early years of no-fault divorce, advocates and researchers often called it *nonadversary divorce*. The California *Family Law Act* of 1969 went so far as to alter the entire divorce lexicon to reflect that anticipated nonadversarial nature. *Divorce* was replaced by *dissolution* and *plaintiff* by *petitioner*, to name two examples. In practice, however, no-fault law simply transferred the hostility from proving fault to establishing claims over property and children; it is no longer considered nonadversarial.

The most common intellectual argument against fault-based divorce law, however, was that it forced individuals to lie and perjure themselves. This is the position taken by Judge Posner, stating:

> [C]onfining divorce to grounds...[leads to investing] resources in manufacturing them....At this point internal goals of the legal system — the goals of economizing on judicial resources and of reducing perjury — become decisive in favor of allowing either consensual divorce or divorce at will." (1992, 252.)[12]

Along the same lines, Humphrey states: "To require an adversary proceeding and fabrication of a statutory excuse to legally justify the marriage dissolution makes a mockery of matrimonial law" (1972/73, 111).

Whatever lay behind the demand for no-fault divorce, the report of the Archbishop of Canterbury's Group on the Divorce Law (1966) was instrumental in bringing a no-fault law to the state of California and played a role in the few discussions in Canada as well. Here was a major religious source of authority, acting independently of North American legislative bodies, drawing the same conclusions that divorce reformers sought. The Canterbury report views marriage as a lifelong commitment in which society has a stake. In order to mitigate suffering, it says, marriages that are no longer functional should be recognized as such and allowed to dissolve. It is a serious job of the *courts* to make this decision. Courts decide, on a careful consideration of all evidence, what the outcome of the marriage should be; for this reason, the writers of the report ironically reject the notion of mutual consent:

> The fatal defect of the consensual principle is...that it subjects marriage absolutely to the joint will of the parties, so making it in essence a private contract. Since it gives the court, as representing the community, no effectual part in divorce, it virtually repudiates the community's interest in the stability of mar-

---

12 In a forthcoming publication, I provide an alternative hypothesis. I argue that the change in law was the result of changes in female work force participation rates. As more women entered the work force, estimating their marital contributions became more difficult, increasing the number of bad marriages. These bad marriages created a demand for divorce reform.

riage....Dissolution of marriage ought always to require a real exercise of judgment by the court, acting on the community's behalf. (1966, 34.)

In practice, of course, no-fault divorce becomes unilateral divorce: one party to the contract exercises control — at the expense not only of the community and the courts but often of the other spouse and children as well.[13] Given that the Anglican church was promoting divorce reform, that no major churches were actively against it, and that there was no intellectual opposition, it is not surprising that the laws passed quite uneventfully.

The Canadian experience appears typical. A reading of the parliamentary debate on the 1968 Canadian act reveals little opposition. After the introduction of the bill, the leader of the opposition stated, "Mr. Chairman, in just a few words I should like to indicate that we on this side of the chamber approve of reforming the divorce law, and look forward to receiving the bill" (Canada 1967, 5017). The debate that followed offered no opposition. Members from both sides simply repeated that adultery and separation were not the only factors that could terminate a marriage, and that the time had come for a new way.

Jacob (1988), writing mostly on the California experience, also argues that no-fault divorce arrived with little resistance. And thus most western countries quietly altered their divorce laws.[14]

The Silent Revolution

Today it is useful to ask: why did no one anticipate the problems that might arise from the no-fault law?[15] The Canterbury report provides

---

13 Foster and Freed state: "It is not an over-simplification to say that such statutes convert the system from one where divorce most often is a matter of mutual consent into one where it is available upon unilateral demand" (1973/74, 446).

14 The list of no-fault jurisdictions includes: Australia, Bermuda, Canada, China, Denmark, England and Wales, Finland, France, Germany, Greece, Hungary, Israel, the Netherlands, New Zealand, Northern Ireland, Scotland, South Africa, Sweden, Switzerland, and the United States.

15 A number of people deal with this question. The phrase *silent revolution* comes from Herbert Jacob (1988), who ironically argues that the law had no major...

a hint in its failure to consider the economic incentives that would
significantly change with a new divorce law — a failure that occurs
over and over in the history of no-fault divorce debates. Reformers,
both legal and sociological, tend toward an idealized view of marriage, the law, and human motivation. Quite often, the picture
painted is that men and women are either compatible or not; therefore, that a marriage is either good or bad; and if it is bad, that a divorce is inevitable. Individuals, too, are classified dichotomously:
most are good and interested in the welfare of others, but some are
bad and hopeless. Finally, reformers often view the law as completely binding — that is, whatever it states in principle will be the
actual outcome. For example, if it decrees that marital property will
be split equally on divorce, such a split will occur.

This outlook fails to account for the economic realities of marriage and the law. Economists view the world in terms of the rights
people *actually* possess and of their ability to make decisions based
on this possession, not just under the law.[16] Furthermore, economists view marriage as a long-term exchange shaped in an effort to
police the *self-interested* motives of the husband and wife. One implication of the economic approach is that individuals change their
behavior when they face different sets of incentives.

A Spectrum of Marriages

A key mistake that no-fault divorce advocates made in arguing for
the law — one that must have biased interpretations of the early

Note 15 - cont'd.

> ...impact on the divorce rate or the welfare of women. He argues that the laws
> changed quietly because the reformers couched everything in neutral bureau-
> cratic language. Reading him, one gets the impression that the law almost came
> about by accident. Others argue that the change was silent because it was simply
> a question of making the law more honest. But again, why was there no anticipa-
> tion of what was to come?

16 For example, a sailboat in Vancouver's English Bay may have a legal right of way,
   but when a large motorboat bears down on it and forces a change of course, the
   navigator of the larger boat holds the economic right. Economic rights, though
   they overlap legal rights, are closer to Hobbesian rights of nature. Legal rights enhance economic rights, which is why they are so valuable.

evaluations — was the assumption that marriages are either good or bad, and the number of each is independent of the law. Whitehead quotes an early twentieth-century advice writer as saying "[N]o good purpose is achieved by keeping people together who have come to hate each other" (1997, 19). The implication seems to be that hatred is exogenously imposed on the couple by the gods.

Sheppard, in defending the no-fault system, states:

> The idea, embraced by the no-fault separation ground, [is] that unhappy marriages are not worth retaining....It seems to me self-evident that an unwanted marriage...can be a source of enormous family harm....Surely the state has no principled interest in refusing to recognize this. (1990, 148–149.)

Similarly, Zuckman and Fox say:

> [T]here are relationships which cannot easily be altered to make the marriage smoother. Divorce provides a quick and unequivocal termination of such marriages. (1972/73, 536.)

Sentiments like these are commonplace in the pro-no-fault literature.

One can more usefully think of a spectrum of marriages: some healthy, generating large positive amounts of surplus utility to each spouse; others unhealthy, generating large negative amounts of utility; and a continuum in between. The number in any category is not exogenously given. Most reformers advocated a change in divorce law because they thought that they were freeing a fixed number of bad marriages that were bad independent of the law. They ignored the fact that for any given law many marriages are *marginal*, just barely in the parties' interests in keeping together. In other words, maintaining a marriage depends on the costs and benefits of staying together, and changes in these costs and benefits can lead good marriages into marginal ones, and marginal ones into bad ones.[17] For the latter, relaxing the law tips the scale in favor of divorce.[18]

---

17 Or the costs and benefits could change such that the number of good marriages increases.

18 One might think that if the marriages are marginal, then there is no social loss when they end. However, there are also intramarginal marriages, and the losses...

The Economist's View of Marriage

Cohen provides a provocative summary of the economist's view of marriage:

> Marriage...is a marvelous invention....it is not natural....It is designed to harness men's energies to support the only offspring they may legitimately have,...in a world in which marriage is the norm. We lose sight of this truth at our peril. The truth has become less obvious in the last century because the poverty and material insecurity that were virtually universal conditions prior to that time have been alleviated in a number of wealthy Western and Eastern countries. And so we have been seduced by a variety of erroneous and pernicious theories on the function of marriage, specifically notions of marriage as entirely contingent on its origin as the culmination and cementing of romantic love or as an equalitarian partnership. (1995, 2290.)

To the economist, a man and woman enter into a marriage because there are gains from joint production.[19] Marital production, especially children, requires a long time and involves the investment of resources that are specific to the family. Marital law is designed to prevent inefficient breaches of the contract — or to put it another way, to prevent one spouse from taking advantage of the other's weaker bargaining position due to the specific investments in the marriage.[20]

A key aspect of the economic approach to marriage is that, at any given stage of a marriage, the husband and wife are not likely equal in terms of their bargaining power or, in practice, equal under the law. Before 1970, many US states and most Canadian provinces

---

Note 18 - cont'd.

...of their dissolution may be considerable. (An intramarginal marriage is one in which the benefits of staying married are greater than the cost. When the law changes, many marriages that had been intramarginal become marginal.)

19 The economist does not deny love. But it plays a role in the choice of the partner, not in the design of the contract.

20 See Cohen (1987); Allen (1990); and Becker and Murphy (1988) for economic theories of marriage that elaborate on the hazards of joint family production.

allocated marital property based on title if divorcing spouses did not reach a property agreement. Under a fault-based law, this approach posed little problem. If the husband wished to leave the marriage, he had to "pay" his wife in terms of the family home, child custody, and alimony in order to get her agreement to a fault. However, under the no-fault law, when the husband could leave unilaterally but still held title to most family assets, they usually went automatically to him.[21]

Even today, husbands and wives are not equal in the timing or nature of their contributions to marriage. Cohen (1987) discusses the implications that result from women's making large, sunk investments early in many marriages, mostly in the form of children. Under such circumstances, husbands have an incentive to exploit a larger share of the gains from marriage under the threat of leaving.

Nor are husbands the only spouses interested in terminating a marriage. Wives, in fact, are more likely to file for divorce than husbands. The motivation for wives' filing often involves the children. If a wife wants more or complete control over the children and if she anticipates receiving it through a divorce, she may, in effect, file for divorce in order to obtain custody. Given the economically "lumpy" (one-time) nature of children and the fact that the utility a father derives from them may critically depend on the presence of a mother to look after them, no-fault divorce again allows for the possibility of one spouse's absconding with marital wealth.

---

21 The most famous such case in Canada is *Murdoch v. Murdoch* (1975, 1 SCR 423; 1974, 41 PLR (3d) 367). A divorcing couple had farmed in Alberta for 25 years, during which Mrs. Murdoch had made significant contributions to the farm. However, since she had made no financial contribution and her husband held title to the property, she walked away with basically the dress on her back.

The situation was similar in many US states. Kargman says:

> Many of the states that have changed their grounds from fault divorce to no-fault divorce, have failed to make the necessary changes in the property relationships between husbands and wives. As a consequence, laws of property geared to a fault based divorce system interfere with the intent of no-fault divorce reform to make divorce a non-adversary procedure. (1974, 44.)

In a 1990 study, I examine the effect of US title laws and show that they encouraged divorce under no-fault laws. Title laws in both Canada and the United States had all changed by the 1980s.

The Effect on the Divorce Rate

Divorce reformers so little anticipated these problems because they had a flawed theoretical view of the world. It was implicitly predicated on the idea that the changes in the law would bring about no changes in behavior, only legal recognition of what already existed in practice. The earliest attempts at evaluating the effect of no-fault divorce also fell victim to this bias. The first empirical studies, which were little more than visual inspections of divorce rate graphs,[22] were almost unanimous in concluding that the law had had no effect on the divorce rate.

Unfortunately, idealized views of marriage that do not reflect the true underlying economic forces are still around. Annamay Sheppard, a die-hard advocate, correctly notes that no-fault divorce is theoretically premised on the idea that men and women are equal:

> In that new model, the assumed economic dependence of married and divorced women has been replaced by an assumption that marital partners are equal in all matters, including matters of family economics. (1990, 145.)

Although Sheppard fully acknowledges that no-fault laws appear to have increased divorce rates ("as a statistical matter, it is a fact that the rising divorce rate has overlapped and coincided with divorce reform" [p. 146]), and have been detrimental to women ("[a]s these statistics make clear, women without husbands confront financial problems of extraordinary magnitude — problems from which women with intact marriages are shielded, at least in part" [p. 148]), she nonetheless concludes that the solution is simply to transfer wealth to those harmed by divorce, using income assistance, day care, work training, and so on. But she makes these recommendations without any consideration of their potential feedback to the decision to divorce or to any other behavior that could result from changing more costs and benefits.

---

22 I am referring here to the preregression era of data analysis. Now it seems hard to believe, but examination of early no-fault divorce studies shows a strong willingness to draw conclusions from a dearth of information.

My purpose here is not to consider such reforms but to stress that failure to recognize the difference between principle and reality has led to the surprise over higher divorce rates and the feminization of poverty. The tragic truth is that men and women are *not* equal in terms of biology, earnings, or feelings toward children, and, as a result, the two partners are usually not equal in terms of bargaining strength throughout the marriage.[23]

Divorce in Theory

Although unrealistic views of the world may have been the reason why so few of the impacts of no-fault divorce were anticipated and why the early evaluations of no-fault on the divorce rate were mistaken, analysts developed some strong economic theory after the fact to justify the approach.

Utility

In order to elaborate the sophisticated argument about why no-fault divorce should have had no impact on the divorce rate, I must introduce the distinction between an *efficient* and *inefficient* divorce.

Suppose, as only an economist can, that one can place dollar values on marriage and on being divorced — numbers that reflect the utility that the husband and wife obtain from their marriage or from being single.[24] If the joint value of being single (that is, the sum of the husband's and wife's single values) is greater than the joint value of being married, then a divorce is efficient. When the opposite

---

23 Weitzman recognizes this, saying "the unanticipated and probably unintended consequences of the no-consent rule have fallen most heavily on the older and economically weaker wife" (1985, 27). But although she focuses mostly on the welfare of the wife after divorce and concludes that "divorce is a financial catastrophe for most women" (p. 339), she spends little time on divorce rates.

24 I stress that this dollar value is *not* a reflection of the financial value of the marriage; it is just a convenient measure of the total utility the husband and wife obtain from being in a particular marriage or from divorcing in particular circumstances. Even expressing utility in dollars is an arbitrary convenience; one might use units of imaginary *utils*.

is true — that is, when the joint value of staying together is greater than being apart — and yet the couple still divorces, this divorce is inefficient. Presumably the law should allow efficient divorces because they raise social values (utility), and it should discourage inefficient divorces because they lower social value.

In viewing marriages as simply good or bad and in thinking that only bad marriages end in divorce, the proponents of divorce reform had concluded that no-fault divorce was efficient. They received theoretical justification in an influential article published in 1977 by Becker, Landes, and Michael, which argues that only efficient divorces occur.[25] Consider the dollar values in Table 1 as representing the values of a couple in and out of marriage. In panel A, the total value of the marriage is greater than the total value of the couple when they are divorced; thus, this marriage is efficient, and the couple should not divorce. Suppose the two live in a jurisdiction with a fault-based divorce law. The husband must come to his wife and purchase the right to divorce. It would leave him better off by $10, but the wife would be worse off by $20. In other words, the husband is willing to pay $10 for the right to divorce, but the wife will not accept anything less than $20. As a result, a divorce will not happen, and the socially efficient result occurs.

Now suppose the jurisdiction's divorce law is no-fault. The husband need not purchase the right to divorce — he can just leave. But the wife is willing to pay him to stay. Clearly there is room for bargaining since the $20 the wife is willing to pay exceeds the $10 that the husband requires. Once again the marriage remains together. In other words, it does not matter which type of law is in place; the same efficient outcome will occur.

Moreover, if the marriage is inefficient — that is, if row labels in Table 1 are reversed (see panel B) — then the marriage will end in divorce under both types of law. If the wife in panel B seeks and obtains a divorce under a fault-based law, she is better off by $20 to divorce, compared with her husband's loss of $10. If she pays her husband

---

25 Becker, a future Nobel Prize winner, based the argument on the work of Ronald Coase (1960), another Nobel Prize winner.

Table 1:   ***Sample Payoffs in Marriage***

	Husband	Wife	Total
	(dollars)		
A. An Efficient Marriage			
Married	50	50	100
Divorced	60	30	90
B. An Inefficient Marriage			
Married	60	30	90
Divorced	50	50	100

Source: Adapted from Allen 1995.

even $11, they are both better off with a divorce. If the law is no-fault, she leaves and the husband is unwilling to compensate her for staying. Once again, the law has no effect on the divorce outcome.

This point bears reiterating: regardless of the type of divorce law, only efficient divorces occur when parties are free to bargain. The empirical implication is that the change in divorce law should have had no effect on the divorce rate.

Transaction Costs

This result is powerful, and it gave theoretical justification to the preliminary assessments of the new laws. Yet something about it rings untrue. It involves the critical assumption that property rights (ownership) are complete; in economists' jargon, for the result to hold, the transaction costs — the costs of establishing and maintaining property rights[26] — must be zero.

The problem is that marriage is an exchange in which the transaction costs are quite high. Thus, divorces that happen in no-fault situations may be inefficient.

The number and types of transaction costs that may result in inefficient divorces under no-fault divorce laws seems to be quite

---

26 See Allen (1991) for an elaboration.

large. First, as already mentioned, quirks in property laws at the time of divorce can easily create situations whereby efficient marriages dissolve. For example, if a wife has contributed to the education of her husband but the courts do not consider his degree as property, then her contribution is not considered in the marital property settlement. Likewise, pension funds, insurance policies, and lost work force opportunities may or may not be considered property in a given jurisdiction. Some US states automatically split marital property 50:50, ignoring which spouse brought it into the marriage. In others, the courts make an effort to establish each spouse's contribution to the marriage.

In every case, authorities make imperfect rules that allow some spouses to gain an advantage. The history of divorce legislation since the enactment of no-fault divorce has been the adoption of one band-aid remedy after another. No sooner is one type of asset ruled marital property than another example emerges. As long as laws are costly to write, none will ever define property accurately enough, and the possibility of inefficient divorces arises.

A second reason for inefficient divorces is government failures to enforce rulings of support payments for children and spouses, thereby allowing instigating parties to avoid some of the costs of their actions.[27] Hence the private values of the party leaving the marriage can be out of line with the joint value of the marriage. The phenomenon of the deadbeat dad imposes costs not only on the mother and children but also on the state, which is often required to assist the family through welfare. To the extent that welfare creates its own set of disincentives, the wife and children are further made worse off.

Third, many family assets may be difficult and costly to bargain over at the time of divorce because they are indivisible or they are public goods — goods whose consumption by one person does not hinder consumption by another. With children, for example, the fact

---

27 Moir (elsewhere in this volume) makes the case that failure to make payments may reflect more the fact that one man cannot support two households than a lack of responsibility on the part of the husband.

that a father gets utility from them does not mean the mother cannot also gain utility.[28] This situation affects divorce because it means that the husband can leave a marriage and still get utility from being a father. And a mother who attempts to use children as an enticement to get the father to stay is limited by the fact that they are partly public goods. Zelder (1993) makes the case that children are always quasi-public goods, and as a result their presence almost always makes divorce inefficient.

Fourth, a spouse's violent reactions may make renegotiating the terms of the marriage too costly, and an inefficient divorce or marriage may occur. Inefficient bargains are always the result of a failure to respect the property rights of others. Given the physical difference between husbands and wives and given the privacy in which they interact, violence is often a possibility. Either party may be capable of threats of violence in order to forcibly dissolve a marriage and enforce a property settlement that does not reflect the true contributions of the parties. Likewise, if the two stay together for a time, either may force a divorce by destroying the marital capital by being abusive and irresponsible or by dissipating financial assets. Similarly, one party may be able to maintain a marriage through threats of force. When violence or threats of violence are involved, inefficient divorces and marriages are likely.

Finally, the fact that contracts based on a promise not to leave are essentially unenforceable in court restricts the bargaining ability of the person who least wants to leave. The result can be inefficient divorce.[29] This restriction is particularly a problem for women. Of the many contributions wives make to marriage, a major one is the bearing and rearing of children. Although a mother may also work,

---

28 Of course, to the extent that utility from children is tied to access, this tie reduces the public good nature of children. Unfortunately, for many fathers this does not appear to be the case.

29 This last point is made by Brinig and Buckley (forthcoming). Allen and Brinig (1998) provide another reason for bargaining failures: the biological difference between men's and women's lifecycle demands for sex. Marriage is such a complicated contract that the list of transaction costs that could lead to breach is probably very long.

the presence of a child causes major disruptions in work force participation and hence a reduction in her financial contribution to the household. Because child bearing and rearing take place early in a marriage, the wife makes a sunk investment in the marriage, placings herself in considerable jeopardy. The husband, on the other hand, makes no such investment. In fact, the typical male's income increases throughout his working life. Middle-aged husbands, then, can realistically expect to find a new spouse after divorce, while the same is not true for middle-aged wives.[30] Under these conditions, it is easy to see why the inability to enter a binding contract with the husband is detrimental to wives.

Given all these possibilities for unequal bargaining power, the question of what happens to the divorce rate when the law changes from fault-based to no-fault is ultimately an empirical one that hinges on the level of transaction costs. If transaction costs are high, because, for example, marital property is difficult to define or child payments are hard to enforce, then the divorce rate should increase with the introduction of no-fault laws.

The Evidence

Another side to the fact that no-fault divorce allows for inefficient divorces is that the old fault-based law allowed for inefficient marriages. If transaction costs prevent an unhappy couple from reaching a bargain over divorce, this marriage is considered inefficient. Hence, two critical questions need to be addressed in discussing divorce law. First, did the no-fault divorce act increase the incidence of divorce? Second, which problem is worse: the inefficient marriages that existed in Canada before 1968, or the inefficient divorces that take place now? I now turn to the evidence regarding the first question. The papers by Moir and Brinig (elsewhere in this volume) attempt to address the second.

---

30 After age 40, the male-to-female sex ratio also begins to turn against women, and the increased competition hurts the bargaining position of wives.

In order to understand the empirical evidence on the effect of no-fault laws on the divorce rate, one must divide the literature into those studies published before and after 1986. That year saw the publication of Elizabeth Peters' work in the *American Economic Review*, the capstone of a series of papers that conclude no-fault laws had made no difference in divorce rates. Being the first analyst to use a large data set and sophisticated econometric techniques, Peters appeared to provide the ultimate empirical verification of the work done by Becker, Landes, and Michael (1977) a decade before.

Yet this triumph was short lived. Indeed, its demise had been foreshadowed a year earlier with the publication of Weitzman's *The Divorce Revolution* (1985). Although Weitzman's book contains no random samples or complicated regressions, its commonsense reporting rings true. In contrast to Peters' report, Weitzman's interviews and numbers suggest that divorce rates were higher with no-fault laws and that divorce was a financial disaster for women. Jacob (1988, 162) was one of the last major social scientists to assert that no-fault laws had no impact on the divorce rate, quite tersely stating, "no fault itself did not add to the rising wave of divorce."[31] Since the publication of Peters' work, not a single empirical study on divorce rates has agreed with her finding. In fact, her results have been shown to depend on a misclassification of data.

Early Studies

At least seven studies on divorce rates and no-fault laws appeared before 1986.[32] In retrospect, many of them are reminiscent of the

---

31 He argues elsewhere (Jacob 1989) that no-fault divorce laws had no effect on the welfare of women either, a statement that makes one wonder why he chose *The Silent Revolution* as the title of his book.

　　Parkman, in a book highly critical of no-fault divorce, tersely reviews the literature on the divorce rate. Citing only Becker (1981) and Peters (1986), he concludes that "[n]o-fault divorce did have a feedback effect that led to an increase in the divorce rate for a period shortly after its introduction, but the divorce rate then returned to its earlier trend" (1992, 79). He was unaware of the studies that were about to refute this conclusion.

32 See Zelder (1992) for a critical assessment of these early studies.

blind men who feel different parts of the elephant. They had no computers or software to work with and practically no data!

Goddard (1972), the first, concludes that no-fault laws in California increased the divorce rate because the number of divorces in 1970 and 1971 was higher than "expected." Schoen, Greenblatt, and Mielke (1975) visually compare the California trend in divorce with the US trend and conclude that there was no lasting effect.[33] Gallager (1973) provides another example of simplistic methods. Using a table of divorce decrees for seven years across three counties, he concludes that divorce rates in Delaware soared as the result of no-fault laws.[34] The other studies — by Wright and Stetson (1978); Frank, Berman, and Mazur-Hart (1978); and Sepler (1981) — although better, still amount to simple correlations and visual inspection of graphed divorced rates.

Five years passed between the publication of Becker's work (1981) on California and the Peters (1986) article already mentioned. Unlike the earlier analysts, Peters began with the 1979 Current Population Survey (CPS) published by the US Bureau of Labor, which had a special supplement related to divorce. From this data, she drew a sample of approximately 20,000 women from all 50 states — all had been married just once, and some had been divorced. With these data, she ran logit regressions, controlling for age, number of children, education, region of residence, and so on, along with a vari-

---

33 Becker (1981) repeated this type of experiment using econometric methods and arrived at basically the same conclusion.

34 Gallagher, although a lawyer, does not even get the classification quite right. In analyzing no-fault divorce laws, the most important feature is that the law allow for unilateral divorce. Gallagher is incorrect in stating, "[n]o-fault divorce is a concept that has been recognized in Delaware since 1957 when voluntary separation for three years became a ground for divorce" (1973, 873). Since the separation was to be voluntary, the Delaware divorce law amounted to a mutual divorce law, which is the opposite of a unilateral law. This is seen later in his paper when he states:

> [L]awyers found that a contested voluntary separation action was usually difficult for a plaintiff to win. The controversy often evolved into a claim by the plaintiff that the separation was voluntary against a disclaimer of voluntariness by the defendant. In most contested cases, the plaintiff lost. (Ibid.)

able indicating whether the state had a no-fault divorce law.[35] She finds that the value of no-fault variable is essentially zero: the probability of divorce does not depend on the type of law.

Peters' cross-section regression is very sensitive (see Allen 1992). What made the CPS data so valuable was that they were collected between 1975 and 1978, a time when some states had no-fault divorce laws and others did not, a crucial situation for a cross-section regression. A problem arises, however, over how to classify the states that changed their laws during the 1975–78 period. It turns out that Peters misclassified three states (Massachusetts, Rhode Island, and Wyoming). Although these states accounted for only 38 divorces in the whole sample of 20,000 women, simply correcting the classification error changes Peters' result from the law's having no statistical effect to its having a positive and significant one. Suddenly, all of the evidence to suggest the type of law does not matter is reduced to the earlier crude graphs of divorce rates.[36]

Studies after 1986

Since 1986, a flood of research on the effect of no-fault laws on divorce rates has reflected higher-quality data, better econometric programs, and better legal definitions. Marvell (1989) conducted the first complete, systematic time-series analysis of divorce rates across the United States, using aggregate state divorce-rate data by year, along with other variables that measure average state incomes and so on.[37] He concludes, "[n]o-fault laws...had a significant impact on divorce rates, with the major thrust delayed for a year" (1989, 563).

---

35 Given the primitive state of computers and software in the early 1980s, this regression was quite an accomplishment.

36 Many of these early studies, like Gallager (1973), are plagued with data problems and incorrect classification of states. See Marvell (1989) for a discussion.

37 Data on divorce usually take one of two forms: large individual random samples or state-wide statistics. The advantage of the former is that the analyst can examine individual characteristics, but the data are only cross-sectional and therefore ignore fixed effects. The advantage of the latter is that one can use cross-sectional time-series regressions, which control for exogenous changes in the divorce rate over time and across space, but only crude averages control for demographic variables.

Anderson and Shughart were the first to consider the effect of property laws and the distinction between no-fault laws that allow unilateral divorce and those that do not. Using aggregate time-series data from the United States, they conclude, "[s]tates that do not provide a no-fault divorce option, have lengthy residency requirement, and impose mandatory separation periods tend to have lower divorce rates" (1991, 143).

Other significant studies in recent years have examined more subtle issues. Nakonezny, Shull, and Rodgers look at how no-fault divorce interacts with income, education, and religiosity; they conclude that "the enactment of no-fault divorce law had a clear positive influence on divorce rates" (1995, 487). Weiss and Willis (1989) were the first to use a panel data set that follows a cohort through time, and find that no-fault laws consistently increased the rate of divorce. Finally, Brinig and Buckley, who use aggregate longitudinal data with the most careful legal classification of states thus far, say their

> principal finding is that divorce levels are positively and significantly correlated with state laws which do not penalize marital misbehavior at the time of divorce....Our study of 1980–91 divorce rates provides the strongest evidence to date that no-fault divorce laws are associated with higher divorce levels. (Forthcoming, 16.)

Three More Studies

Although the limits of this essay are too tight to permit analysis of many of the papers described, three recent ones are of particular importance for the argument made here and so deserve more detail.

The first is a new study by Leora Friedberg (1998) that attempts to provide a definitive answer to the question whether divorce laws affect divorce rates. To do so, she amasses a data set that includes "virtually every divorce in the U.S. over the entire period of the law changes" (1998, 613). This set is a panel of state-level divorce rates, so she can both compare differences in divorce rates across states and control for changes in divorce behavior across time. Using a series of state and time dummy variables that control for fixed differences across time and states, Friedberg concludes:

> The estimation reveals a strong influence of unilateral divorce: divorce rates would have been about 6 percent lower if states had not adopted unilateral divorce, accounting for 17 percent of the overall increase between 1968 and 1988. (1998, 626.)

In addition, Friedberg uses the legal definitions produced by Brinig and Buckley (forthcoming) to test the different impacts of the different state laws. Some states have no-fault laws that require mutual agreement, while others have true, unilateral no-fault laws. Friedberg finds:

> [T]he type of unilateral divorce a state adopted mattered. The strictest unilateral divorce, without separation requirements or fault considerations in property division, raised the divorce rate by 0.549 per thousand people — 11.9 percent of the average of 4.6 during the sample period....Overall, the results strengthen conclusions about the impact of switching to any type of unilateral regime. (Ibid., 620.)

The Friedberg study is likely to go down as the definitive answer in the no-fault divorce debate. Some might consider the changes in divorce rates she reports as brought about exclusively by the change in law — about 5 to 10 percent — to be too small to worry about. However, as Friedberg notes, the accumulation was 17 percent of the divorces over the no-fault era.[38] Moreover, changing the law is one of the few instruments available to reduce divorce rates, no matter how small the change. The ultimate issue is not how large the effect is, but whether or not these divorces should be allowed. In other words, is the rise in divorce a result of inefficient or of efficient divorces? If the law contributes to a 10 percent rise in the number of inefficient divorces, then presumably, society should prevent this increase.

---

38 One reason the numbers may appear low is that the United States had and has a spectrum of laws in the fault-based and no-fault eras. Forty years ago, many states had laws that were quite liberal, while today many no-fault states are quite conservative. Hence, in contrast to the situation in Canada, where the change in law was so discrete and profound, the change in US law was less dramatic.

Two studies attempt to identify the presence of inefficient divorces caused by the change in the law. Zelder (1993) argues that because children are a public good in marriages, they can lead to inefficient bargains over divorce. With the presence of public goods, the marriage can be efficient, as already discussed, but if one party unilaterally decides to leave, the *private* transferable wealth of the other spouse may be inadequate to prevent the divorce. The divorce instigator can gain all of the benefits of being single, while still consuming the public goods of the marriage. Such divorces are inefficient.

To test his argument, Zelder constructs a variable that measures the total expenditure on children divided by the nonchild assets in the household, which presumably proxies the importance of children in the marriage. This variable is then multiplied by a no-fault dummy to capture the inefficient divorces. Using the data set from the Panel Study of Income Dynamics, Zelder finds that his variable is positive and significant. He concludes that the presence of children and the bargaining problems they cause at divorce are a significant source of inefficient divorces.

Zelder's finding is of particular importance to the no-fault debate because children are found in virtually all marriages. If children create public goods problems that generate inefficient divorces, then the law should not allow divorce at the will of one party except in cases of childless couples.

In a recent study (Allen 1998), I take a different approach in finding evidence for inefficient divorces. I model costly information about future contributions of potential spouses that results in mistakes in the choice of marriage partners. This paper uses variables that measure pregnancy before marriage, work force participation, and the variance in work force participation, all multiplied by a no-fault dummy to estimate the probability of an inefficient divorce.[39]

My 1998 paper is also the only one to analyze the Canadian experience with no-fault divorce. The fact that divorce is a federal

---

39 The actual econometric technique, though not complicated, would be space consuming to explain, and it is irrelevant to the point being made here. Interested readers can refer to the article.

responsibility provides an alternative opportunity to test the standard question. That Canada's no-fault law raised the divorce rate is unquestionable. Even a glance at the crude divorce rate (see Figure 1) makes it obvious that something significant happened in 1968.

Implications and Resolution

In a tally of divorce rate studies, the crude score is 11 to 7 in favor of the divorce rate's increasing as a result of no-fault divorce laws. If one eliminates studies that contain mistakes in legal classification, miscoded data, visual techniques, or trivial sample sizes, the score is 9 to 0 — an absolute rout. After almost 30 years of analysis, there is no question that divorce rates were affected by the law. There is also evidence that some of the rise in those rates is the result of inefficient divorces. The question now is, should we care?

The answer to this question critically hinges on the issue of how many divorces are efficient versus inefficient under the current law as opposed to some alternative legislation. For an illustration of this point, return to Figure 1, which shows the absolute divorce rate for Canada over the past 70 years. In any year, there has surely been a mixture of efficient and inefficient divorces. For the sake of argument, suppose the number of efficient divorces over time has been constant. Divergences from this constant number reflect inefficient marriages or divorces.

For example, suppose the efficient number of divorces was 100 per 100,000 population. Figure 1 reveals that, until the passage of the *Divorce Act*, the actual divorce rate was lower than this level, so there must have been a number of inefficient *marriages* in existence. And after 1968 the number of inefficient *divorces* must have been very large since the divorce rate is much higher than 100. If the efficient number of divorces was indeed 100, then one could conclude that the introduction of the law caused more problems than it solved.

On the other hand, if the efficient number of divorces was 200 per 100,000 population, then one would arrive at the opposite conclusion: that the level of inefficient marriages before 1968 was much greater than the level of inefficient divorces that followed.

Figure 1: *Divorce Rate, Canada, 1921–94*

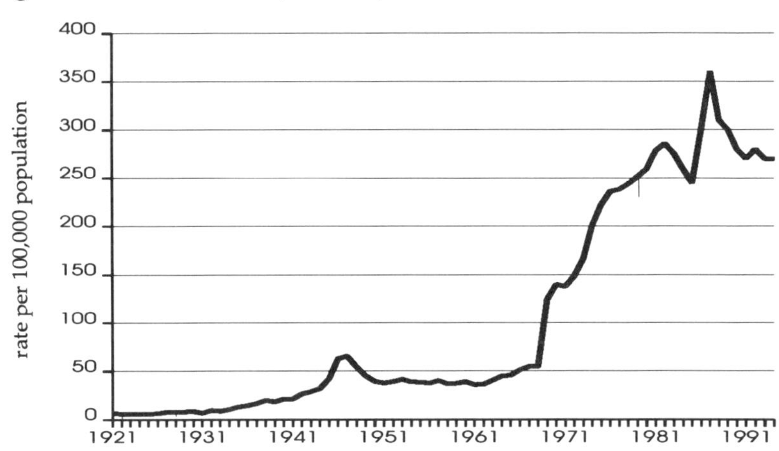

Source: Statistics Canada, Vital Statistics, various years.

Hence the argument regarding whether or not one should care comes down to one's position on the level of the efficient divorce rate. If one believes it to be low, then the recent experiment with no-fault divorce has been a mistake. If one believes it is high, then no-fault divorce, despite the social pathologies it leads to, is still better than the alternative.

Papers by Moir and Brinig (elsewhere in this volume) provide a handle on this issue. Moir strongly argues that the efficient divorce rate is low because of the effect divorce has on children. Zelder (1993) would back up Moir. If children are a major source of bargaining problems that lead to inefficient divorces and if most divorcing couples have children, then most divorces are likely to be inefficient.

Brinig notes that the issue is less clear with respect to wives. Many women are abandoned, but many others abandon their husbands. Current research by Brinig and Allen is finding that husbands often file for divorce when they can abscond with the financial assets of the marriage, while women often file to gain custody and control over the children. This research suggests that both husbands and wives behave opportunistically at the time of divorce, ignoring the interests of the other spouse. Such a finding reflects the unilateral nature of no-fault divorce, and it implies that the efficient divorce rate is much lower than what is currently observed.

The unilateral aspect of no-fault laws means that too often divorce is little more than an act of theft that leaves behind poor wives and children with reduced human capital or husbands with only the nominal title of father. In both cases, the effects are often long lived. The feminization of poverty and the increase in the number of children living below the poverty line are two implications of increased divorce. The rise of fathers' rights and support groups is another. When an inefficient divorce takes place, the *unwilling* party is left worse off.

The effects of no-fault divorce reach far beyond the couples who are actually divorcing. In addition to increasing female poverty and fatherless homes, threats of higher divorce rates escalate private individual efforts to insure against the hazard. When the *opportunity* for inefficient dissolution exists, marriages are postponed, some people undertake more spousal search and others less, prenuptial contracts are made, fathers become less emotionally attached to their children, and wives increase their labor force participation. Many of these behaviors are themselves destabilizing to the marriage. Prenuptial agreements create incentives for spouses to keep their property separate and to resist investing in the marriage when the investment or returns are subsequently commingled into marital property. Women's participation in the labor force can add stress to the marriage and reduces the gains from specialization between household and market production,[40] lowering the gains from marriage and raising the probability of divorce.

Furthermore, the possibility of no-fault divorce alters bargaining relationships within *all* families.[41] Disputes naturally arise in any

---

40 Keep in mind this is work force participation for the purpose of insurance. Hence, the first-best choice of the couple would be for only one person to be in the work force.

41 Parkman notes, "[i]n the two decades since the introduction of no-fault divorce, we have probably seen more changes in the structure and stability of the U.S. family than in any other period in U.S. history" (1992, 2). He does not think these changes were favorable.

family. Husbands and wives often have different objectives, which manifest themselves in different opinions on how and when to spend money, raise and discipline children, divide household chores, and all the other thousands of aspects of married life. Bargaining within a marriage, then, is necessary and cannot be done completely before marriage, given that nothing can be fully anticipated. Which spouse wins in any specific dispute depends on relative bargaining power, which, in turn, partly depends on the opportunities outside marriage. Because of their unilateral nature, no-fault laws increase the bargaining power of the spouse with the best out-of-marriage opportunities. Quite often this is the husband, given that child bearing is so specific to a given marriage, but it may be the wife. The point is that no-fault laws affect all marriages this way — even those with a low chance of divorce. No-fault divorce laws have altered the relative bargaining strengths of each party. No-fault divorce allows husbands to gain financially from divorce, but it also allows wives to gain emotionally and perhaps to gain complete custody of children. Which spouse gains in power depends on wives' financial options and husbands' emotional attachment to the children.

If, as seems likely, no-fault laws have increased the divorce rate *and* the efficient level of divorces is on the low side, the question then arises, what is to be done? The days of fault-based laws are long gone and will never come back. Very few believe that the solution is a return to a system that encouraged perjury and that was based on a fixed number of faults.

What made the fault system workable, however, was that it forced most divorces to be mutual. It has been estimated that 90 percent of divorces in the fault-based era were by mutual consent (Fain 1977, 34). The essence of a mutual divorce is that no divorce can occur without its making both parties better off; in other words, it eliminates the theft element of divorce.

Mutual agreement is predicated on mutual respect for the individual rights of each party to contract *freely*. One party may, of course, try to use violence to force a termination or continuation of a marriage. To reduce this possibility, violence should be a fault for divorce *and* a consideration for property settlement. In other words, if the husband threatens his wife with violence if she attempts to negotiate a divorce, then this threat should be considered a ground for divorce and should influence the property settlement in her favor.

The introduction of mutual divorce law would eliminate inefficient divorces.[42] No one would be able to leave a marriage without the consent of the other party, and no consent would be given unless welfare was improved. Furthermore, because property negotiations would take place within the family, issues regarding the legal definition of property would become irrelevant. Because the effective right to grant a divorce would be held by the party who most wanted to remain married, both parties could make specific investments in the marriage in the confidence that they could not be stolen or destroyed by the unilateral departure of a spouse.[43]

To the extent that child poverty is a simple byproduct of divorce, a mutual divorce law would get to the crux of the problem by thrusting the obligation to pay for divorce back on the party instigating it.[44] Thus it would reduce poverty without adding to government expenditures.

Furthermore, a mutual divorce law would achieve all of this while still maintaining the spirit of honesty that was sought for in the initial divorce reforms. With such a law, couples would not need to fake a marital fault and perjure themselves. At the same time, a mutual divorce law would allow truly dead marriages to be terminated.

---

42 On the down side, what a mutual divorce law creates is the possibility of inefficient marriages. It is conceivable that individuals may stay in dead marriages because of high transaction costs. It is, however, difficult to imagine what these transaction costs might be. Since destroying a marriage is always easier than nurturing it, this problem seems minimal. One implication of a mutual divorce law is that both individuals would be careful in the selection of their spouse.

43 Also protected would be problems that can arise over some fathers' being less bonded to their children than the mothers. Strategic bargaining in which the father threatens to seek custody in order to obtain a lower property settlement (a common action with no-fault divorce) would be eliminated with mutual divorce.

44 Consider too that a large number of single parents have never been married. No-fault divorce, by lowering the value of marriage and making spouses with specific marital investments vulnerable, has lowered the attractiveness of being married. A mutual divorce law would encourage more marriages, as well as reduce divorces.

Finally, a mutual divorce law would involve no complicated policies but rather a minimal alteration in the current legislation. It is very seldom that such a simple solution arises to so many complex problems.

Conclusion

One would be hard pressed to find another example of a single piece of legislation that has had as much impact on families as the introduction of no-fault divorce. It has increased the divorce rate — in a way that left many in poverty, both emotionally and financially.

Despite these problems, no-fault divorce laws remain an invisible cancer in our society. There are no rallies for their repeal, no constituency lobbies against them, and no massive intellectual force opposes them. The reason for this silence about no-fault divorces, as for its silent introduction, is the faulty view of the family that most seem to believe in. In understanding that only a fixed number of married couples seek divorce in a year, people ignore the fact that individuals change their behavior when their circumstances change. The no-fault experiment has provided an opportunity to test this theory of the family, and in rejecting the noneconomic view, society can provide a better foundation for future family policy. The road to better divorce law leads to mutual consent.

References

Allen, Douglas. 1990. "An Inquiry Into the State's Role in Marriage." *Journal of Economic Behavior and Organization* 13(2): 171–191.

———. 1991. "What Are Transaction Costs?" *Research in Law and Economics* 14 (Fall): 1–18.

———. 1992. "Marriage and Divorce: Comment." *American Economic Review* 82 (June): 679–685.

———. 1995. "Some Comments Regarding Divorce, Lone Mothers, and Children." In Martin D. Dooley et al., *Family Matters: New Policies for Divorce, Lone Mothers, and Child Poverty.* The Social Policy Challenge 8. Toronto: C.D. Howe Institute.

———. 1998. "No-Fault Divorce in Canada: Its Cause and Effect." *Journal of Economic Behavior and Organization.* 37 (2): 129–149.

————, and Margaret Brinig. 1998. "Sex, Property Rights and Divorce." *European Journal of Law and Economics* 5 (June): 211–233.

Anderson, Gary, and William Shughart II. 1991. "Is Breaking Up Hard to Do? Legal Institutions and the Rate of Divorce." *Journal of Public Finance and Public Choice* 2: 133–145.

Archbishop of Canterbury's Group on the Divorce Law. 1966. *Putting Asunder: A Divorce Law for Contemporary Society.* London: Society for the Promotion of Christian Knowledge.

Becker, Gary. 1981. *A Treatise on the Family.* Cambridge: Harvard University Press.

————, Elizabeth Landes, and Robert Michael. 1977. "An Economic Analysis of Marital Instability." *Journal of Political Economy* 85: 1141–1187.

————, and Kevin Murphy. 1988. "The Family and the State." *Journal of Law and Economics* 31 (April): 1–18.

Brinig, Margaret, and Frank Buckley. forthcoming. "No-Fault Laws and At-Fault People." *International Review of Law and Economics.*

Canada. 1967. Parliament. House of Commons. *Debates.* Ottawa: Queen's Printer.

Coase, Ronald. 1960. "The Problem of Social Cost." *Journal of Law and Economics* 3 (October): 1–44.

Cohen, Lloyd. 1987. "Marriage, Divorce, and Quasi Rents; Or, 'I Gave Him The Best Years of My Life'." *Journal of Legal Studies* 16 (June): 267–303.

————. 1995. "Rhetoric, The Unnatural Family, and Women's Work." *Virginia Law Review* 81: 2275–2303.

Fain, Harvey. 1977. "Family Law — Whither Now?" *Journal of Divorce* 1: 31–42.

Frank, Alan, John Berman, and Stanley Mazur-Hart. 1978. "No Fault Divorce and the Divorce Rate: The Nebraska Experience — An Interrupted Time Series Analysis and Commentary." *Nebraska Law Review* 58 (1): 1–99.

Foster, Jr., Henry, and Dorothy Freed. 1973/74. "Divorce Reform: Brakes on Breakdown?" *Journal of Family Law* 13: 443–493.

Freed, Dorothy, and Henry Foster, Jr. 1979. "Divorce in the Fifty States: A Overview as of 1978." *Family Law Quarterly* 13: 105–128.

Friedberg, Leora. 1998. "Did Unilateral Divorce Raise Divorce Rates? Evidence from Panel Data." *American Economic Review* 88 (3): 608–627.

Gallagher, John. 1973. "No-Fault Divorce in Delaware." *American Bar Association Journal* 59: 873–875.

Goddard, Wendell. 1972. "A Report on California's New Divorce Law: Progress and Problems." *Family Law Quarterly* 6: 405–408.

Humphrey, Stephen. 1972/73. "Kentucky Divorce Reform" *Journal of Family Law* 12: 109–150.

Jacob, Herbert. 1988. *Silent Revolution: The Transformation of Divorce Law In the United States*. Chicago: University of Chicago Press.

———. 1989. "Another Look at No-Fault Divorce and the Post-Divorce Finances of Women." *Law and Society Review* 23 : 95–115.

Kargman, Marie. 1974. "Family Law in Flux." *Et Al.* 3: 41–49.

Lecky, William. 1869. *History of European Morals: From Augustus to Charlemagne*. New York: Appleton and Company.

Martingale-Hubbel Law Digest. 1991. New Providence, NJ.

Marvell, Thomas. 1989. "Divorce Rates and the Fault Requirement." *Law and Society Review* 23 (4): 543–567.

Milton, John. [1643] 1959. *Complete Prose Works of John Milton*. New Haven: Yale University Press.

Nakonezny, Paul, Robert Shull, and Joseph Rodgers. 1995. "The Effect of No-Fault Divorce Law on the Divorce Rate across the 50 States and Its Relation to Income, Education, and Religiosity." *Journal of Marriage and the Family* 57: 477–488.

Parkman, Allen, M. 1992. *No-Fault Divorce: What Went Wrong?* Boulder, Col.: Westview Press.

Peters, H. Elizabeth. 1986. "Marriage and Divorce: Informational Constraints and Private Contracting," *American Economic Review* 76 (June): 437–454.

Posner, Richard. 1992. *Sex and Reason*. Cambridge, Mass.: Harvard University Press.

Rheinstein, Max. 1972. *Marriage, Stability, Divorce, and the Law*. Chicago: University of Chicago Press.

Schoen, Robert, Harry Greenblatt, and Robert Mielke. 1975. "California's Experience with Non-Adversary Divorce." *Demography* 12: 223–243.

Sepler, Harvey. 1981. "Measuring the Effects of No-Fault Divorce Laws across Fifty States: Quantifying a Zeitgeist." *Family Law Quarterly* 15: 65–102.

Sheppard, Annamay. 1990. "Women, Families and Equality: Was Divorce Reform a Mistake?" *Women's Rights Law Reporter* 12 (Fall): 143–152.

Talbot, Margaret. 1997. "Love, American Style." *The New Republic*, April 14.

Weiss, Yoram, and Robert Willis. 1989. "An Economic Analysis of Divorce Settlements." Population Research Center, University of Chicago. Mimeographed.

Weitzman, Lenore. 1985. *The Divorce Revolution: The Unexpected Social and Economic Consequences for Women and Children in America*. New York: The Free Press.

Whitehead, Barbara. 1997. *The Divorce Culture*. New York: Knopf.

Wright, Gerald, and Dorothy Stetson. 1973. "The Impact of No-Fault Divorce Law Reform on Divorce in American States." *Journal of Marriage and the Family* 40: 575–581.

Zelder, Martin. 1992. "Did No-Fault Divorce Law Increase the Divorce Rate? A Critical Review of the Evidence." Northwestern Law School. Mimeographed.

———. 1993. "Inefficient Dissolutions as a Consequence of Public Goods: The Case of No-Fault Divorce." *Journal of Legal Studies* 22 (June): 503–520.

Zuckman, H., and W. Fox. 1972/73. "The Ferment in Divorce Legislation." *Journal of Family Law* 12: 515–605.

The Effects of
Divorce on Wives

Margaret F. Brinig

Divorce naturally affects both husbands and wives in a number of ways: financial, social, and psychological. Spouses of different genders do not, however, experience these changes in the same way or to the same degree. Divorce tends to be a good thing financially for men: they are often better off than they were while married (Galerneau and Sturrock 1997; Galerneau 1998; Duncan and Hoffman 1985; Peterson 1996).[1] They can take this relatively great wealth and attract a new spouse, if they desire, and many do. Their greatest problems seem to be psychological ones resulting from the lack of contact with (or, for some, the loss of) their children and the corresponding duty of paying child support (Chambers 1995; Umberson and Williams 1993). These costs manifest themselves in physiological ways as well (Riessman and Gerstel 1985).

Women feel the effects of divorce in other ways. Canadian and US women, who in most cases have primary custody of minor children of the marriage, are often financially much worse off than they were during the marriage, both in terms of liquid assets and income. They are more likely than their former husbands to remain single for many years, and many (particularly African-Americans) never remarry (Clarke 1995, 5). Divorced wives apparently succeed on the psychological front more than do their ex-husbands, however. Although living alone and bringing up children is hard, draining work, many divorced women feel a sense of release from their un-

---

1 Throughout this essay, data and references refer to the United States unless otherwise noted. In this citation, the first source is Canadian, the rest are US.

happy marriages and of pride in being able to succeed on their own (Whitehead 1997, 184).

In this paper, I review the data comparing women's experiences in marriage to those after they divorce. It concludes that divorce, and particularly no-fault divorce, harms the average woman, perhaps even more than it does the average man. The no-fault aspect contributes to women's problems in both procedural and substantive ways, primarily because women tend to transfer financial wealth in order to secure custody of their children.

The Divorce Process

The tendency to rely on private agreements has been hailed as one of the real achievements of no-fault divorce, and has undoubtedly lowered the processing costs of divorce for many couples (see Allen, elsewhere in this volume). By process, I mean the legal steps that must be taken to dissolve a marriage. Although not everyone believes that these lower costs are a good thing, the relaxed proof requirements mean that lawyers do not necessarily have to be involved in divorce proceedings. The divorce itself can often be accomplished by filing simple forms, sometimes even over the Internet. If there are more complicated financial and custodial problems, theoretically they can be sorted out by the couple, perhaps with the help of a trained counselor or mediator.

Despite the prevailing optimism about it, some analysts are concerned that no-fault divorce has merely removed conflict from the divorce process to other areas (Wardle 1991). As one author wrote recently,

> disputes over property and custody are often battlegrounds on which spouses indirectly work through their feelings about the end of marriage. We must ask whether the provision of an explicit mechanism for dealing with marital misconduct in certain instances might better channel and control these impulses. (Reagan 1992, 139.)

Empirical studies of divorce since the introduction of the no-fault option have shown a relationship between lowering the procedural costs for divorce and increasing some other costs, many of them nonfinancial: the incidence of spouse abuse and of other marital opportunism, such as "theft" of professional degrees earned during marriage (Brinig and Crafton 1994, 892). If the spouses' contributions to the marriage occur at different times, and it is easier for most husbands to begin anew than for their wives, husbands have the ability to exploit wives' reluctance to leave marriage. Easier divorce may also increase the gap between the hours worked (in and out of the paid labor force) by men and women (Parkman 1998).

However, whatever its limitations, no-fault divorce has definitely changed the way two parties negotiate a divorce. No-fault divorce energized the divorce mediation movement, which was heralded as an opportunity to provide "divorcing couples with an opportunity to nurture" their necessarily continuing relationships, particularly in the cases where there were minor children, (Mnookin and Kornhauser 1979). In particular, feminists heralded mediation because it promised to consider disputes in the language of relationships rather than individual rights (Rivkin 1984, 23; Menkel-Meadow 1985, 53). This context tends to be more important for wives, whose self-esteem is often more centered in relationships than their husbands'.

Most recently, now that the legal profession seems to have adjusted to mediation, some feminists in both the United States and Canada have reversed course and attacked the process. Their objections are twofold: Some writers argue that because women, more than men, seek connection through relationships (Grillo 1991, 102), they systematically fare worse because they trade financial or custodial property for stronger relationships with their ex-spouses. In other words, according to these writers, women will try to be "nice" and leave the relationship on good terms, even if doing so means settling for a smaller property settlement or a less-than-satisfactory joint custody arrangement. Others argue that women might trade away money to preserve custody in order to avoid litigation because, at least where custody is concerned, they are more risk averse than their husbands (Ellis 1992). In any case, some trading, or at least bargaining, occurs during the divorce process (Brinig and Alexeev

1993). Regardless of how mothers feel about the relationship between money and custody, to trade one for the other is probably not in the children's best interests. There is also a more generalized fear among both Canadian and US authors that, in bargaining without the buffer of the formal judicial process, face-to-face without lawyers present, husbands will take advantage of their wives' lack of power within the marital relationship.[2] The mediator will not take the wife's side because he or she is merely a facilitator trying to help the couple reach agreement. An attorney, on the other hand, can be the wife's "mouthpiece," and has a professional obligation to zealously promote her interests.

Despite these concerns, studies in US jurisdictions to date have not shown that women systematically fared worse than men, in terms of either financial or custodial outcomes or of their satisfaction with the process (see Brinig 1995 for a review). Regardless of the system of divorce laws in any jurisdiction and of whether or not mediation is used as a means of settlement, wives (and children in their custody) receive on average between 45 and 55 percent of the total marital assets — including court-ordered child support, which may never be collected — and half custody of the children for between 71 and 75 percent of the time. Women thus receive roughly half of the monetary assets of the marriage but have more mouths to feed. This situation may please many women, but it may well harm their children.

Alfini et al. (1994) point out that it is not clear that women systematically fare worse because of risk aversion. It is entirely possible, as we will see below, that the controlling factor in this bargaining is not men's and women's different attitudes toward risk but their different preferences about custody.

The outcome of bargaining between two spouses depends on the divorce laws of their particular jurisdiction as well as on what the spouses want, or what their partners think they want. Four significant legal variables play their part. The first is the statutory prefer-

---

2 For examples, see Shaffer (1988, 181, 185); Bryan (1992); Ilich and Jones (1980); and Weigers (1992).

ence for child custody arrangements. Most jurisdictions currently either provide for joint custody,[3] or presume that the primary care-taker before separation, usually the mother, is the best custodian following divorce.[4] The second variable involves allowable grounds for divorce. US jurisdictions have either a combination of fault and no-fault, or no-fault alone; all of Canada is a no-fault jurisdiction. The third variable concerns the basic rationales for alimony: whether for support of a dependent former spouse or temporary payments for rehabilitative purposes. The final, and no less signifi-cant, legal variable is the approach to property, which may be based on either equitable distribution or the division of community prop-erty. Equitable distribution jurisdictions, including provinces such as Manitoba, Newfoundland, Nova Scotia, and Ontario, award spouses whatever share of property seems "fair."[5] Community prop-erty jurisdictions, including Quebec and British Columbia, presume that both spouses are equal partners in the marital "community."[6] The two approaches may yield very little difference in terms of ac-tual settlements, but there is generally far more discretion in an equitable distribution than in a community property system.

Interestingly, the amounts of both property and custodial time after bargaining occurs tend to be relatively constant across jurisdic-tions. The fact that settlements are substantially similar across US

---

3 See, for example, Va. Code Ann. section 107.2 (1992), which defines joint custody in three ways: (i) joint legal custody where both parents retain joint responsibility for the care and control of the child and joint authority to make decisions concern-ing the child, even though the child's primary residence may be with only one parent; (ii) joint physical custody, where both parents share physical and custo-dial care of the child; or (iii) any combination of joint legal and joint physical cus-tody that the court deems to be in the best interest of the child.

4 *Garska v. McCoy*, 278 S.E.2d 357 (W. Va. 1981), at 357.

5 See Alberta's *Marital Property Act* C M-9; Ontario's *Family Law Act* c. 4 section 4, which provides for equal division unless to do so would be unconscionable; Manitoba's *Marital Property Act* CCSM CM45, which divides marital property un-der a presumption of equality; Nova Scotia's *Marital Property Act* c. 275, which equally divides the marital home and provides that a fair division will be equal unless proved otherwise; and Prince Edward Island's *Family Law Act*, Cap F-3, which has deferred community.

6 See Quebec, C.Q. 414 (family patrimony) and C.P. 722 (community); British Co-lumbia, *Community Marriage Act*.

states seems most peculiar, especially considering that one spouse frequently settles for less than he or she could have obtained in court (Brinig and Alexeev 1993, 283). Wives seem to "trade" property shares from theoretically reasonable amounts (half the property, perhaps alimony, and certainly child support) in order to obtain more than half the custodial time. In fact, women seem to be willing to forgo up to 20 percent of the marital estate (usually in the form of alimony or child support) to secure large custody shares.

Because of the larger number of divorces that occur since the introduction of the no-fault option and because women receive smaller financial settlements through bargaining, by objective measures, then they would have had if they had gone court, they seem to be doing worse than under the old divorce laws. Since a no-fault system allows unilateral divorce, the spouse who wants to preserve the marriage has nothing to bargain with to keep the other spouse from divorcing, even if the former wants to stay together more than the latter wants to leave. The result is that couples may now divorce "inefficiently." When a mediocre marriage ends before the spouses have accumulated much property, the custodial parent is most often a wife who finds herself without a high income (or the ability to acquire one), substantial financial assets, or even a secure stream of child support payments. The rents or benefits that wives receive from children are thus being extracted by husbands during the divorce. The result is that many divorced women and the children who live with them become impoverished.

Financial Effects

Divorce has always been financially difficult for women. Since no-fault divorce was introduced, the negative monetary consequences have been large enough to create widespread public concern (Peters 1986). Divorced women, particularly those with children, make up a very large proportion of those below the poverty level in both the United States and Canada (Finnie 1993, 205). Bane and Ellwood (1986) estimate that only about 25 percent of all poor divorced women were poor prior to the breakup of their marriages; the other three-quarters became impoverished because of, or following, divorce. Historically, divorced women have received the majority share of public assistance payments (Carbone 1994; McLanahan and Garfinkel 1989). And because they are relatively poor, children of divorce and their custodians disproportionately live with the consequences of poverty: worse schools, reduced access to medical care (at least in the United States), less appealing and less permanent living conditions, more exposure to crime, and fewer amenities generally than those who are financially better off (McLanahan and Sandefur 1994, 24).

Even the most conservative estimates of custodial versus noncustodial shares of wealth note that custodial parents (mostly former wives) and their children experience a drop in living standards following divorce, while noncustodial parents do better on a per capita basis than they did while they were married (Peterson 1996; Duncan and Hoffman 1985; McLanahan and Sandefur 1994, 86–88). In Canada, Ross Finnie's study of a sample of taxpayers reveals that marital splits are associated with

> (1) large *differences* in economic well-being between men and women, (2) low income *levels* for woman, including a large proportion in poverty, and (3) associated relative and absolute economic deprivation of *children*. (Finnie 1993, 205.)

A similar set of results was obtained in the United States in 1991 using the Survey of Income and Program Participation: on average, families lost 22.6 percent of their income when the husband left the home, and many fell below the poverty level (about 18.5 percent of two-parent families live in poverty, compared with about 31 percent of households headed by single mothers four years after divorce; see Bianchi and McArthur 1991). Poverty among families headed by divorced women is not only more prevalent than it is among two-parent families, it is also more likely to be chronic, lasting an average of seven years compared with the general average of less than three years (Bane and Ellwood 1986).

In general, fathers earn more than mothers, partly because they enjoy greater human capital development and partly because they receive greater returns to this capital (Landes 1978; Allen 1992; Brinig 1997). Custodial parents, which means mothers in a very large proportion of custody cases, must accept employment in the kind of job that is flexible enough to handle their children's emergencies (Blau and Robins 1989). In general, these jobs are lower paying than those employing the "ideal worker" with no children (Silbaugh 1996). Meanwhile, the combined parents' income must now be stretched over two households rather than one. McClanahan and Sandefur (1994, 24) calculate that, in the United States, a family of four needs US$14,228 to live above the poverty line when children and both parents live together. If the parents live in separate households and both children live with the mother, the family needs US$18,603 to maintain the same standard of living for all members: US$11,603 for the mother and children and US$7,299 for the father. Further, more men than women remarry, and those who do so remarry sooner. According to Da Vonza and Rahman (1994), divorced men in the United States are three times more likely to remarry than are women, a discrepancy that seems to hold true in Canada as well (Wu 1994). The remarried family is wealthier because it can take advantage not only of dual earnings but also of the division of tasks into those of wage earner and homemaker.

This difference in post-divorce needs and finances raises several questions. Are the current rules for dividing marital assets at divorce optimal or should spouses share in the earning capacity of the higher-paid partner? Is there a need for some continuing connection between spouses after divorce or does divorce in fact end the marriage for all purposes? Is divorce so financially hazardous for women that the law should be changed to alter their bargaining power? This section considers each of these questions in turn.

Should an Ex-Spouse Share in Earning Capacity?

The question of whether divorced spouses should continue to share enhanced earning capacity continues to fill legal periodicals (Parkman 1995; Brinig 1997; Singer 1997; Krauskopf 1980). When two people marry, they share; they benefit not only from mutual affection, but also from the savings provided by a relative abundance of time. It is readily apparent that one household is cheaper to keep than two, but it is also true that, in a married household, only one spouse need stay home to let in the appliance repair person or the exterminator. The marriage commitment, at least in jurisdictions where divorces assigning fault still exist, gives assurance that the spouse who stays home will not be taken advantage of by the one in the labor force (Cohen 1995) — an assurance not available to an unmarried couple that lives together. The marriage commitment assumes that a couple is in a relationship "for the long haul." It means that they are legally bound to support each other (Scott and Scott 1998).

The allocation of time and its relation to marriage is the subject of a pathbreaking 1965 essay by Gary Becker. He sees workers as dividing their time between labor and leisure. They have only 24 hours to divide; their goal is to maximize both the amount of leisure they have and the financial resources they can enjoy it with. When one spouse stays out of the job market to raise children or manage the household, the couple gives up the opportunity cost of the time. Presumably, to the couple deciding to take this route, the benefits of putting this time into the household are more valuable than whatever they would gain (financially or otherwise) if that spouse remained in the labor force. On average, the value of a nonworking spouse's household production is equal to about 70 percent of the household's money (or market) income after taxes. Thus, even if he or she remains out of the paid labor force, the at-home partner generates 40 percent of the household's full income (Gronau 1980). For the same reason, married men with similar qualifications do better in the business world than women and have better health than single men. Someone else is supplying them with the time (and freedom from distractions) to allow them to perform at their best and to invest in their own human capital. A good analogy for the stay-at-home spouse is a residential college, which assumes most of the housekeeping functions in a dormitory.

Thus, marriage forms a "firm" in which the couple maximize, among other things, their total earnings (Starnes 1993). A greater investment in one spouse may be optimal for the couple. For example, if they remained single, two people might get college degrees that earn each $500,000 over the course of their lifetimes. If the two marry, one spouse may well forgo the degree while the other earns an MD that raises his or her lifetime earnings to $2 million. The optimal "joint" strategy for such a couple during the marriage is for one spouse to stay home (or otherwise provide assistance and support) while the other pursues the degree. This strategy would not be optimal without a marriage, which protects each spouse against opportunistic behavior on the part of the other (Cohen 1995). Because married people share in whatever their spouses earn or acquire, the wife who supports her husband in this way will have something to show for her investment — as long as the couple remain married.

A husband is worth more if highly educated and properly employed. But like the entity represented by a stock share, his greatest financial value as a marital partner lies in the expectation that he will do well (Parkman 1992, 99–101). The spouse who weds the young graduate of Harvard Business School pays more—invests more, in terms of the other suitors she gives up—than the one marrying the high school dropout pumping gas. Marriage (not so much the promise but the conduct that follows it) is both an investment and a sacrifice.

The spouse's reward for this investment is not only the capacity for current purchases and living standards (the dividends) but also the promise of future income based on the incremental increase in that investment (the capital gain). This feature of the marital investment is troubling in divorce settlements because it cannot be predicted with certainty; the courts already address it when they divide pensions. Perhaps the high-earning spouse will work for the same employer until retirement age, or perhaps the employer's pension fund may not do as well as was expected at the time of the divorce. Hence, some jurisdictions estimate the present value of the pension and award the nonemployed spouse some share in it, to be paid when the employed spouse begins to receive the annuity. It should be possible to follow this procedure to compensate for investments in earning capacity as well, since the cost of not rewarding the investment is to increase the temptation for the spouse who benefited by the investment to take the enhanced career and leave the marriage. In other words, since earning capacity is not divided at divorce, a spouse who thinks the marriage may be in trouble has every incentive not to put money into common assets but instead to invest in his or her own career.

Because courts cannot predict the employment future with any accuracy, to ensure a fair award they must make adjustments to the payments made by the breadwinning spouse in the future. Adjustments are possible under the alimony system (Landes 1978), since periodic maintenance payments can be modified in cases of "changed circumstances" such as lower- or higher-than-expected earnings. There is some controversy over how often such alimony were made even before no-fault divorce was introduced. Now, in many jurisdictions, alimony is ordered only in exceptional cases, and only for a limited time to "rehabilitate" the career of the previously dependent spouse. Periodic, long-term alimony contradicts the "clean-break" divorce theory of no-fault advocates (Kay 1987). Thus, in California, for example, property distribution has become the primary way in which financial situations are adjusted following a divorce. Simplification was supposed to be the hallmark of no-fault divorce, yet it has transformed the relatively simple alimony process (which required some continuing contact) into the more complex one of property valuation and division (which ends all contact at divorce).

The theoretical and practical problem with distributing property from a marital "estate" is that many divorcing couples have few tangible assets to divide. Their most valuable possessions are various claims on future income, such as pensions and returns on human capital. The more risk-averse spouse, usually the woman, might well prefer to accept a lump sum smaller than the expected value of the future benefits. But if there is no way, practically speaking, to reduce these benefits to present value and pay the adjustment in a lump sum, all a court can do is order the higher-earning spouse to pay at some time in the future when he or she realizes the income. This arrangement means that a link between the former spouses continues past the divorce. Such continued contact creates an economic moral hazard: if the wage earner knows that his ex-wife will share in future wage increases, he will take more leisure time. This behavior is socially counterproductive. Yet many jurisdictions, including the US government, assign pension earnings in this way, paying when the pension actually is paid out. Besides, as I demonstrate in the next section, divorce is far from the clean break reformers contemplated.

The emphasis on marriage as a less-than-permanent phenomenon — one from which each spouse must emerge independent and self-sufficient if it ends in divorce — encourages both partners to invest in themselves and their careers rather than in the other spouse or in the marriage itself. Marriage, therefore, comes to look more like cohabitation. A rational wife, for example, frequently makes sure she stays working full time because she may well end up divorced (Parkman 1998). She therefore does not have as much time to devote to herself or to joint enterprises such as housework and children. Both spouses, frenetically busy, may simply "burn out" emotionally, increasing stress when they must do time-intensive household activities (Hochschild 1997).

Thus, women fare worse at divorce (and, sometimes, during marriage) in part because their investments in their husbands are not realized when they should be. The abandonment of permanent alimony in most breakup situations has meant that wives are unable to share in marital wealth. Because they do not receive the proper return on their investments, they do worse today than they did in the age of fault-based divorce. Ultimately, both spouses end up making less-than-optimal investments.

The answer to the question heading this section, therefore, is that spouses should indeed share in earning capacity.

Does the Financial "Clean Break" Theory Work?

No-fault divorce, together with modern maintenance and property distribution laws, was supposed to facilitate easy exit from marriage and create a clean break from the terminated relationship (Ellman 1990). These aspects of current family law typify a contractual view of marriage. Taken together, they make it more difficult for an intact marital relationship to resemble a community in which intimacy is shared (Brinig 1994b).

The malaise that numerous divorced people and commentators today feel about aspects of this difficult topic stems, at least in part, from a sort of cognitive dissonance: the judge says the marriage is over and the ex-partners must begin life anew, but the ex-partners' lives may still be hopelessly entangled. Marital assets are so difficult to split because they are connected to the future as well as the past. By explicitly recognizing investments in such marital assets as earning capacity, one can make marriage less a contract and more a permanent arrangement that does not just "end."

Marriages that continue some form of connection after a divorce often have the tie of minor children, although some childless marriages also fall into this category, especially those that have lasted for many years. As a result, what Starnes (1993) calls the "displaced homemaker" has presented a difficult problem for courts and scholars discussing the role of alimony. In many situations, she (it was almost always the wife in marriages before the introduction of the no-fault regime) married and raised children under a system in which it was expected that she invest in human capital that would aid her in household production, remaining in the home rather than the labor market. If a no-fault divorce ends her marriage without her fault or consent, she may be left with few marketable skills, no reasonable prospect of "rehabilitation," and a life in shambles (Schneider and Brinig 1995, 59).

In many cases, the ex-wife is therefore an obvious candidate for some sort of maintenance payment arrangement — if, for example, the marriage occurred before the introduction of no-fault divorce and produced children who have now grown. Income sharing, which is the arrangement she is likely to end up with, ties the former partners together unless she remarries. Even if there are no offspring, the couple may have shared so much life in common that the marriage itself — memories, perhaps a career, as well as whatever goods the two have accumulated together — becomes a permanent tie (Brinig 1996). Women in this situation constitute the most troublesome category for feminists who want to discourage dependence, but as a transitional and humane matter, they must be protected (Kay 1987). Feminists are then led to ask whether the kind of investment that necessarily creates dependence should be encouraged in the first place.

Perhaps this is the point on which two categories of marriage should be identified for divorce settlement purposes: those that are without children and last only for a short time and those that are "covenant marriages," to use the new terminology, each type having its own divorce rules and compensation schemes.[7] In a longer marriage with children, dependence stemming from a substantial marital investment is likely, and ought to be protected. In such marriages, at least, there can be no clean break.

When minor children are involved, divorce becomes sticky for another reason. The presence of children usually means that at least one caretaker must sacrifice leisure time and employment time for them (Fineman 1995). The financial impact on the caretaker's career is permanent whether the children are born early or late in the marriage, and is estimated at 1.5 percent of total future earnings per year out of the job market (Hoffman 1987; Cox 1984). If the custodial parent must find some kind of flexible employment following the divorce because, for example, money is not available to hire a full-time nanny, then the loss accepted during the marriage (at the time the child is conceived or born) continues after divorce. Further, children necessitate ongoing contact between divorcing parents to accommodate child support and visitation. These connections preclude a clean break. Studies (see Weiss and Willis 1985; Aquilino 1994; Zill, Morrison, and Coir 1993) show, however, that in nearly all

---

7 In the Louisiana and Arizona statutes, for example, divorcing couples elect whether to participate in a no-fault system or one requiring a lengthy separation period plus either counseling or proof of fault. Proposals currently being debated in Virginia and Pennsylvania would make the system not one of choice, but of whether or not the marriage has produced children. For a review of this issue, see Brinig (1998).

cases, the more involved both parents remain, the better off is the child, so that one must question the advantage of a clean break following divorce. Noncustodial fathers who have substantial contact with their children not only enrich their children's lives through their more significant attachment but also tend to be more faithful in paying child support (Seltzer 1997).

As one writer notes, child support payments "chain a divorced couple together," producing a continual conflict: "the father often resents them and the mother is often angry because they seem to her to be too little or too late" (Lobsenz 1971, 140). Further, women more than men seem to bear the burden of their children's suffering, holding themselves responsible for the child's emotional and physical well-being (Whitehead 1997, 63).

All these factors indicate that a marriage, particularly a marriage with children, cannot be simply and cleanly ended. Legal and social policy must therefore recognize that a relationship continues after a divorce. A few policy proposals are briefly outlined at the end of this essay.

How Much Worse Off Are Women under the No-Fault System?

The no-fault liability rule, while it frees couples from the restrictions of fault-based divorce, has proved troublesome for alimony and custody rules, as we have seen. Once a fault on the part of one spouse, which had previously been the trigger for awarding alimony, was no longer necessary for divorce, alimony ceased being a form of damages and became a mechanism to provide for the needy spouse who could not support himself or herself because of a lack of job training or education or the competing burdens of child care. Alimony under the no-fault system was to be rehabilitative, not compensatory. Economic equality was to be secured through property distribution, which, as the Chief Justice of the Supreme Court of Canada has argued (L'Heureux-Dubé 1994), could be made without regard to fault and with a recognition that each spouse contributed to the marriage as a partner.

These changes in the financial aspects of divorce settlements have not, however, completely solved the problems they were meant to address. Since many women do not earn as much as their husbands, they have lower opportunity costs, and frequently remain primary caretakers for their children despite gender-neutral custody laws. Rehabilitative schemes may compensate for a woman's monetary investments in a marriage, but cannot make up for her nonmonetary contributions. A divorced woman also finds it more difficult to remarry than does a man. If their marriages did not last long enough to accumulate significant tangible property, many divorcing women find themselves worse off than divorcing women were before the advent of no-fault divorce. This presumably unintended consequence of no-fault divorce has been noted by many writers (see Brinig and Crafton 1994, 878–879).

A closely related matter concerns the division of property upon divorce. In a fault-based system, the at-fault party is penalized through equitable distribution. In a no-fault jurisdiction, in contrast, any fault is by definition irrelevant. Although the system used for dividing property in a no-fault divorce may be called "equitable distribution," in practice courts have paid attention primarily to *financial* contributions to the marriage when making awards, since valuing homemaking seems difficult. If husbands were more often at fault than were wives, wives should have fared better prior to the no-fault system. There is little evidence, however, that the move to a no-fault system affected the distribution of the matrimonial assets. An early study of no-fault divorces used panel data to show that alimony awards were indeed lower in states that had adopted the new divorce laws (Landes 1978). More recently, however, several writers have reported that property settlements did not change much with the introduction of a no-fault system: an empirical study of divorces in the state of New York found that no-fault settlements differed little from those of the earlier, fault-based, divorce era (Garrison 1991); a national study of panel data found little difference in divorce settlements between fault and no-fault states (Weiss and Willis 1993); and Brinig and Alexeev (1993) compared 1987 divorce settlements in

Virginia (a fault state) and Wisconsin (a no-fault state), and found nearly identical payouts.

Landes' important (1978) theoretical and empirical article on the economics of alimony has been replicated more recently by Garrison (1991), by Weiss and Willis (1993), and by Brinig and Alexeev (1993). These works deal not only with alimony but also with property distribution. To the extent, then, that women and the children in their custody are disadvantaged by divorce, as both US and Canadian empirical studies have found (Peterson 1996; Finnie 1993), the persistent "feminization of poverty" should decrease in jurisdictions undergoing a partial or full return to fault-based divorce. The decrease would come primarily from the lower rates of divorce (since married families are by all accounts financially the best off), and only secondarily from any incremental difference fault-based settlements might bring. Of course, women found to be at fault would do less well, at least where alimony was concerned (Brinig 1997).

The unavoidable financial changes caused by the necessity for the custodial parent to have at least some flexibility in employment, and the loss of the marital household's economies of scale, are exacerbated by the fact that many noncustodial parents do not pay the full amount of child support owed. This fact has sparked a controversy over whether the rate of default on support is the primary problem, or whether the fault lies with a sex-biased system of divorce and custody (Leving 1997, 2). There may be many reasons why noncustodial parents fail to pay support: their distaste for their former spouses may exceed their felt obligation to their children (*Kujawinski v. Kujawinski*;[8] Brinig and Buckley 1996; Schneider and Brinig 1996, 971); they may be involved with the children of new relationships (Seltzer, Schaeffer, and Chang 1989, 55); or they may be unwilling to hand over money when they cannot monitor how it is spent (Weiss and Willis 1985; Lerman 1989, 219, 223). In any case, noncustodial parents (most of whom are fathers) pay a disgracefully small part of their court-ordered support (Zweibel and Shillington 1994; Brinig and Buckley 1998; Lerman 1989, 226). In the United

---

8 *Kujawinski v. Kujawinski*, 376 N.E.2d 1382 (Ill. 1978).

States, only about half make complete payments, even after private and federal collection efforts. Collection rates vary widely, ranging in 1990 from nearly 100 percent in Iowa to 15 percent in Florida — for an examination of this phenomenon, see Brinig and Buckley (1996, 217). Payment levels vary almost as widely in Canada (Pulkingham 1994). Many welfare programs in both countries reduce welfare payments dollar for dollar by the amount of maintenance, and collect support payments directly from the higher-earning spouse.

The custodial parent — most often the woman — loses too, since raising children is not easy. If a child's father effectively abandons the child, the mother must raise the children on her own, a doubly difficult task. In cases where the parents are unable to cooperate on issues such as child support and visitation, the resulting strain hurts both mother and child.

Social Effects

Although the severe social stigma that used to cling to divorce has disappeared since the no-fault "divorce revolution," a divorce may in fact still reduce social esteem, especially for older women in Canada (Davies 1988). For many women who married before the introduction of no-fault divorce, social life revolves around their husbands' social acquaintances.[9] Older women are also the most likely to be economically dependent on their husbands (Cohen 1987). Even couple who have married more recently are likely to socialize mostly with other married couples, so that if they divorce the social group must "choose sides." In the readjusted group of friends, women who remain married may feel competition from the woman who is divorced. If the divorced wife is the custodial parent, she now faces babysitting costs if she wants to go out with her friends — costs that in marriage were subsidized by her husband.

In the 1970s, rates of remarriage began to decline in the United States, dropping by 38 percent for divorced women between 1970 and 1990. Divorced women, except for those aged 20 to 24, are less

---

9 *Kozlowski v. Kozlowski*, 80 N.J. 378, 403 A.2d 902 (1979) gives an example, although it involves a cohabiting couple.

likely to remarry than divorced men (Clarke 1995, 3). Further, half of these new marriages end in divorce before the children of the first marriage turn 18 (Whitehead 1997, 96).

Former wives and their children are also discomfited by the residential instability that accompanies divorce (ibid., 93). Although US Bureau of the Census statistics show that about a fifth of US households make a substantial move during any two-year period, a disproportionate number of dislocations are caused by divorce (United States 1995). One measure of this instability is the increasing number of cases filed by noncustodial divorced parents wanting to block the custodial parent's move out of the area (American Law Institute 1997, section 2.20, Reporter's Notes 377–389; Levmore 1998). Most, but not all, of these suits are brought by fathers seeking to maintain stable relationships with their children. In such cases, former wives may retort that they lost their freedom to move for employment, child care, or social reasons, while their husbands did not. Similar objections have been raised to suits by noncustodial divorced fathers who attempt to regulate the religious upbringing of their children. Even if the parents agreed before the marriage that the child would be brought up in a particular religious tradition, the courts are unlikely to decide in favor of such suits (Silbaugh 1996, 30).

In sum, although society no longer attaches stigma to divorce, detachment from marriage does not hold many social advantages for women. Nonetheless, all the negative consequences divorce holds for women discussed so far seem to be counteracted by a very strong psychological gain, at least for women who initiate the divorce.

Psychological Effects

Not surprisingly, the spouse who sues for divorce most often feels best about the process and the result. In most cases, it is the woman who brings suit (Friedman and Percival 1976, 69; Gunter and Johnson 1978; Brinig 1993, 466), perhaps because if the husband leaves, the wife must begin divorce proceedings to enforce his support duties and formalize custody arrangements (the so-called first mover advantage) (Brinig and Carbone 1988, 863–864). However, while they show initial enthusiasm for the divorce, in the long run divorced wives tend to have a much harder time in many objective ways than do their former husbands.

Americans sometimes associate divorce with psychological liberation. In fact, one study reveals that after leaving a marriage more than half of the women in the sample, particularly those separated for less than a year, were pleased to have "the freedom to be [themselves]," and felt "more like a free person" (Riessman 1990,165). Some strains of feminism hold that women suffer from low self-esteem, lack assertiveness, are overeager to please, and sometimes show an excessive concern for the needs of others; thus, if divorce promotes greater self-confidence and self-awareness, it can reduce psychological inequalities between men and women (Whitehead 1997, 78; Mahoney 1996). Furthermore, women seem to benefit from egalitarian, emotionally satisfying marriages, while men benefit most from traditional, specialized marriages, even those that are emotionally less fulfilling (Nock forthcoming).

The major objection feminists are likely to have about more restrictive divorce laws is that such laws would enhance the power imbalances these writers find in so many current marriages (Wax 1997). Women who are deeply troubled in their relationships and who would otherwise obtain no-fault divorces might not be able to prove fault, or might be afraid to seek a divorce based on fault grounds, particularly cruelty. Because they generally have less secure financial positions than their husbands (ibid., 4–12), they might not be able to get good legal assistance for the divorce proceedings, including the expert witnesses they might need to prove cruelty or intoxication, for example. These women might therefore have to "trade" property or other financial resources in order to simply escape. Or, some feminists claim, they might have to endure increasing amounts of abuse from their husbands. How often such "bad marriages" occur is an open empirical question; Virginia data for 1995 show that only about 5 percent of divorces in that state cited cruelty, one of the fault possibilities available, as grounds for the suit. Some feminist writers, notably Demie Kurz (1995), claim that half of divorcing couples have experienced marital violence.

Conclusion

Women, and the minor children who live with them, suffer significant financial harm as a result of divorce. They lose more than their former husbands, perhaps because they lose in the bargaining process itself, but more likely because the man's human capital (earning capacity), which is enhanced during the marriage, is more portable than theirs (housework and child care skills), and because as they are usually the custodial parents they will have to work at lower-paying employment because they require flexibility.

Divorce also hurts women socially, even though it no longer carries the stigma it once did. In addition to the loss of social station that may accompany their financial losses, women are less likely than their former husbands to remarry.

Despite these negatives, some divorced women seem remarkably happy about their situations. Kurz, in a survey of 129 randomly selected divorced women in Pennsylvania, found that 61 percent had positive feelings about their divorces, while another 12 percent were ambivalent (1995, 188–189). Similarly, Braver, Whitley, and Ng (1993) found that both wives and husbands identified wives as the "dumpers" in a large percentage of the divorces (see also Scott 1990). Perhaps this paradoxical result is related to what Allen says (in this volume) about the "theft," or transfer, of resources to men (during marriage as well as after it) that has accompanied no-fault divorce. In other words, perhaps women leave marriages because their husbands have mistakenly extracted too great a share of the benefits of the relationship, or perhaps wives are unhappy because, as Parkman (1998) finds, they must work so hard to preserve their marriages and to insure against their ending. Divorce, even with the increase in responsibility that it brings, at least allows women the illusion of choice. Women who file for divorce obtain a "first mover" advantage, as petitioners are often able to secure custodial and other rights for the future. For women, unlike for men, the divorce process secures rewards that are not primarily financial.

It is clear that the current system of easy, no-fault divorce has major flaws, often leaving women — especially those with children

— in dire straits financially and with losses to their earning potential that most will never recoup, however much emotional relief they must feel on release from an unhappy marriage. The notion that divorces can end relationships completely with a "clean break" is false, and legal and social policy should recognize this fact.

Laws must be rewritten to encourage investments during marriage (in finances and in children) that will reap rewards regardless of whether or not the legal relationship ends and the spouses are free to remarry. At minimum, laws that need amending include those allowing recoupment of earning capacity and joint custody. They might also include laws making divorce itself more difficult, for example, through requiring mutual consent.

On the other hand, since women seem to be the ones seeking relief from marriage through divorce, a more ambitious reform program from the woman's perspective would aim at marriage instead of divorce. One such proposal would treat household work in much the same way as is employment outside the home: as a basis both for taxation and for eventual pensions (Staudt 1994). More commonly, feminist writers suggest that husbands and wives should be able to contract explicitly about financial rewards for household services (Silbaugh 1996; Wax 1998). Less drastic results, which might change the outlook on marital investment, would compensate women through shares in their husbands' enhanced earning capacities on divorce (Brinig 1997; Parkman 1995). Finally, many of the troubling results outlined in this essay might be ameliorated with changes in custody laws. Brinig and Buckley (1998) find that increasing noncustodial fathers' expected contact with their children (through joint custody or more extensive visitation) not only encourages more faithful payment of child support, but also reduces the divorce rate.

References

Alfini, James J., et al. 1994. "What Happens When Mediation Is Institutionalized? To the Parties, Practitioners, and Host Institutions." Panel discussion. *Ohio State Journal on Dispute Resolution* 94 (9): 307–332.

Allen, Douglas. 1992. "'What Does She See in Him?' The Effect of Sharing on the Choice of Spouse." *Economic Inquiry* 11: 57–67.

American Law Institute. 1997. *Principles of the Law of Family Dissolution.* Preliminary Draft 7. Chestnut Hill, Penn.: American Law Institute.

Aquilino, William S. 1994. "Impact of Childhood Family Disruption on Young Adults' Relationships with Parents." *Journal of Marriage and the Family* 56: 295–313.

Bane, Mary Jo, and David Ellwood. 1986. "Slipping Into and Out of Poverty: The Dynamics of Spells." *Journal of Human Resources* 21: 1–23.

Becker, Gary S. 1965. "On the Allocation of Time." *Economics Journal* 75 (September): 493–517.

Bianchi, S., and E. McArthur. 1991. "Family Disruption and Economic Hardship: The Short-Run Picture for Children." United States, Department of Commerce, Bureau of the Census, Current Population Reports, Series P-70, No. 23. Washington, DC: US Government Printing Office.

Blau, David M., and Phillip K. Robbins. 1989. "Fertility, Employment and Child-Care Costs." *Demography* 26: 289–299.

Braver, Sanford L., Marnie Whitley, and Christine Ng. 1993. "Who Divorced Whom? Methodological and Theoretical Issues." *Journal of Divorce and Remarriage* 20 (1, 2): 1–19.

Brinig, Margaret F. 1993. "The Law and Economics of No-Fault Divorce." *Family Law Quarterly* 26: 453–470.

———. 1994. "Status, Contract and Covenant." *Cornell Law Review* 84: 1573–1602.

———. 1995. "Does Mediation Systematically Disadvantage Women?" *William and Mary Journal of Women's Rights* 2: 1–34.

———. 1996. "The Family Franchise." *Utah Law Review* 1996: 393–428.

———. 1997. "Property Distribution Physics: The Talisman of Time and Middle Class Law." *Family Law Quarterly* 31: 93–118.

———. 1998. "The Law and Economics of Covenant Marriage." *Gender Issues* 1: 1–30.

———, and Michael Alexeev. 1993. "Trading at Divorce: Preferences, Legal Rules and Transaction Costs." *Ohio State Journal on Dispute Resolution* 8: 279–297.

———, and F.H. Buckley. 1996. "The Market for Deadbeats." *Journal of Legal Studies* 25: 201–232.

———, and F.H. Buckley. 1998. "Joint Custody: Monitoring and Bonding Theories." *Indiana Law Journal* 73: 393–427.

———, and June Carbone. 1988. " The Reliance Interest in Marriage and Divorce." *Tulane Law Review* 62: 870–882.

———, and Steven Crafton. 1994. "Marriage and Opportunism." *Journal of Legal Studies* 23: 869–894.

Bryan, Penelope E. 1992. "Killing Us Softly: Divorce Mediation and the Politics of Power." *Buffalo Law Review* 40: 441–523.

Carbone, June. 1994. "Income Sharing: Redefining the Family in Terms of Community." *Houston Law Review* 31: 359–415.

Chambers, David M. 1995. "Fathers, the Welfare System, and the Virtues and Perils of Child-Support Enforcement." *Virginia Law Review* 81: 2575–2605.

Clarke, Sally C. 1995. "Advance Report of Final Marriage Statistics, 1989 and 1990." *Monthly Vital Statistics Report* (National Center for Health Statistics) 43 (12).

Cohen, Lloyd. 1995. "Marriage, Divorce, and Quasi-Rents: 'I Gave Him the Best Year of My Life'." *Legal Studies* 16: 267–323.

Da Vonza, Julie, and Omar M. Rahman. 1994. "American Families: Trends and Correlates." *Population Index* 59 (3): 350–386.

Davies, Christine. 1988. "Divorce and the Older Woman in Canada." *The Cambrian Law Review* 19: 17–25.

Duncan, Greg J., and Saul D. Hoffman. 1985. "A Reconsideration of the Economic Consequences of Marital Dissolution." *Demography* 22 (November): 485–497 .

Ellis, Jane. 1992. "Surveying the Terrain: A Review Essay of Divorce Reform at the Crossroads." *Stanford Law Review* 44: 471–508.

Ellman, Ira M. 1990. "The Theory of Alimony." *California Law Review* 77: 1–81.

Fineman, Martha A. 1995. *The Neutered Mother and Other Twentieth-Century Disasters*. New York: Routledge.

Finnie, Ross. 1993. "Women, Men, and the Economic Consequences of Divorce: Evidence from Canadian Longitudinal Data." *Canadian Review of Sociology and Anthropology* 30: 205–241.

Galerneau, Diane. 1998. "Income after Separation: People without Children." *Perspectives on Labour and Income* 10 (2): 32–37. Statistics Canada cat. 75-001-XPE.

———, and Jim Sturrock. 1997. "Family Income after Separation." *Perspectives on Labour and Income* 9 (2): 18–28. Statistics Canada cat. 75-001-XPE.

Garrison, Marsha. 1991. "Good Intentions Gone Awry: The Impact of New York's Equitable Distribution Law on Divorce Outcomes." *Brooklyn Law Review* 57: 621–754.

Grillo, Tina. 1991. "The Mediation Alternative: Process Dangers for Women." *Yale Law Journal* 100: 1545–1610.

Gronau, Reuben. 1980. "Home Production — A Forgotten Industry." *Review of Economics and Statistics* 62: 408–416.

Gunter, B.G., and D.P. Johnson. 1978. "Divorce Filing as Role Behavior: Effect of No-Fault on Divorce Filing Patterns." *Journal of Marriage and Family* 40: 571–587.

L'Heureux-Dubé, Claire. 1994. "Economic Consequences of Divorce: A View from Canada." *Houston Law Review* 31 (Summer): 451–498.

Hochschild, Arlie. 1997. *The Time Bind: When Work Becomes Home and Home Becomes Work*. New York: Henry Holt and Company.

Ilich, John, and Barbara S. Jones. 1980. *Successful Negotiating Skills for Women*. Reading, Mass.: Addison-Wesley.

Kay, Herma Hill. 1987. "An Appraisal of California's No-Fault Divorce Law." *California Law Review* 75: 291–319.

Krauskopf, Joan M. 1980. "Recompense for Financing Spouse's Education: Legal Protection for the Marital Investor in Human Capital." *Kansas Law Review* 28: 379–417.

Kurz, Demie. 1995. *For Richer, For Poorer: Mothers Confront Divorce*. New York: Routledge.

Landes, Elisabeth. 1978. "The Economics of Alimony." *Journal of Legal Studies* 7: 35–78.

Lerman, Robert I. 1989. "Child Support Policies." In Phoebe H. Cottingham and David T. Ellwood, eds., *Welfare Policy for the 1990s*. Cambridge, Mass.: Harvard University Press.

Leving, Jeffery M., with Kenneth A. Dachman. 1997. *Fathers' Rights*. New York: Basic Books.

Levmore, Saul. "Joint Custody and Strategic Behavior." *Indiana Law Review* 73: 429–440.

Lobsenz, Norman M. 1971. "How Divorced Young Mothers Learn to Stand Alone." *Redbook*, November 1971, p. 140.

McLanahan, Sara, and Irwin Garfinkel. 1989. "Single Mothers, the Underclass, and Social Policy." *Annals of the American Academy of Political and Social Sciences* 501: 92–104.

————, and Gary D. Sandefur. 1994. *Growing Up with a Single Parent: What Hurts, What Helps*. Cambridge, Mass.: Harvard University Press.

Mahoney, Kathleen E. 1996. "Gender Issues in Family Law: Leveling the Playing Field for Women." *Family and Conciliation Courts Review* 34: 198–218.

Menkel-Meadow, Carrie. 1985. "Portia in a Different Voice: Speculation on a Woman's Lawyering Process." *Berkeley Women's Law Journal* 1: 39–65.

Mnookin, Robert, and Lewis Kornhauser. 1979. "Bargaining in the Shadow of the Law: The Case of Divorce." *Yale Law Journal* 77: 959–998.

Nock, Steven L. Forthcoming. *Marriage in Men's Lives*. Oxford: Oxford University Press.

Parkman, Allen. 1992. *No Fault Divorce: What Went Wrong?* Boulder, Col.: Westview Press.

————. 1995. "Human Capital as Property in Celebrity Divorces." *Family Law Quarterly* 29: 141–169.

———. 1998. "Why Are Married Women Working So Hard?" *International Review of Law and Economics* 18 (1): 41–50.

Peters, H. Elizabeth. 1986. "Marriage and Divorce: Informational Constraints and Private Contracting." *American Economic Review* 76: 437–454.

Peterson, Richard R. 1996. "A Re-evaluation of the Economic Consequences of Divorce." *American Sociological Review* 61 (3): 528–536.

Pulkingham, Jane. 1994. "Private Troubles, Private Solutions: Poverty among Divorced Women and the Politics of Support Enforcement and Child Custody Determination." *Canadian Journal of Law and Society* 9 (Fall): 73–97.

Regan, Milton C. 1992. *Family Law and the Pursuit of Intimacy.* New York: New York University Press.

Riessman, Catherine Kohler. 1990. *Divorce Talk: Men and Women Make Sense of Personal Relationships.* New Brunswick, NJ: Rutgers University Press.

———, and Naomi Gerstel. 1985. "Marital Dissolution and Health; Do Males or Females Have Greater Risk?" *Social Science and Medicine* 20 (6): 627–635.

Rivkin, Janet. 1984. "Mediation from a Feminist Perspective." *Law and Inequality* 2: 21–35.

Schneider, Carl E., and Margaret F. Brinig. 1996. *An Invitation to Family Law.* St. Paul, Minn.: West Publishing Company.

Scott, Elizabeth S. 1990. "Rational Decisionmaking in Marriage and Divorce." *Virginia Law Review* 76: 9–94.

———, and Robert Scott. 1998. "Marriage as a Long-Term Relational Contract." *Virginia Law Review* 84: 101–176.

Seltzer, Judith A. 1997. "Father by Law: Effects of Joint Legal Custody on Nonresident Fathers' Involvement with Children." National Survey of Families and Households Working Paper 75. Madison: University of Wisconsin, Center for Demography and Ecology.

———, Nora C. Schaeffer, and Chang Hong-wen. 1989. "Family Ties after Divorce: The Relationship between Visiting and Paying Child Support." *Journal of Marriage and the Family* 51 (November): 1013–1032.

Shaffer, Martha. 1988. "Divorce Mediation: A Feminist Perspective." *University of Toronto Law Journal* 46: 162–200.

Silbaugh, Katherine. 1996. "Turning Work into Love: Legal Responses to Home Labor." *Northwestern University Law Review* 91: 1–86.

Singer, Jana. 1997. "Husbands, Wives, and Human Capital: Why the Shoe Won't Fit." *Family Law Quarterly* 31: 119–131.

Starnes, Cynthia. 1993. "Divorce and the Displaced Homemaker: A Discourse on Playing with Dolls, Partnership Buyouts, and Dissociation under No-Fault." *University of Chicago Law Review* 60: 67–139.

Staudt, Nancy. 1996. "Taxing Housework." *Georgetown Law Journal* 84: 1571–1647.

Umberson, Debra, and Camille L. Williams. 1993. "Divorced fathers; Parental Role Strain and Psychological Distress." *Journal of Family Issues* 14 (3): 378–400.

United States. 1995. Department of Commerce. Bureau of the Census. "Annual Geographic Mobility Rates, by Type of Movement, 1947–94." *Current Population Survey* (August).

Wardle, Lynn D. 1991. "No-Fault Divorce and the Divorce Conundrum." *Brigham Young University Law Review* 1991: 79–142.

Wax, Amy S. 1998. "Bargaining in the Shadow of the Market: Is There a Future for Egalitarian Marriage?" *Virginia Law Review* 84 (4): 509–672.

Weigers, Wanda. "Economic Analysis of Law and Private Ordering: A Feminist Critique." *University of Toronto Law Journal* 42: 170–206.

Weiss, Yoram, and Robert J. Willis. 1985. "Children as Collective Goods and Divorce Settlements." *Journal of Labor Economics* 3: 268–292.

Whitehead, Barbara Dafoe. 1997. *The Divorce Culture*. New York: Alfred Knopf.

Wu, Zheng. 1994. "Remarriage in Canada: A Social Exchange Perspective." *Journal of Divorce and Remarriage* 21: 191–224.

Zill, Nicholas, Donna Ruane Morrison, and Mary Jo Coiro. 1993. "Long-Term Effects of Parental Divorce on Parent-Child Relationships, Adjustment, and Achievement in Young Adulthood." *Journal of Family Psychology* 7 (1): 91–103.

Zweibel, Ellen, and Richard Shillington. 1994. *Child Support Policy: Income Tax Treatment and Child Support Guidelines*. Waterloo, Ont.: Wilfrid Laurier University, Faculty of Social Work, Centre for Social Welfare Studies.

A New Class of
Disadvantaged Children:
Reflections on "Easy" Divorce

Donald S. Moir

Thirty years ago Canada abandoned law that sought to sustain the institution of marriage, to the extent the civil law could.[1] The old law was replaced by the federal *Divorce Act* of 1968, which, as it developed, looked on marriage not as an institution[2] but as no more than an essentially private relationship between adults terminable at the will of either.

It seems doubtful that this outcome was the intent of the drafters of the 1968 act.[3] Yet, in practice, it became the fact. The change

---

I use the phrase *"easy" divorce* in preference to the more common *no-fault divorce* as being the more accurate description. What distinguished "easy" divorce from what preceded it was recognition of divorce by consent of the parties; in practice, a unilateral decision to divorce had become lawful, although it still required the formalistic imprimatur of the court. Divorce itself may be "easy" under the new law, but the incidents of it under federal and provincial jurisdiction, especially in the division of property and the allocation of custody and support, are more difficult, complex, and disputatious than they were under the old law. The strictures of the old law were sometimes evaded. Cynics said of it that there were two grounds for divorce: adultery and perjury.

1 Principally, the English *Divorce and Matrimonial Causes Act* of 1857. Quebec and Newfoundland had no law of divorce until passage of the federal act in 1968. Ontario had none until 1930. In Quebec and Newfoundland (and Ontario until 1930), divorce was by petition to the Senate — a costly and rare proceeding.

2 I use the term *institution* throughout to reflect the fact that the interests in a marriage extend to the children of that marriage, the extended family, the community, society, and the state. That is, marriage brings into being an organization to serve interests beyond those of the two parties.

3 See, for example, the Report of the Special Joint Committee of the Senate and House of Commons (Canada 1967b). A never-followed case (*Harding v Harding*,...

was profound. The old law had recognized the stake of children, the extended family, society, and the state in a marriage; that is, that marriage was institutional and dissoluble only for grave, objectively determinable cause. Under the new law, marriage became no more than a private two-party "contract" dissoluble at the will of either wife or husband.

The change in the law of divorce was reinforced by all the provinces' adoption, in the late 1970s and early 1980s, of legislation to govern the division of property and awards of custody and of spousal and child support.[4] These laws' broad remedies are available on the unchallengeable application of either spouse.[5]

In 1985, a new federal *Divorce Act* replaced the 1968 act. In summary, the 1985 act provides for divorce on the grounds of "marriage breakdown": adultery, cruelty, or separation for one year. In practice, it contemplates termination at the will of either party; that is, breakdown on the grounds of separation can be the choice of one party.

The notable aspect of the 1968 and 1985 acts is their disregard of the interests and welfare of children. In the 154-page 1967 report of Parliament's special joint committee on divorce, less than a page re-

---

Note 3 - cont'd.

...(1972) 8 RFL 236) noted that the new law changed the nature of the marriage covenant, but that recognition did not permeate the case law for some years.

4   It is the combined effect of the *Divorce Act* of 1985 and the provincial family property legislation that has given rise to the now-large divorce industry — that agglomeration of judges, lawyers, accountants, psychiatrists, psychologists, social workers, evaluators, economists, appraisers, actuaries, tax specialists, mediators, and so on needed under the legislation to serve the industry.

5   The public clamor for revised matrimonial property legislation came about principally because of a misinterpretation of the Supreme Court of Canada's 1974 decision in *Murdoch v Murdoch* [1974] 1 W.W.R. 36 (SCC), which was later superseded by other decisions of the Court. Although Mrs. Murdoch had worked for 25 years on small prairie farms together with her husband and children, she did not hold title to the property, and the Court denied her any trust interest in the farm. Mrs. Murdoch was a Catholic and morally reluctant to petition for divorce. Had she done so, she could have sought half the farm as lump-sum maintenance. The public was, however, correctly outraged at Mrs. Murdoch's plight and saw the remedy in revised provincial marital property legislation, rather than divorce.

fers to children, entreating the court (without legislative direction) "to see that the members of the family do not suffer the rupture of family life more than is necessary" (Canada 1967b, 151). The principal concern is to do no more than regulate the termination of relationships between autonomous adults; under the legislation, children are but adjuncts — neither participants in nor protected by an institution. In proposing to the House of Commons what became the 1968 act, then justice minister Pierre Trudeau said nothing about children (Canada 1967a, 5083–5089). More remarkably, when then justice minister John Crosbie proposed the 1985 act, he said nothing about consequences for children (Canada 1985, 4932–4936); by that time there was strong evidence of the harm being done to children by the divorce of their parents.

The legislators had discounted what was and remains fundamental to Canadian society: marriage is the principal *institution* for raising children (Popenoe 1996, 1–51). If it is undermined, children will suffer and are suffering. In the end, society and the state will be afflicted and are being afflicted.

In following the legislative trail, I do not suggest that the civil law is omnipotent. It is not. Except when the law is invoked, adults conduct their intimate affairs in light of an interrelated web of influences, cultural, social, and economic, of which the law is one strand. Marriage is a creation more of the culture than of the law.[6] As I argue in this paper, marriage at law differs from the culture's perception of it.[7] Canada's present law of divorce is countercultural. Weitzman is correct in her observation that it is the law of divorce with its ancillary remedies that defines the nature of the marriage covenant at law (1985, 366). The culture's perception of marriage may be something else. In fact, there is little evidence that the changed law was the re-

---

6 In these comments on the interrelation and dichotomy of the law and the culture (and throughout the paper), I am indebted to, *inter alia*, Barbara Dafoe Whitehead, *The Divorce Culture* (1997); and Mary Ann Glendon, *Abortion and Divorce in Western Law* (1987).

7 Compare the words of the marriage vows, religious and civil, and the law (*Bracklow v Bracklow* (1995), 13 RFL (4th) 184, (Boyle, J.); June 10, 1997, CA 0200133, BCCA; leave to appeal to SCC granted).

sult of a broad change in social attitudes. There is evidence that the changed law was the product of a limited elite, including academics and lawyers, and of the therapeutic culture that, in turn, enmeshed the mainline Protestant churches.[8] Moreover, there is reason to speculate that a majority of the public may remain traditional in its concepts of marriage and the family.[9]

Contemporaneously with the abandonment of the concept of marriage as an institution and the exaltation of the autonomy of adults over the welfare of children has come a roughly fivefold increase in the rate of divorce,[10] a new class of disadvantaged children — the children of divorce — and a concomitant cluster of social ills.

---

8 Jacob documents this point for the United States in his *Silent Revolution* (1988). In the absence of the same measure of documentation, one can reasonably suppose that influences in Canada were much the same. Jacob makes it clear that "the divorce revolution" (the title of Weitzman's book) was a "silent revolution" that did not concern, involve, or consult the public — not even the then-nascent women's movement.

9 A recent study by Statistics Canada (cat. 11-008-XPE, 11) finds that Generation Xers (ages 15–26) — those Canadians who as children have experienced "easy" divorce — have a more traditional view of marriage as a lifelong commitment than do baby boomers (ages 30–49) or their elders (ages 50 and over). A National Opinion Research Center survey reports that in 1982 a majority thought that divorce laws should be more strict (1982, 162). A recent US survey finds a high level of sexual fidelity among both married men and women (Lauman 1996). Marriage remains a major festival in much of our society.

10 The rate of divorce is a vexing and disputed subject, partly because analysts express that in different ways. Those differences, though relevant to precise determinations, are of little relevance in this context. For convenience, I express the rate here in the number of divorces per 1,000 population.
    Statistics Canada notes:

    A small proportion of [the] impressive rise [in the rate of divorce since 1968] is attributable to the growth in the number of married couples. A much larger portion results from a higher propensity among couples to divorce, and the increasing ease of obtaining a divorce. (1992, 53.)

    The rate of divorce in Canada was 0.548 in 1968; 1.938 in 1970; 2.59 in 1980; 2.94 in 1990 (Statistics Canada 1993, 17); and 2.7 in 1994 (Statistics Canada, cat. 84-214-XPB [1995], 4). In considering the changes, note the bulges in the rates following passage of the 1968 and 1985 acts.
    Having reached its apogee of 3.551 in 1987, the rate of divorce is now somewhat reduced and appears to be on a plateau. No one knows whether this decrease reflects a reduced propensity to divorce or changes in the rate of marriage and in the age of the population.

Our society and its economy afflict children in many ways with far-reaching consequences. "Easy" divorce is one such affliction. The focus of this paper is law reform. I argue that the law influences the rate of divorce and, further, that unless the law of divorce is corrected, other measures to address the afflictions of children will be impeded, if not thwarted. Furthermore, any correction of the law of divorce is achievable in a reasonable time without requiring the spectrum of remedies needed to reduce the other afflictions of children, many of which flow from the loss of family structure.[11]

I propose that we consider the law of divorce (remembering that it defines the nature of the marriage covenant at law) from a new perspective: the perspective of children, not that of adults. To put the same thought in another way, the law should recognize and sustain marriage as an institution whose primary function is the raising of children. It is beyond the scope of this paper to propose specific legislative revision. I do no more than suggest the nature of legislation that would put the interest of children first while, arguably, enhancing the institution for adults.

The law of the separating family, federal and provincial, is beset with complexities and contradictions. It is a realm of the "expert." This paper is no more than an overview, an attempt to make plain the follies of present law and to prompt discussion of their correction. As an overview, it is necessarily terse, without the detailed explanation that individual subjects may warrant.

The Children of Divorce

The children of divorce are a new class of disadvantaged children. In 1995, the parents of 47,118 Canadian children were divorced (Statistics Canada, cat. 213-XPB [1995], 20). Almost 50,000 additional children *a year* are now being exposed to risks encountered on their parents' divorce, risks they would not face if their families remain in-

---

11 The term *family structure* has entered the language. It seeks to distinguish among intact families of biological parents and children, separated or single-parent families, and stepfamilies. The first offers the best chance of optimal child development. I take any departure from that configuration to be a loss.

tact. All of these children are at risk (although some are escaping risk from families in which there has been abuse or undue turmoil). Studies in the United States[12] suggest that all of these children will be delayed in their development; that a significant minority — one-third[13] in samples analyzed by Wallerstein and Kelly, Hetherington, and Guidubaldi — will be chronically disadvantaged, cognitively, socially and financially (but see Amato (1994).[14]

The longitudinal studies of the children of divorce are few and must be read carefully with regard to the methodology, nature of the survey, sample size, gender, age, and so on. From the available data, one cannot be sure of the proportion of children of divorce who are chronically disabled in their functioning; it appears, however, to be a significant minority of the total population of children.[15]

Compared with children in intact families, children whose parents have divorced are much more likely to drop out of school, to engage in premarital sex, and to become pregnant outside of marriage. These effects are found even after taking into account parental and marital characteristics before the divorce (Furstenberg and Teitler 1994). The data show that children of single parents are twice as likely as children from intact families to be delinquent or criminal;

---

12 See Wallerstein and Kelly 1980; Hetherington 1984; 1989; Hetherington, Cox, and Cox 1982; 1985; Guidubaldi 1988; Guidubaldi et al. 1983; Guidubaldi and Perry 1985; Guidubaldi, Perry, and Clemenshaw 1984.

13 In Wallerstein and Kelly, this proportion was noted five years after divorce. Later, at 10 to 15 years after divorce, it was found that some children who had done reasonably well at the five-year mark had become symptomatic (Wallerstein and Blakeslee 1989). For further difficulties 25 years after divorce, see Wallerstein and Lewis (1998); and Madam Justice L'Heureux-Dubé (1998).

14 For a review of four of these studies, see Moir (1992). For reference to other studies, see Moir (1993; 1996). Few comparable studies have been done in Canada. I assume, however, that society, the economy, and law in the United States are sufficiently similar to those in Canada to make it probable that consequences for children in the two countries are similar.

15 I stress that the data throughout are in the aggregate. Notwithstanding that children of divorce face risks that children brought up in intact families do not, one cannot assume that a given child of divorce is necessarily condemned to chronic impairment. Admirable children of admirable single parents in favorable circumstances can and do beat the odds. Further, some children can benefit from the divorce of their parents when there has been undue family turmoil or abuse.

that children brought up by other than their biological parents[16] are twice as likely to do poorly in school and one and a half times more likely to have difficulty in joining the job market; and that girls are twice as likely to have teenage pregnancies.

All this is so even when the data are controlled for race, income, education of parents, age, and place of residence (McLanahan and Sandefur, *Growing Up with a Single Parent* [1994, esp. p. 91]). For example, a study of 17,000 children controlled for age, sex, race, maternal employment, and family income reports that children living with a parent and a step-parent or only a divorced mother are 20 to 30 percent more likely to have an accident, 40 to 50 percent more likely to repeat a grade at school, and 70 percent more likely to be expelled from school than are children living with both biological parents.[17] In *Putting Children First: A Progressive Family Policy for the 1990's*, Kamarck and Galston, drawing on a spectrum of studies, find:

> The relationship between family structure and crime is so strong that controlling for family configuration erases the relationship between race and crime and between low income and crime. (1990.)

Divorce is associated with increased rates of poverty, crime, and mental and physical illness for both adults and children and increased mortality in adults (Tucker et al. 1997).

The list of facts is almost endless: children who exhibit violent misbehavior at school are 11 times as likely not to live with their fathers (Sheline, Skipper, and Broadhead 1994); the proportion of single-parent households in a community predicts its rates of violent crime and burglary, but the community's poverty level does not (Smith and Jarjoura 1988); 72 percent of adolescent murderers grew up without fathers (Cornell et al. 1987); and 70 percent of juveniles in

---

16 Children adopted in early infancy are so small a proportion of the total that they do not appear in the data. This paper equates infants adopted early with those who live with their biological parents.

17 Deborah Dawson, National Center for Health Statistics, May 1990, as reported in "Non-traditional homes can hurt kids' health," *Wall Street Journal*, July 5, 1990.

state reform institutions grew up in single- or no-parent situations
(Beck, Kline, and Greenfield 1988).

Remedies

There can be no doubt that with high rates of divorce has come an
historically new and large class of disadvantaged children: the children of divorce. Professionals are not unaware of these children.
Elaborate, expensive, and problematic remedies to ameliorate their
plight exist in all provinces. However, these remedies treat the
symptoms, not the disease.

The principal remedies sought are through therapeutic intervention and various regimes of custody and access.

Therapy

The early reformers in the United States, followed by those in Canada, assumed that divorce was a neutral factor for children. In this,
they were guided by the clinicians[18] of the time, some of whom,
without any evidence beyond wishful thinking, touted divorce as
good for children.[19] The clinicians were wrong. The proponents of
"easy" divorce among them were not dissuaded by the accumulat-
ing evidence of the harm being done to children of divorce. They
proposed (and still propose) "easy" divorce but with therapeutic intervention to "correct" the distress of children whose parents divorce. Indeed, some say that children who have difficulty adjusting
to the loss of a parent through divorce are clinically impaired and in

---

18 Here and throughout, *clinicians* refers to mental health professionals of whatever
stripe: psychiatrists, psychologists, social workers, and so on.

19 For example, Gettleman and Markowitz claim that children can learn from step-
parents to "break away from excessive dependence on their biological parents"
(1974, 86–87); Krantzler says that children of divorce can learn "more co-operation
and respect, more regard for differences as well as similarities" and "grow into
the unique individuals they are capable of becoming" (1974); and Kraus (1979,
111) speculates that increased parental personal autonomy will lead to the development of better relationships with children.

need of therapy — therapy, they imply, that they are competent to give (see Dineen, *Manufacturing Victims* [1998]).

As a result, all jurisdictions in Canada and the United States have well-intentioned, elaborate programs of court-connected and private therapy, conciliation, joint custody, mediation, and the like.[20] There is no evidence of their efficacy beyond the well-intentioned endorsements of the clinicians who conduct them. There is no evidence that such programs resolve the harm to children of divorce in the long run. Wallerstein and Lewis (1998) report evidence that the harm persists as late as 25 years after the divorce of the parents.

Custody and Access

Although the welfare of children is not a consideration at law in the decision to divorce, it is sought to be a consideration, although adjunctive, in the determination of children's living arrangements after parents separate. Wallerstein and Kelly (1980) say that, in their sample of children of divorce, those who did best were those who maintained the closest relationship with their noncustodial parents.[21]

In slow response to Wallerstein and Kelly's findings and the understandable promptings of fathers' rights activists, the *Divorce Act* of 1985 and the practice have evolved. It now appears to be an article of faith in most jurisdictions and before most judges that the court ought to do what it can to maintain relationships between children and their nonresidential parent.[22]

However desirable that concept, it can seldom be given effect over time. A court can do little to maintain relationships beyond the short run. Furstenberg and Nord (1985) find that a majority of children had not seen their separated fathers in a year; that 20 percent

---

20 It is beyond the scope of this paper to analyze each of these differing interventions.

21 This simplistic statement is at risk of obscuring the complexities and interrelations of the many variables involved — complexities the authors did not ignore.

22 I cannot detail here the various measures of joint custody, parenting plans, and the like and their efficacy. There is, however, a substantial literature.

had not seen him in five years; and that when any relationship existed,[23] it was social, not instrumental.[24]

To all intents and purposes, divorce condemns most children to loss of a parent. Children who lose a parent by death appear to have significantly less trauma than if the loss is by divorce (Whitehead 1997, 98, 110). In a 1992 study titled "Psychological and Structural Factors Contributing to the Disengagement of Non-Custodial Fathers after Divorce," Kruk reports that a principal reason for divorced fathers' dropping out is their frustration and agony over a truncated relationship; that is, in many cases, the more caring the father before separation, the more tempted he is to disengage afterward.[25]

Conclusion

In summary, without having yet considered the loss to children of reduced economic circumstances following divorce, one can see that divorce puts the children of adequate parents at risk.[26] And little can be done to mitigate that risk — even the best-intentioned provisions for custody and access, with elaborate programs of joint custody, shared parenting, parent education, counseling, mediation and the like, are thwarted by actualities in most cases in the longer run.

Do Fathers Matter?

Following consideration of six nationally representative data sets involving more than 25,000 children in the United States, McLanahan and Sandefur (1994) conclude that postdivorce poverty accounts for

---

23 Overwhelmingly, mothers, not fathers, get custody, even where there is said to be joint custody. Hereafter, my reflections assume divorced mothers are the custodial parents and fathers the noncustodial parents.

24 As I suggest later, the child-support guidelines adopted in Canada in 1997 may make continuing relationships more difficult than they were for less well-to-do fathers.

25 For a review of US studies that roughly parallel Kruk's findings, see Dudley, "Noncustodial Fathers Speak about Their Parental Role" (1996).

26 As already pointed out, children in families in which there is abuse or undue family turmoil are already at risk. Divorce may be an amelioration.

half the dysfunction of children of divorce. The remaining half is accounted for by loss of family structure. Moreover, as already mentioned, even if the policy of the law is to maintain relationships between children and their absent postdivorce fathers, in practice,

> marital disruption effectively destroys any on-going relationship between children and their biological parents living outside the home in a majority of cases. (Furstenberg and Nord, "Parenting Apart: Patterns of Child Rearing after Marital Disruption" [1985, 895].)

In most circumstances, a noncustodial father ceases to be a father. At best he becomes little more than a "weekend sugar daddy." In disrupted families, only one child in six, on average, saw his or her father as often as once a week in the past year, and close to half did not see him at all (National Commission on Children 1991). As time goes on, contact becomes even more infrequent. Ten years after a marriage breaks up, more than two-thirds of children report not having seen their father for a year (ibid.).

Even for fathers who maintain regular contact, the pattern of father-child relationships changes. Nonresidential fathers behave more like relatives than like parents. Instead of helping with homework or carrying out a project with their children, they are likely to take them shopping, to the movies, or out to dinner. Instead of providing steady advice and guidance, divorced fathers become "treat" dads (Furstenberg and Cherlin, *Divided Families: What Happens to Children When Parents Part* [1991, 10]). The conclusion that divorce sentences a child, for all intents and purposes, to loss of a father in the majority of cases appears inescapable. (There are, of course, bad fathers. Divorce is a remedy, not a loss, in those cases.)

Fathers and mothers are not androgynous in their roles as nurturers of children or even in those children's perceptions. Penelope Leach says, "Children between the ages of two and five are looking out for what it means to be male and female, and are eager to identify with models of their own sex" (1997, 520). Nor, it appears, is this early search for gender identity the result of socialization. There is a substantial literature on the role of fathers beyond that of providers.[27] The role of a father in the life of his daughters differs from his role in the life of his sons. Nor is that difference simply the result of socialization; it appears to be inherent in humankind. And we know that girls denied the affection of a father seek it through early intimacy.

Popenoe concludes that the evidence is such that

> [A] strong case can be made that paternal deprivation, in the form of physical, economic, and emotional unavailability of fathers to their children, has become a form of child maltreatment in America today. (*Life without Father* [1996, 9].)

One final, noteworthy aspect of the role of fathers is that stepfathers and biological fathers are not substitutes. Although one of every four children growing up in the 1990s will eventually enter a stepfamily, according to one survey (Whitehead 1993, 47), nearly half of all children in step-parent families will see their parents divorce again by the time they reach their late teens. But even when a second divorce does not occur, the evidence suggests that remarriage neither reproduces nor restores the intact family structure, even when it brings more income and a second adult into the household. In fact, children living with step-parents appear to be even more disadvantaged than children living in a stable single-parent family (ibid.; Zill and Rogers 1988). According to Hashima and Amato (1994), children reared in stepfamilies are more likely to experience harsh parental discipline than children reared in intact two-parent families; this relationship holds even after taking into account household income, family size, education, and race.

The Finances of Divorce

Important among the risks arising from the loss of a parent is poverty. Seventy-one percent of single-mother families have incomes below Statistics Canada's low income cut-off (LICO); the compara-

---

27 One regrets that today's society needs such a literature. It is a response to what Blankenhorn calls the "devaluation" of fatherhood (1995, 16). On the role of fathers, complementary to and overlapping that of mothers, see, for example, Leach (1994); Popenoe (1996); and Blankenhorn (1995).

ble share of two-parent families is 16.4 percent (Canada 1996, 87).[28] Poverty has long been looked on as the most important indicator of dysfunctional child development. As already noted, a broad and careful study estimates that, although half of the dysfunction of children of divorce is attributable to loss of family structure, the other half is the result of poverty (McLanahan and Sandefur 1994).

Divorce is a financial disaster for most children. The complacent assumption of the Canadian reformers appears to have been that the child support provisions of the divorce acts of 1968 and 1985 would adequately address the problem. They did not. As discussed below, the support of children of divorce brings to the fore one of the principal contradictions of "easy" divorce.

Child Support

Until May 1, 1997, the amount of child support was left to be decided on a case-by-case basis, responsive in theory to the particular circumstances of the family in a particular locality. The transaction costs were high. It was said that awards were inconsistent among judges and from place to place and that they were often inadequate in amount.

In an attempt to correct the flaws of discretionary awards, a 1997 amendment to the *Divorce Act*[29] brought into effect fixed child-support guidelines — fixed, that is, in the absence of "undue hard-

---

28 The sample included families headed by both divorced and never-married women. The income amounts do not include spousal support but do include paid child support. Recall that LICO is a measure of comparative, not absolute, poverty (Fellegi 1997).

29 At the same time, Parliament reversed the long-standing tax policy whereby child support was deductible by the payer and taxable in the hands of the recipient (almost always the mother), which usually permitted some measure of tax splitting. "No deduction — no inclusion" became the new law. The net annual revenue windfall from the changed policy is about $330 million, according to a Department of Finance estimate quoted in Finnie (1995, 163). As Finnie notes, the total loss to divorced parents who lose out under the new scheme is much larger ("say, $630 million"), but there are winners (more-affluent parents with approximately equal incomes). The windfall to the government is at the expense of money otherwise available to support children.

ship" (section 15.1 (3)), a term whose meaning we do not yet know, notwithstanding the attempt at definition in the regulations.[30] Desirable as guidelines may be, Canada does not yet have enough experience with them to know whether they will increase the amount of awards. In the United States, guidelines have not significantly increased the amounts awarded, although their advocates had predicted increases of two and a half times. Much of the statistical increase of about 15 percent in the United States has been attributable to fewer zero awards (see Pearson, Thoennes, and Tjaden 1989; Tjaden, Thoennes, and Pearson 1989; Thoennes, Tjaden, and Pearson 1991).

One result of the guidelines adopted in Canada is a heavier burden on less-affluent fathers than on those who are better off. Noncustodial fathers must pay in child support a fixed proportion of income, regardless of its amount, except in the highest brackets. Supporters of a flat-rate income tax may approve; those who endorse a progressive tax should not. Bear in mind that a father's ability to maintain a relationship with his noncustodial children depends, *inter alia*, on the income he has available after paying child support and income tax.

An anomaly of "easy" divorce has been its failure to provide through legislation policy direction on the perplexing issues of the competing financial needs of the children of divorce and their absent fathers, of the competing needs of first and second families, or of the extent to which the resources of a second spouse should be taken into account. The new regulations attempt to fill the gaps. Whether they will, through judicial interpretation, is yet to be seen. The regulations and their complexities offer ample busy work for lawyers and go some way to defeat the intent of the guidelines — that is, to reduce transaction costs.

At best, child-support guidelines are no more than a band-aid (and an inadequate one at that) for the poverty of children of di-

---

30 In a lecture on or about May 7, 1997, to judges in British Columbia on the guidelines and their regulations, a Department of Justice spokesperson said wryly that they are "as simple as the *Income Tax Act*."

vorce[31] — even if the experience in Canada is better than that in the United States. They do not and cannot address a fundamental flaw of "easy" divorce — namely, that in only the most affluent families is there enough money to go around for two households. Most separated families have to adjust to a lower standard of living. The weight of the decline appears to fall more heavily on women and the children under their care than on men. But, strangely, there seem to be no reliable data that take into account fathers' appropriate living expenditures including the costs of separated parenting.

Meanwhile, divorce *is* an economic disaster for the great majority of children, and there are no effective remedies in the context of "easy" divorce. Such remedy as there is, is a reduction in the incidence of divorce — that is, in the diseconomies of divorce.

Spousal Support

Obviously, the economic welfare of a child of divorce depends on the economic welfare of the custodial parent — the mother in the great majority of cases.

Divorce and the inadequacies of the remedies of "easy" divorce are often cited as a principal cause of the feminization of poverty. In 1985 (the year of Canada's revision of its *Divorce Act*), Lenore Weitzman published her *Divorce Revolution*, reporting that in California, on average, divorced men were 42 percent better off and women were 73 percent worse off a year after divorce than they had been during marriage (p. 338). That finding caught broad public and professional attention and gave rise to widespread commentary. That divorce substantially enriched men and gravely impoverished women became an article of faith — even of the Supreme Court of Canada.[32]

The only problem is that the figures were wrong by a wide margin. In 1996, Peterson, a US sociologist, reanalyzed Weitzman's data and found a mathematical error; using the same data as had

---

31 The accompanying tax change is, of course, detrimental to children of divorce.

32 See *Moge v Moge* [1992] 3 SCR 345. The majority said, in effect, that judicial notice of the "fact" could be taken.

Weitzman, he reports that divorced women suffered a 27 percent decline in their standard of living and men a 10 percent increase (1996, 534). Weitzman acknowledges her error (ibid., 537–538).

A more recent US study (McKeever and Wolfinger 1997) finds that single women experienced a 12 percent decline in their standard of living after divorce; the authors attribute the betterment over past years to increased labor force participation. The most recent Canadian data (Statistics Canada 1997, 7–8, 10–11) are not as optimistic. They show a 23 percent decline in adjusted family income of divorced women and a 10 percent increase in divorced men's income.

The perception of a grave imbalance between the financial outcomes of divorce for women and for men prompted by Weitzman's error deflected policy analysts toward measures to correct the imbalance and away from consideration of the across-the-board diseconomies of divorce facilitated by the law.[33] As noted above, an imbalance exists but it is not nearly as large as Weitzman led policy analysts to suppose. Moreover, there is an increase in the adjusted family income of separated women over time; after five years, the initial median decrease of 23 percent is reduced to 5 percent (Dooley 1995, 48–49).

Not the imbalance but the absolute level of the support of former wives is, of course, critical for children in their care. Preponderantly, the children of separated parents remain in the care of their mother. If she is poor, so will be the children. Nor can child support correct the situation.[34] The supposition, prompted by Weitzman, that

---

33 Although it was not prompted by Weitzman's book, section 15 (7) of Canada's 1985 *Divorce Act* is an example. It requires a court to recognize any economic advantage or disadvantage to a spouse arising from a marriage or its breakdown. A careful determination of the dollar cost (or benefit) of advantages and disadvantages is prohibitively expensive and indeterminate. In *Moge v Moge*, the Supreme Court sought to relieve that cost and indeterminacy by directing that judicial notice could be taken of the "fact" that in most circumstances men substantially benefit from divorce and women are gravely deprived by it. Such provisions as section 15 (7)(a) are, of course, to the benefit of the divorce industry.

34 I omit consideration of joint residential custody (a concept beloved of theorists), whereby children of separated parents live alternately with each parent. Few families can afford two principal homes.

most fathers are substantially enriched by their divorce is wrong. None but the most affluent separated fathers can afford adequate child support if that means providing economic benefits equivalent to what a child would have enjoyed had her or his parents not divorced. Child support from the less affluent can do little to relieve poverty even if noncustodial fathers are to be thrust into penury.

We have no study of the reasonable needs of noncustodial fathers including the cost of maintaining relationships with their absent children. Unfortunately, the Federal/Provincial/Territorial Family Law Committee on Child Support Guidelines did not undertake such a study. The essence of the matter is that there is seldom enough money to go around. The majority of intact families live on a financial knife-edge and cannot afford the cost of separated living and separated parenting. The myth of a prevalence of deadbeat dads is just a myth; there are deadbeat dads but not, I suggest, a prevalence of them. Yet it is the policy of the law to facilitate family separation.

Legislators and policy analysts propound what are essentially administrative, makeshift solutions (for example, child-support guidelines), which themselves give rise to yet further anomalies (for example, to impede all but better-off fathers of first families from seeking to enter into new relationships — a "right" supposedly accorded by "easy" divorce).

A fundamental flaw of "easy" divorce is this: it seeks to facilitate, if not encourage, divorce in the supposed interest of adults; on the other hand, divorce contributes to a very high incidence of child poverty. Legislators and policy analysts pursuing administrative solutions overlook or ignore the simple fact that there is not enough money to go around. The diseconomies of separated parenting are apparent, though they have never been adequately measured.[35] The law is at war with itself.

---

35 Finnie (1994) estimates that, if the costs of divorce were equally split, each of the households would have 80 percent of the predivorce standard of living. The study is not convincing. It seems probable that the costs of two adequate households are significantly higher. I base these assertions on exposure to the budgets of a few hundred separated families in the course of my practice.

The Impact on
Society and the Economy

Logically, if divorce results in a high incidence of harm to children, the impoverishment of separated women and the children in their care, diseconomies of separated families, the loss of cognitive capacities, the higher incidence of early pregnancy, the loss of fathers, and so on, it must affect not only the persons involved but society as a whole and the economy.

We have little hard data on the extent of the impact. There is, however, a basis for informed inference. We know, for example, that the proportion of single-parent households — but not the poverty level — predicts a community's rates of violent crime and burglary. We know that girls of divorced families are much more likely to have early unwedded pregnancies than are girls of intact families, regardless of poverty level. We know that children of divorce have lower academic achievement and are much more likely to drop out of school before graduation than their peers from intact families.[36] But we do not know the eventual impact on our economic potential in the sense of having measured it.

Daniel Patrick Moynihan, the distinguished US sociologist and now senator, predicted in 1965:

> From the wild Irish slums of the 19th century Eastern seaboard to the riot-torn suburbs of Los Angeles, there is one unmistakable lesson in American history: a community that allows a large number of young men to grow up in broken families, dominated by women, never acquiring any stable relationship to male authority, never acquiring any set of rational expectations about the future — that community asks for and gets chaos. Crime, violence, unrest, unrestrained lashing out at the whole social structure — that is not only to be expected; it is very near to inevitable. (Self-quoted in Moynihan, "Defining Deviancy Down" [1993, 26].)

---

36 I stress again that the data speak in the aggregate; an individual child disadvantaged by divorce may overcome his or her disadvantage in favorable circumstances.

In 1993, Moynihan wrote, "[T]he inevitable, as we now know, has come to pass" (ibid.). In 1965, he had been speaking primarily about black communities. In 1993, the phenomena encompassed increasing elements of the white community.

Blankenhorn predicts that if present trends of fatherlessness continue,

> After the year 2000, as people born after 1970 emerge as a large proportion of our working-age adult population, the United States will be a nation divided into two groups, separate and unequal. The two groups will work in the same economy, speak a common language, and remember the same national history.[37] But they will live fundamentally divergent lives. One group will receive basic benefits — psychological, social, economic, educational, and moral — that are denied to the other group. (*Fatherless America: Confronting Our Most Urgent Problem* [1995, 16].)

John Richards, in his important *Retooling the Welfare State*, relates the loss of family structure to increased need for welfare. He argues, correctly in my view, that legal policy should discriminate in favor of a secure family structure (1997, 254 ff).

It may be trite to observe that we are in an age demanding an ever-increasing measure of human capital. It is not trite to observe that with "easy" divorce we have adopted a regime of law that does what it can to diminish human capital. For the most part, human capital depends on investment — both financial and nurturing — in children (Romer, "Economic Growth and Investment in Children" [1994]). Divorce is likely to limit a separated father to the financial contributions to his children that he is required to make. An absent father's capacity to nurture is severely constrained (Furstenberg and Cherlin 1991). One can speculate, as well, that during marriage the uncertainties of tenure in an era of "easy" divorce may inhibit emotional and financial investment in children. Clearly, the human

---

37 One wonders if Blankenhorn is correct that children of divorce and children from intact families will "remember the same national history." It seems that the family has a part in transmitting national history and national values and that an intact family can better transmit them. Further, the loss of cognitive capacity of children of divorce may inhibit transmission in school.

capital of children of divorce is less than it otherwise might be. But we do not know how much less or the proportion of the loss from the potential pool of human capital.

In order to discuss the erosion of social capital — perhaps the most insidious effect of "easy" divorce — one must go beyond empiric data into the realm of social theory. In his seminal essay on "Social Capital and the Creation of Human Capital," James S. Coleman (1988) distinguishes among physical capital, human capital, and social capital. Social capital manifests itself in a variety of ways. It exists in *relations* among persons. Like physical capital and human capital, social capital facilitates productive activity. Coleman notes, for example,

> [A] group within which there is extensive trust-worthiness and extensive trust is able to accomplish much more than a comparable group without that trust-worthiness and trust. (Ibid., S101.)

That is, benign relations among persons — social capital — have value.

The essential elements of social organization that permit the development of social capital include trustworthiness, reciprocity, and a network for transmission and enforcement of norms. In some cases, it is community pressure and the risk of exclusion that may enforce the norm. In the case of the family, it is ultimately the law if there is to be a norm of fidelity to family. If the law recognized such a norm (and it does not now), community pressure can encourage that norm without the need for the law's intervention.

Coleman identifies the family as the most fundamental form of social capital (ibid., S109–S113). It is in the family that children learn to trust or not to trust, that they learn or do not learn about reciprocal obligations and entitlements. Initially, children's network for transmission of norms and their enforcement may be limited to the family. Later, the network will extend to the community, but children will bring to the extended network lessons learned within the family. The lesson may be trustworthiness if the children are secure in their parents. It will not be if they lose a parent through divorce.

Coleman notes that a child's intellectual development depends in substantial part on the human capital of his or her parents provided they are an important part of that child's life.

> [I]f the human capital possessed by parents is not complemented by social capital embodied in family relations, it is irrelevant to the child's educational growth that the parent has a great deal, or a small amount, of human capital. (Ibid., S110.)

That is, if a parent is not there to transmit his or her human capital, it will not avail the child.

In "Bowling Alone: America's Declining Social Capital," Putnam documents the decline of civic engagement in the United States and with it the loss of social capital. He notes, as well, the family as the most fundamental form of social capital and the loss of family structure as a contributor to social decapitalization (1995, 73).

The distinguished US political philosopher Jean Bethke Elshtain takes the argument a step further. In "Marriage in Civil Society," she notes that

> where [the] norms and networks of civic engagement [that is, social capital] are robust, education improves, families are more likely to stay together, poverty diminishes, crime is inhibited and, even, it seems, mortality rates improve. (1996, 1.)

Identifying marriage and family as the most vital forms of civic association, which she calls "the locus of private life [but] critical to public life, to the life of community and civic association" (ibid., p. 4), Elshtain concludes,

> [W]e must reweave the bonds of democratic community by rebuilding our primary institutions. And we must begin with the institutions of marriage and the family. (Ibid.)

Those who thought to reform the law of divorce in the 1960s, 1970s, and 1980s were so intent on their narrow agenda that they failed to give thought to the family's fundamental place in society and its contribution to the economy. The price has been high, and it may become higher still.

Why Did the Reformers Go Wrong?

Even with a written record from only 30 years ago, one cannot today be confident beyond doubt of getting into the minds of the reformers of the 1960s. Nor can one be sure of the limitations of their knowledge. However, before I outline where I think the law of divorce should go, I look back through the lens of three decades' experience of "easy" divorce.

In introducing what became the *Divorce Act* of 1968, then justice minister Pierre Trudeau said

> I think one of the fundamental tasks we must achieve in this Parliament is to avoid mixing sacred and the profane. We must realize we are living in a pluralistic society, and even though some laws may be repugnant to the morals of individual members they must realize that we are all here to legislate not our own personal morals upon the country but to seek solutions to evils which arise in a civil society and which must be solved by civil or criminal laws. (Canada 1967a, 5084.)

The evils to which Trudeau referred were the miseries of adults caught up in unhappy marriages. It is interesting to note that, while he and the reformers deplored the sacred's imposition of its values on what he said was a pluralistic society, the reformers had no hesitation in imposing the profane on society. If one spouse looks on marriage as a solemn commitment, indissoluble except for grave cause, and the other spouse does not, the law imposes on the committed spouse the values of the uncommitted.

Whatever Trudeau had to say about the sacred, mainline Protestant churches and the "Canadian Catholic Conference" (the justice minister's term) proposed as the sole ground for divorce *marriage breakdown*, meaning that one spouse or the other was unhappy in the marriage. Robert McCleave, a member of Parliament's joint committee, commented in the House of Commons with respect to the churches' proposal:

> Those who advocated it [marriage breakdown as the sole ground for divorce] most strenuously could never believe that one party to a marriage could unfaithfully treat the other party to a mar-

riage; that one party to a marriage could brutally abuse the other party to a marriage. Those who adopt the principle of marriage breakdown but want to be kind to both parties to a marriage that is in difficulty are living in the strange twilight world of today's morality, where there are no blacks or whites. (Ibid., 5089.)

One cannot know to what extent in the 1960s the religious ceremony of marriage had ceased to be a matter of conviction and become a matter of custom. Nevertheless Trudeau was wrong in categorizing the legal choices as between the sacred and profane. That which is labeled *sacred* is often no more than a manifestation of experience that society has found beneficial. A long history had found committed marriage as best for children and society.

The flaw in the thinking of Trudeau and the reformers of the 1960s was, of course, that they saw marriage as no more than a relationship between two adult individuals and overlooked the stake children and society have in marriage. One can surmise that the reformers, captive of the hubris of the time (as were many of us), supposed that the law affecting society's fundamental institution could be fundamentally changed without unanticipated and untoward results.

Trudeau (and the legal profession generally) was on firmer ground in deploring the existing and "very hypocritical procedure of fabricating evidence and arranging proof for a divorce, which is also a hypocrisy and a sham" (ibid., 5083). To the extent that divorces were obtained under the old law through fabricated evidence, they were unquestionably a blight on the administration of justice.

The reasons for divorce reform in the United States (in the same direction as that in Canada) are explicitly stated in the prefatory note to part IV of that country's *Uniform Marriage and Divorce Act* as the elimination of "perjury" and the avoidance of "bitterness" (9 U.L.A., 148).[38] The theory was no fault, no fabrication and no fault, no bitter-

---

38 Marriage and divorce law is a matter of state jurisdiction in the United States. In an effort to bring state laws in line with one another, the National Conference of Commissioners of Uniform State Laws makes recommendations that are reported, with commentary, in *Uniform Laws Annotated*. States rarely adopt the recommendations without amendments; as a result, marriage and divorce laws, among others, vary among the states.

ness. What is open to question is whether the remedy to the blight adopted in legislation — namely, expunging any concept of fault in marital relations — is the only possible remedy for perjury and bitterness. The reformers' choice of expunging any concept of fault was influenced by the therapeutic culture.[39]

The Influence of the Therapeutic Culture

"Easy" divorce was and is substantially influenced by what Bellah and his colleagues, in *Habits of the Heart: Individualism and Commitment in American Life* (1985) call the "therapeutic culture."[40] Indeed, it can be said that, in large part, "easy" divorce was a product of the therapeutic culture. It has a significant influence on the mainline Protestant religious community. It is a culture that not only refuses to take a moral stand but looks on morality as pathology. Bellah et al. note that people in general are not nearly as selfish as the therapeutic culture seeks them to be (ibid., 129).[41]

In an op-ed article in the *New York Times*, Peter Kramer, a psychiatrist, succinctly expresses the ideology of the therapeutic culture: "enhanced autonomy [is] the goal of psychotherapy" (1997, A15). What he means, of course, and what his culture means, is autonomy for *adults*. Children cannot be autonomous while they are children. Adults who seek to care for children cannot be autonomous from them. Nor can two adults who seek to best nurture their children be autonomous from one another. Yet the law of "easy" divorce adopts the therapeutic culture's goal of adult autonomy.

---

39 Canada's "easy" divorce is more purely "no fault" than is the law in most US states. In the majority of them, courts have discretion to take "conduct" into account in the division of property, the award of alimony, or both (see Wardle 1991.)

40 The authors reflect on the extent to which our society looks to the value system of the mental health professions — which is to say adult self-interest — and abandons other sources of values.

41 And see Glendon, *Abortion and Divorce in Western Law* (1987, 108). This is not to disparage the therapeutic professions' empirical contributions, which have been valuable. It is to caution against theorists who go beyond the data yet command a wide audience, both professional and public, and influence both the law and its practice. One suspects they command an audience because their message is comforting — comforting, that is, for adults. (See Dineen 1998.)

Some people put adult autonomy ahead of other obligations. This point is well illustrated by a recent public lecture by a Canadian essayist of note who had left his wife and children. He declared divorce to be "morally legitimate" because it "accords respect to an individual's need against the devouring claims of family life" (Ignatieff 1998a, 25). In response to criticism (Zyla 1998), Ignatieff rationalized that the "key issue is not whether parents live under the same roof but whether they provide children with sustained devotion" (Ignatieff 1998b, 21).

Even in those rare circumstances that do not preclude the "sustained devotion" of separated parents over time, the evidence, as opposed to therapeutic theory, is plain: the best — and, one would hope, the most rewarding — child rearing is a hands-on, daily responsibility of husband and wife. The task (if it can be called a task and not life's most fulfilling endeavor) is doubly difficult in an economy that requires both parents to have paid employment in most circumstances and in a society in which family gender roles are only in the process of adapting to changed economics.

The therapeutic culture and the value system that prompts it have a crucial influence on the development and practice of family law. That culture is a hidden hand behind "easy" divorce and its practice. There is reason to suppose that the value system of the therapeutic culture — a value system that puts the supposed interests of adults ahead of those of children — is not that of a majority of people. If Canadian society is to be child centered, as opposed to adults first, an initial step is to correct the law.

Does the Law Matter?

This paper sketches the law of "easy" divorce and the afflictions of children and of society that have followed it. But it cannot be said that the law alone "caused" them nor that a change in the law alone would correct them. The law is only one of many cultural, social, and economic influences on human affairs (see Haveman and Wolfe 1995).

The essential arguments here are that the law has *some* influence on family structure and that the loss of family structure is at the root of many of the afflictions we witness. For some time, however, it was the counterintuitive but conventional wisdom that the legislation of "easy" divorce had had no influence on the incidence of divorce in the successive US states that adopted it. Studies of various degrees of elaboration backed this conclusion. (For a consideration of such studies, see Allen elsewhere in this volume; Allen 1992; and Moir 1992.)

Newer studies, as Allen explains in his paper in this volume, establish that "easy" divorce does increase the incidence of divorce, although, as he notes, analysts do not know the extent to which the law operates as an isolated factor. The studies are content to look for a correlation between the incidence of divorce and the adoption of "easy" divorce laws. What they miss is that, if divorce is easy, one disaffected spouse can resort to it. If, however, divorce is not easy and can bring penalties, there is reason to suppose (and it is the experience of the law) that self-interest will inhibit some recourse to it.

Another consideration is that the law has a function beyond the regulation of human affairs. It is a statement of the values of society, an appeal to and a code for our better natures. If it says, as present law does, that marriage is a transitory relationship severable at the will of either spouse without cause and that the assumed interests of adults take priority over the welfare of children, one cannot expect people to disappoint it. (Indeed, it is remarkable that the majority of people still disappoint the law and stay married.) If, on the other hand, the law were to embody what I believe to be the cultural ideal of marriage as a solemn commitment — a commitment under which the welfare of children is best served — then the law should do what it can to encourage people to reach for that ideal. It follows that, in this context as in others, the law has two functions: one positive, the other negative. Its positive function is to do what it can to encourage conduct between adults that serves children's interests. Its negative function is to do what it can to discourage conduct that does not.[42]

---

42 These statements are self-evident. I make them because of those who argue for the law's irrelevance in this context and because present law gets matters backward: it discourages conduct the data tell us is benign and encourages conduct we know to be adverse to the interests of children and, arguably, adults.

Family Law Reform: Policy Considerations

What kind of divorce law would best serve its positive and negative functions? The data make it plain that a secure family structure is critical to the well-being of society and of its children. "Easy" divorce contributes to the loss of family structure. Thus, the aim of reformed law should be a reduction in the incidence of divorce, a principal element of the loss of family structure.

In the hope of encouraging broad discussion of the specifics of reformed legislation, I offer some basic precepts of law to reinforce family structure.

The Nature of the Law

The law should recognize commitment in marriage[43] and do what it can to encourage and enforce that commitment. In other words, the law should regard marriage as an institution indissoluble except for grave cause — an institution in which others than the adult partners, particularly their children, have an interest.

At law, commitment is to be recognized, encouraged, and identified by condemning its breach. Adultery and, in some jurisdictions, cruelty have long been recognized as grounds for divorce. In my view, child abuse is also a compelling ground for divorce. Deser-

---

43 In 1997, the Louisiana state legislature passed, with only one dissenting vote, a most striking and, indeed, ingenious measure for family law reform. It enacts what it calls *covenant marriage* as an option to marriage under the state's still-existing "easy" divorce law. Couples about to be married have a choice between the two forms of marriage, and couples in an existing marriage can opt for covenant marriage.

The covenant is to be entered into most solemnly and recorded. There are no penalties for breach of covenant, but a covenant marriage is severable only for egregious misconduct on the part of a spouse — cruelty, adultery, child abuse, and the like — or after a two-year separation. Provision for division of property (Louisiana is a community-property state), spousal support, and custody remain as they were. Overall, the provisions for covenant marriage are not dissimilar from those for marriage under the old law except for the absence of penalties and two-year separation as a ground for divorce.

Professor Katherine Spaht, the initiator of covenant marriage, has told me that proposals for covenant marriage are now before "more than" 20 state legislatures.

tion is an ultimate breach of commitment, but including it as a ground for divorce would need a careful consideration of its terms.

It follows from the recognition of commitment that *only* a committed spouse could petition for divorce against a spouse alleged to be in breach; that is, a spouse in breach of commitment would be precluded from petitioning. (I leave for discussion the perplexing issue of entitlement to petition when both are in breach.)

Remedies: Compensation and Penalties

The law's recognition, encouragement, and enforcement of commitment in marriage would necessarily involve awarding the spouse who had fulfilled the commitment and any children in her or his care such compensation as is possible; that the "innocent" spouse (and children) should be saved harmless so far as is possible from the financial consequences of the other spouse's breach.

In considering the remedies of the innocent spouse (apart from the divorce itself) under a regime of law that recognized commitment, one must bear in mind that the nature of the legal issues between divorcing wife and husband as to property division and spousal support would be quite different than they are now under "easy" divorce. Under present law, the aim is equality without regard to conduct; under the proposed law, the aim would be compensation for loss.

The experience of the law suggests that legislation that did what it could to encourage commitment would, at least in time, have some effect in reducing the incidence of divorce. I have some expectation (and it is the experience of the law) that a law that penalized a spouse in breach of commitment would, in some measure, discourage breaches and thereby reduce the incidence of divorce.

I also expect that if the issues between a divorcing husband and wife were the fact of breach of commitment and compensation (issues that only the innocent spouse could raise), they would be easier to resolve than issues of achieving equality. This expectation is reasonable since the finding of specific faults is easier for courts to deal with than the more nebulous notion of equity. Moreover, the division of property and spousal support would not be more complex determinations than they are under present law and would be better directed to the actual needs of separating families.

Division of Property

The division of what is recognized as family property is among the most contentious of issues of "easy" divorce and productive of busy work for the divorce industry.[44] Law that recognized commitment would abandon spousal equality as the criterion for property division — a criterion that is productive of litigation.[45] In contrast, law that recognized commitment in marriage would seek to use property division to save financially harmless, to the extent possible, the spouse (and any children in her or his care) who had fulfilled the commitment. It would be a matter of nice judgment in the legislation, a developing case law, or both to determine the extent to which it would be fair and expedient to penalize the spouse in breach in the division of property. A special difficulty would be the now well-established assumption that division of property on divorce is within provincial jurisdiction in Canada. The potential of this consti- tutional barrier suggests that some measure of federal-provincial accord may be required if property is to be looked to for compensation. In the context of federal jurisdiction over divorce, however, there is a long-established jurisdiction to look indirectly to property as a source of lump-sum support.

Spousal Support

A second source of financial compensation for a spouse who had fulfilled the commitment (and for any children in her or his care) would

---

44 "Busy work" because it does not address the real needs of separating families or expressly recognize the stake of children in family property.

45 The tortured rationales for property division under "easy" divorce are well illustrated in articles by eminent US scholars in a special issue of *Family Law Quarterly* (1989).

be spousal support — with adequate guarantees of enforcement. Spousal support, often a source of compensation preferable to property division, is an anomaly of "easy" divorce (see O'Connell, "Alimony after No-Fault: A Practice in Search of a Theory" [1988]). The social need is clear, yet to serve it is inconsistent with the current goal of adult autonomy. The law's recognition of commitment in marriage would remove the anomaly. Awarding spousal support to save harmless the committed spouse to the extent possible, would be consistent with the intent of the law. As in the case of property division, however, a nice judgment of the extent would be necessary.[46]

Child Support

A regime of law that does not recognize fault limits child support to concepts of equality between separated spouses. A recognition of commitment would free the determination of child support from that limitation. (Recall, however, that equality of responsibility for the support of children of separated parents is not the motivating factor of child-support guidelines, as it was before their introduction.)

Custody and Access

One of the most strikingly unjust anomalies of "easy" divorce is the way it can, without an objectively determinable cause, deprive a child of an otherwise adequate parent and that parent of an effective relationship with his child. Under the current divorce law, one parent (most often the mother) can gain custody of the child, taking him away from the other parent without cause.

---

46 It would be no easy task to formulate law and develop case law to determine the extent to which it was just, fair, and expedient to penalize in either property division or spousal support a spouse in breach in the interest of compensating a committed spouse and the children in her or his care. Clearly, the circumstances in which the committed spouse could be fully compensated for her or his economic loss would be rare. The precedents of the past are of little guidance in today's world. I make no attempt to suggest a direction.

If the law were to recognize commitment in marriage as a factor influencing the determination of custody and access, it would remove the anomaly, although the change might be a most contentious policy issue.[47] That the determination should be in the best interest of the child (without regard to the conduct between husband and wife) is one of the most deeply entrenched dogmas in family law. It is a statutory requirement in Canada and in most US states.

Yet the late Meyer Elkin, dean of court-connected family counselors, said "the best interest of the child" is a phrase that comes "trippingly off the tongue" with little meaning. In the case of an adequate mother and father and in the absence of undue turmoil between them, "the best" usually means that the parents stay together, as can be inferred from the data.

To analyze the flaws of the best-interest-of-children doctrine in the determination of custody would be beyond the scope of this essay. In brief, the use of that doctrine under present law and more so in a law to encourage commitment in marriage can be questioned on several grounds. If both parents are adequate, no one, not even the most expert, can know which of the two will be the better parent in the future. Except when the inadequacy of one parent is plain, mother custody and father custody will differ, but no data can predict which will be "better."[48] The application of the best-interests doctrine is an exercise in bias weighted against fathers. A rebuttable presumption that custody go to the committed parent, with such access to the parent in breach as is appropriate, seems unlikely to put children at risk, and it would be consistent with the recognition of commitment. (The presumption would not preclude parents from making such living arrangements as they reasonably think best for the children.)

---

47 I use the old language for convenience, but I intend it to encompass various other living arrangements for children of separated parents. A new language may be available when Parliament's Special Joint Committee on Child Custody and Access reports.

48 For a brief analysis, see Moir 1996 (especially the letter from Janet R. Johnson quoted on p. 20); Joan Kelly's "The Best Interests of the Child: A Concept in Search of a Meaning" (1997); and Dineen, *Manufacturing Victims* (1998).

Moreover, if the law were to encourage commitment in marriage, that purpose would be defeated were the best-interests doctrine to give the uncommitted spouse unrestricted grounds to litigate custody.

The Intentions
of the Proposed Law

The intentions and attributes of the law I propose would be, for the most part, implicit, not express. It would seek to encourage commitment, in contrast to present law which seeks to facilitate divorce. Although the law of divorce and its corollary remedies can never be simple, an enactment along the lines proposed seems likely to simplify the matter by eliminating many of the anomalies and inconsistencies of "easy" divorce that are so productive of contention.

The proposed law would bring the law of divorce in line with what appears to be the cultural perception or at least the ideal of society: that marriage is a life-long commitment in the absence of grievous breach. And that ideal, one can say confidently, is the one that gives children their best chance.

The goal of the proposal is for the law to do what it can to reduce the incidence of divorce, an essential measure if the welfare of children is to take precedence over the assumed interests of adults. Would the strictures of the proposed law be evaded as they were in the past (although we have no idea of the extent of the evasion that occurred)? Evasion or attempts at it would be probable. Their extent might depend, in part, on the measure of judicial supervision and enforcement. The makers of policy would have to judge between the harm of possible evasion and the harm of "easy" divorce to children.

A significant function of law in general is to offer a framework for the settlement of differences with a minimum of judicial intervention (see Mnookin and Kornhauser, "Bargaining in the Shadow of the Law: The Case of Divorce" [1979]). The divorce law I propose would, in comparison to present law, reduce the issues in number. It would endow the spouse who is more reluctant to divorce with the better bargaining chips and, at the same time, offer a spousal victim (of cruelty, for example) such financial relief as may be possible.

The proposed law would be gender neutral, as it ought to be. Whatever inequalities may exist between women and men are not to be resolved in the context of divorce. Inequalities are for resolution over time through socialization, economics, and, where appropriate, law other than family law. Similarly, it is not for the law of divorce to level the playing field of custody and access for fathers (provided there is adequate enforcement). Rather, the proposed law would bind both men and women to a standard of conduct in the interest of children.

A fundamental contradiction of "easy" divorce is that, although its principal rationale is to free adults as individuals to do as each wishes, to liberate them from Ignatieff's "devouring claims of family life" (1998a, 25), its result has been a degree of state intrusion into family affairs that would have appalled an earlier generation. In the context of divorce, the state regulates the acquiring and disposition of property. A separated custodial parent can be inhibited in her choice of abode or occupation lest it impede the right of access to children of the noncustodial parent. (The courts are, in practice, reluctant to use this power.[49]) In particular, children of divorce are under court order as to the times they must spend with their absent fathers, regardless of their own associations. And in practice, court-appointed clinicians can regulate child-rearing practices, although one cannot assume they have knowledge (Dineen 1998). An aim of the proposed law is to limit and channel state intrusion except where it is imperative.

Would the proposed law reduce the incidence of divorce? The civil law can offer only penalties and rewards. I suggest that the experience of society is that people are responsive to them, at least to a degree. Moreover, if the law expresses the ideals of society, not its least common denominator, there is surely some hope that people will reach for them.

---

[49] *Goertz v Gordon* [1996] 2 SCR 27).

It's All Family

The information we now have is making it increasingly clear that a secure and benign family structure is of itself fundamental to optimal child development and, in turn, to the well-being of society and the economy. Law that does what it can to encourage secure and benign family structures is an essential.

In his tribute to the eminent if politically incorrect US sociologist James S. Coleman on his death in 1995, Senator Daniel Patrick Moynihan, himself an eminent sociologist, recalled Coleman's exhaustive study, *Equality of Educational Opportunity* (Coleman et al. 1966). It had been commissioned under the *Civil Rights Act* of 1964. Schools, especially for blacks, were unequal to those in more upscale communities. Everyone knew that that was the reason for unequal educational results. Everyone was wrong. Differences in family structure most accounted for unequal educational results.

Seymour Martin Lipset summed up of Coleman's findings:

"All family."[50]

References

Allen, Douglas W. 1992. "Marriage and Divorce: Comment." *American Economic Review* 82 (3): 679–685.

Amato, Paul R. 1994. "Life-Span Adjustment of Children to their Parents' Divorce." *The Future of Children* (Los Altos, Cal.: David and Lucile Packard Foundation, Center for the Future of Children) 4 (1): 143–164.

Beck, Allen, Susan Kline, and Lawrence Greenfield. 1988. *Survey of Youth in Custody, 1987*. Washington, DC: US Department of Justice, Bureau of Justice Statistics.

Bellah, Robert N., et al. 1985. *Habits of the Heart; Individualism and Commitment in American Life*. Berkeley, Cal.: University of California Press; reprinted in Perennial Library, New York: Harper & Row, 1986.

Blankenhorn, David. 1995. *Fatherless America: Confronting Our Most Urgent Problem*. New York: Basic Books, 1995.

Canada. 1967a. Parliament. House of Commons. *Debates*. Ottawa: Queen's Printer.

---

50 In his tribute in the *New York Times Magazine*, "Moved by Data, Not Doctrine" (Moynihan 1995, 25), Senator Moynihan quotes Lipset's oral statement to him.

————. 1967b. Special Joint Committee of the Senate and House of Commons. *Report*. Ottawa: Queen's Printer.

————. 1985. Parliament. House of Commons. *Debates*. Ottawa: Queen's Printer.

————. 1996. Statistics Canada and Department of Human Resources Development. *Growing Up in Canada*. National Longitudinal Survey of Children and Youth. Cat. 89-550-MPE; no. 1. Ottawa.

Coleman, James S. 1988. "Social Capital and the Creation of Human Capital." *American Journal of Sociology* 94 (supplement): S95–S120.

Cornell, Dewey, et al. 1987. "Characteristics of Adolescents Charged with Homicide." *Behavioral Sciences and the Law* 5: 11–23.

Dawson, Deborah. 1990. National Center for Health Statistics. Reported in "Nontraditional home can hurt kids' health." *Wall Street Journal*, July 5.

Dineen, Tana. 1998. *Manufacturing Victims*. Montreal: R. Davies Publishing.

Dooley, Martin D. 1995. "Lone-Mother Families and Social Assistance Policy in Canada." In Martin D. Dooley et al., *Family Matters: New Policies for Divorce, Lone Mothers, and Child Poverty*. The Social Policy Challenge 8. Toronto: C.D. Howe Institute.

Dudley, James R. 1996. "Noncustodial Fathers Speak about Their Parental Role." *Family and Conciliation Courts Review* 34 (3): 410–426.

Elshtain, Jean Bethke. 1996. "Marriage in Civil Society." *Family Affairs* 7 (1–2): 1–5.

Family Law Quarterly. 1989. Special issue on property division at divorce. 23: 147–381.

Fellegi, Ivan. 1997. "To measure poverty, you must first wield the right ruler." *Vancouver Sun*, September 18, p. A19.

Finnie, Ross. 1994. *Child Support: The Guideline Options*. Montreal: Institute for Research on Public Policy.

————. 1995. "The Economics of Divorce." In Martin D. Dooley et al., *Family Matters: New Policies for Divorce, Lone Mothers, and Child Poverty*. The Social Policy Challenge 8. Toronto: C.D. Howe Institute.

Furstenberg, Frank, Jr., and Andrew Cherlin. 1991. *Divided Families: What Happens to Children When Parents Part*. Cambridge, Mass.: Harvard University Press.

————, and Julien O. Teitler. 1994. "Reconsidering the Effects of Marital Disruption: What Happens to Children of Divorce in Early Adulthood?" *Journal of Family Issues* 15: 173–190.

————, and Christine Winquest Nord. 1985. " Parenting Apart: Patterns of Child Rearing after Marital Disruption." *Journal of Marriage and Family* 47: 893–904.

Gettleman, Susan, and Janet Markowitz. 1974. *Courage to Divorce*. New York: Simon and Schuster.

Glendon, Mary Ann. 1987. *Abortion and Divorce in Western Law*. Cambridge, Mass.: Harvard University Press.

Guidubaldi, John. 1988. "Differences in Children's Divorce Adjustment across Grade Level and Gender: A Report from the NASP–Kent State National Project." In Sharlene A. Wolchik and Paul Karoly, eds., *Children of Divorce*. New York: Gardner Press.

———, et al. 1983. "The Impact of Parental Divorce on Children: Report of the Nationwide NASP Study." *School Psychology Review* 12: 300–323.

———, and Joseph D. Perry. 1985. "Divorce and Mental Health Sequelae for Children: A Two Year Follow-Up of a Nationwide Sample." *Journal of the American Academy of Child Psychiatry* 24 (5): 531–537.

———, Joseph D. Perry, and Helen K. Clemenshaw. 1984. "The Legacy of Parental Divorce." In B.B. Lahey and A.E. Kazdin, eds., *Advances in Clinical Child Psychology* 7. New York: Plenum Press.

Hashima, Patricia Y., and Paul R. Amato. 1994. "Poverty, Social Support, and Parental Behavior." *Child Development* 65: 394–403.

Haveman, Robert, and Barbara Wolfe. 1995. " The Determinants of Children's Attainments: A Review of Methods and Findings." *Journal of Economic Literature* 33 (4): 1829–1878.

Hetherington, E. 1994. "Stress and Coping in Children and Families under Stress." In Anna-Beth Doyle, Dolores Gold, and Debbie S. Moskowitz, eds., *Children in Families under Stress*. New Directions for Child Development 24. San Francisco: Jossey-Bass.

———. 1989. "Coping with Family Transitions: Winners, Losers, and Survivors." *Child Development* 60 (1): 1–14.

———, Martha Cox, and Roger Cox. 1982. "Effects of Divorce on Parents and Children." In Michael E. Lamb, ed., *Non-Traditional Families: Parenting and Child Development*. Hillsdale, NJ: L. Erlbaum Associates.

———, Martha Cox, and Roger Cox. 1985. "Long Term Effects of Divorce and Remarriage on the Adjustment of Children." *Journal of the American Academy of Child Psychiatry* 24 (5): 518–530.

L'Heureux-Dubé, Madam Justice Claire. 1998. "A Response to Remarks by Dr. Judith Wallerstein." *Family and Conciliation Courts Review* 36 (3): 384–391.

Ignatieff, Michael. 1998a. "The Liberal Imagination: A Defence." The Keith Davey Lecture, Toronto, January 8.

———. 1998b. "Moral intelligence and new family forms." Letter to the editor. *Globe and Mail* (Toronto), January 21, p. A21.

Jacob, Herbert. 1988. *Silent Revolution: The Transformation of Divorce Law in the United States*. Chicago: University of Chicago Press.

Kamarck, Elaine, and William Galston. 1990. *Putting Children First: A Progressive Family Policy for the 1990's.* Washington, DC: Progressive Policy Institute.

Kelly, Joan B. 1997. "The Best Interests of the Child: A Concept in Search of a Meaning." *Family and Conciliation Courts Review* 35 (4): 377–387.

Kramer, Peter D. 1997. "Divorce and our national values." *New York Times,* August 29, 1997, p. A15.

Krantzler, Mel. 1974. *Creative Divorce: A New Opportunity for Personal Growth.* New York: Signet Books, New American Library.

Kraus, Sharon. 1979. The Crisis of Divorce: Growth Promoting or Pathogenic?" *Journal of Divorce* 3: 107–119.

Kruk, Edward. 1992. "Psychological and Structural Factors Contributing to the Disengagement of Non-Custodial Fathers after Divorce." *Family and Conciliation Courts Review* 30: 81–101.

Lauman, Edward O. 1996. *A Social Organization of Sexuality: Sexual Practices in the United States.* Chicago: University of Chicago, National Opinion Research Center.

Leach, Penelope. 1994. *Children First: What Our Society Must Do — and Is Not Doing — for Our Children Today.* New York: Alfred A. Knopf.

———. 1997. *Your Baby and Child: From Birth to Age Five.* 3rd ed. New York: Alfred A. Knopf.

McKeever, Matthew, and Nicholas Wolfinger. 1997. "Reexamining the Economic Costs of Marital Disruption for Women." Paper presented at the annual meeting of the American Sociological Association, Toronto, July 15.

McLanahan, Sara, and Gary Sandefur. 1994. *Growing Up with a Single Parent.* Cambridge, Mass.: Harvard University Press.

Mnookin, Robert, and Lewis Kornhauser. 1979. "Bargaining in the Shadow of the Law: The Case of Divorce." *Yale Law Journal* 88 (5): 950–997.

Moir, Donald S. 1992. No Fault Divorce and the Best Interests of Children." *Denver University Law Review* 69 (3): 663–685.

———. 1993. "No Fault Divorce: An Emperor without Clothes." Paper presented at the International Society of Family Law annual conference, Jackson Hole, Wy., June 3. A draft copy is available from the author.

———. 1996. "Putting Children First: A Reconsideration of Family Law." Paper presented at the International Society of Family Law annual conference, Quebec City, June 14. A draft copy is available from the author.

Moynihan, Daniel Patrick. 1993. "Defining Deviancy Down." *The American Scholar* 62: 17–30.

———. 1995. "Moved by the Data, Not Doctrine." *New York Times Magazine,* December 31, p. 25.

National Commission on Children. 1991. *Speaking of Kids: A National Survey of Children and Parents.* Washington, DC.

National Conference of Commissioners of Uniform State Laws. *Uniform Laws Annotated*, vol. 9. Washington, DC.

National Opinion Research Center. 1982. *General Social Survey (1972–1982).* Chicago: University of Chicago, National Opinion Research Center.

O'Connell, Mary E. 1988. "Alimony after No-Fault: A Practice in Search of a Theory." *New England Law Review* 23: 437–513.

Pearson, Jessica, Nancy Thoennes, and Patricia G. Tjaden. 1989. "Legislating Adequacy: The Impact of Child Support Guidelines." *Law and Society Review* 23 (4): 569–590.

Peterson, Richard R. 1996. "A Re-Evaluation of the Economic Consequences of Divorce." *American Sociological Review* 61: 528–536.

Popenoe, David. 1996. *Life Without Father: Compelling New Evidence that Father and Marriage Are Indispensable for the Good of Children and Society.* New York: The Free Press.

Putnam, Robert D. 1995. "Bowling Alone: America's Declining Social Capital." *Journal of Democracy* 6 (1): 65–78.

Richards, John. 1998. *Retooling the Welfare State: What's Right, What's Wrong, What's to Be Done.* Policy Study 31. Toronto: C.D. Howe Institute.

Romer, Paul M. 1994. "Economic Growth and Investment in Children." *Daedalus* 123 (4): 141–154.

Sheline, Jonathon L., Betty J. Skipper, and W. Eugene Broadhead. 1994. "Risk Factors for Violent Behavior in Elementary School Boys: Have You Hugged Your Child Today?" *American Journal of Public Health* 84: 661–663.

Smith, Douglas A., and G. Roger Jarjoura. 1988. "Social Structure and Criminal Victimization." *Journal of Research in Crime and Delinquency* 25: 27–52.

Statistics Canada. 1992. *Marriage and Conjugal Life in Canada.* Cat. 91-534-XPE. Ottawa.

———. 1993. *A Portrait of Families in Canada.* Cat. 89-523-XPE. Ottawa.

———. 1997. *Family Income after Separation.* Income Analytic Report 5. Cat. 13-588-MPB. Ottawa.

———. Cat. 11-008-XPE. "Canadian Attitudes to Divorce." *Canadian Social Trends* (Spring 1998).

———. Cat. 84-213-XPB. *Divorces 1995.* Ottawa. Annual.

Thoennes, Nancy, Patricia G. Tjaden, and Jessica Pearson. 1991. "The Impact of Child Support Guidelines on Award Adequacy, Award Variability and Case Processing Efficiency." *Family Law Quarterly* 25 (3): 325–345.

Tjaden, Patricia G., Nancy Thoennes, and Jessica Pearson. 1989. "Will These Children Be Supported Adequately?" *The Judges' Journal*, Fall, pp. 5–42.

Tucker, Joan S., et al. 1997. "Parental Divorce: Effects on Individual Behavior and Longevity." *Journal of Personality and Social Psychology* 73 (2): 381–391.

Wallerstein, Judith S., and Sandra Blakeslee. 1989. *Second Chances: Men, Women and Children a Decade after Divorce*. New York: Ticknor and Fields.

———, and Joan Berlin Kelly. 1980. *Surviving the Breakup: How Children and Parents Survive Divorce*. New York: Basic Books.

———, and Julia Lewis. 1998. "The Long Term Impact of Divorce on Children: A First Report from a 25-Year Study." *Family and Conciliation Courts Review* 36 (3): 368–383.

Wardle, Lynn D. 1991. "No-Fault Divorce and the Divorce Conundrum." *Brigham Young University Law Review*, pp. 79–142.

Weitzman, Lenore J. 1985. *The Divorce Revolution: The Unexpected Social and Economic Consequences for Women and Children in America*. New York: The Free Press.

Whitehead, Barbara Dafoe. 1993. "Dan Quayle Was Right." *The Atlantic Monthly*, April.

———. 1997. *The Divorce Culture*. New York: Alfred A. Knopf.

Zill, Nicholas, and Carolyn C. Rogers. "Recent Trends in the Well-Being of Children in the United States and Their Implications for Public Policy." In Andrew J. Cherlin, ed., *The Changing American Family and Public Policy*. Washington, DC: The Urban Institute.

Zyla, Melana. 1998. "Hacking away at family life." *Globe and Mail* (Toronto), January 16, p. 22.

Marriage and Homosexuals

F.H. Buckley

The great romantic movie of my generation was *Jules et Jim*. The eponymous protagonists both love Kathe, first Jules, then Jim. Without leaving Jules, Kathe chooses Jim, since he is more likely to give her children. An unusual arrangement, but one that appealed to an age whose motto, like Kathe's, was "Nous devons repartir de zéro et redécouvrir les règles" (Truffaut 1971, 103). Yet at the end, the romantic experiment fails. "La terre promise était en vue. La terre promise recula d'un bond" (ibid., 130).

We also thought to restart from zero and to reinvent our rules, and we also saw our promised land disappear. Fifty years ago, divorce bore a social stigma and was uncommon. But as social sanctions crumbled, the divorce rates increased. No-fault divorce laws also weakened marriage. Every US state adopted a no-fault divorce law between 1969 and 1985, and divorce rates doubled during this period. (Brinig and Buckley 1998). The record in Canada is similar (see Allen, in this volume). Since stable marriages reduce the cost of child rearing, the increased likelihood of divorce has increased the cost of children and plausibly resulted in a declining birth rate for married families At the same time, reduced social sanctions have resulted in dramatically increased illegitimacy rates, which in some inner cities are as high as 80 percent (Brinig and Buckley, forthcoming).

There was a time when we might have pretended that these changes were benign and that we could reinvent the rules of marriage without cost. But that time has passed. The results are now in. What they tell us is that children are far better off when raised in a traditional two-parent family. Illegitimate children are more likely to to break the law. They are also more likely to become unwed parents themselves and to pass on the pathologies of illegitimacy to a new generation (Popenoe 1996; Blankenhorn 1995).

These costs extend beyond broken families and illegitimate children to a coarser and less gentle society. An early and prescient observer described the family as a "haven in a heartless world" (Lasch 1977), and without it the world is more heartless still. Families socialize us and teach us to trust and to bind ourselves to broader communities. We begin not as atomistic individuals, loving society in the abstract, but as sons and daughters who learn empathy and compassion for strangers by learning them first from our family.

Given the crisis in the family, one might expect that a detailed legal literature would examine the causes of its decline and the law's responsibility for the change. But legal academics have little interest in such work. What instead is a hot topic is homosexual marriage.

The lack of interest in serious social problems, such as divorce, and the fascination with symbolic issues, such as homosexual marriage, is a modern phenomenon. An older generation of Depression-bred liberals would have had little time for the high preciousness of modern liberalism or for homosexual marriage. They would have noted that homosexuals account for only 2 percent of the population (Posner 1992, 294–295) and that a small number of them would wish to marry.

Why, then, the interest in homosexual marriages? Three answers are possible. First, most states (including Canada) subsidize marriage through special wealth-transfer schemes available only to married couples, and homosexual couples might wish to share in these benefits. Second, marriage might usefully permit homosexuals to commit to each other more credibly than they can now and to make greater investments in their relationships. Third, legalizing homosexual unions would place a societal seal of approval on homosexuality and homosexual relationships.

Of these explanations, the third is likely the most important. It plausibly explains the support for homosexual marriage; it also clarifies the associated costs, which, I argue, justify the ban on same-sex marriage.

In this essay, I first survey the homosexual rights revolution under the Canadian Charter of Rights and Freedoms. Without explicitly recognizing a right of homosexual marriage, Canadian courts have struck down statutory entitlements for married couples that exclude homosexual couples. Next, I consider the argument that, on distributional grounds, homosexual couples should be entitled to share in marriage subsidies. I reject this argument because such subsidies are best regarded as incentives to procreation. I then examine spouses' private efficiency gains from marriage. These benefits are mostly a function of child rearing and so are not strong arguments for the recognition of homosexual marriages. Next, I consider libertarian and conservative arguments for and against homosexual marriages. Libertarians assume that such marriages would not impose social costs, but this begs the question, since conservatives explicitly assume that such costs exist. Data to resolve this dispute are unavailable. Yet prudence dictates caution in reforming a social institution when the status quo does not impose a great burden on anyone and when the change would shock the sensibilities of a large segment of the population.

Finally, I appraise the costs of providing a single statutory regime for heterosexual and homosexual couples. Even if homosexual marriages are not in any way inferior to heterosexual marriages, the two kinds of marriage are different. Subjecting them to the same statutory regime would change the laws of marriage and divorce and result in an institution that suits heterosexuals less well than marriage law does at present.

A Right to Homosexual Marriage?

Despite the growing tendency to grant homosexual couples the same privileges accorded married heterosexual couples, neither Canada nor any other country recognizes homosexual marriage as such. But who can say the same of the future? Canadians have witnessed a remarkable expansion in homosexual rights over the past ten years, and the momentum of the change and the general acceptance of antidiscrimination norms make it possible that Canada will be the first country to sanction homosexual marriage.

Charter Rights

Who could have foreseen that stolid, dour Canada would be in the vanguard of the homosexual rights revolution? Not so long ago the *New Yorker* labeled "Worthwhile Canadian Initiative" the most boring conceivable headline. Even the Charter of Rights and Freedoms, our belated attempt to mimic US jurisprudence, seemed a limited document, hedged by prudential conditions. Yet Canada has, more than most countries, a Tory tradition of respect for authority. When its hierarchies decide on a course, even a radical one, dissenting voices are often weaker here than elsewhere.

When the Charter was adopted, there was little to suggest that it would one day be employed in aid of homosexual rights. Section 15 specifically proscribes nine kinds of discrimination; discrimination on the basis of sexual orientation is not one of them. Given Canada's conservative tradition of statutory construction, no one could have guessed that its courts would read in homosexuality as a protected class. Moreover, section 1 provides that section 15's equality rights are subject to "such reasonable limits prescribed by law as can be demonstrably justified in a free and democratic society."

Despite this, the Supreme Court of Canada has aggressively expanded the scope of equality rights under the Charter. In *Anderson v Law Society of British Columbia*,[1] it held that a requirement that lawyers be Canadian citizens violated section 15, even though citizenship was not one of the enumerated grounds of discrimination. The Court held that the promise of equality extended not only to listed but also to "analogous grounds" of discrimination. How broad these analogous grounds might be has recently become clear in a remarkable series of cases. In *Miron v Trudel*,[2] the Court held that the Ontario *Insurance Act*'s denial of spousal benefits to unmarried heterosexual partners violated section 15. Distinctions between married and common law spouses were invidious and could not be upheld under

[1] *Anderson v Law Society of British Columbia*, [1989] 1 SCR 143, 56 DLR (4th) 1.
[2] *Miron v Trudel*, 124 DLR (4th) 693 (1995).

section 1. Then, in *Egan v The Queen*,[3] a unanimous Court held that homosexuals are protected as an analogous class under section 15.

Modern Equality Rights

A bare majority of the *Egan* Court held that the denial of federal old age pension benefits to partners in a homosexual union could be upheld under section 1. A homosexual couple had applied for an allowance under the *Old Age Security Act*. Although their combined incomes fell below the specified level, the application was denied on the basis that the parties were not "spouses," as that term was used in the act. The lower courts ruled that this did not violate the Charter, and these decisions were upheld by the Supreme Court. Nevertheless, the case represented a strategic victory for the homosexual rights movement. A unanimous Court affirmed the extension of antidiscrimination rights to analogous grounds and found that this extended to homosexuals. A conservative, Burkean wing of four judges held that the statute was saved by section 1, while a liberal wing of four judges dissented. The swing vote belonged to Mr. Justice Sopinka, who held that, although the statute contravened equality rights under section 15, it was nonetheless saved by section 1. As he noted, welfare legislation is necessarily Fabian, proceeding through incremental stages to benefit first this, then that social and economic group. In the case of old age pensions, the target group of beneficiaries was female widows with few marketable skills. If overbroad equality rights prevented Parliament from discriminating among welfare beneficiaries in this way, then fewer wealth-transfer schemes would be enacted.

Mr. Justice Sopinka's voice was that of an older and honorable generation of liberals, who saw the problem of social justice primarily in economic terms and sought to promote economic justice through wealth-transfer schemes. This is the liberalism of T.C. Douglas in Canada and Franklin Roosevelt in the United States. It is not the modern lifestyle liberalism of those who, like the four dissenting

---

3 *Egan v The Queen*, 124 DLR (4th) 609 (1995).

judges, seek to transform social norms and institutions. A just society, in their view, does more than tolerate differences in values; it also celebrates diversity with the goal of according equal respect to every lifestyle choice. Thus, Mr. Justice Cory (with whom Mr. Justices Iacobucci and McLachlin concur) stated:

> In our democratic society, every individual is recognized as important and deserving of respect. Each individual is unique and distinct....[I]ndividuals, because of their uniqueness, are bound to vary in their personal characteristics which may be manifested by their sexual preferences whether heterosexual or homosexual. So long as those preferences do not infringe any laws, they should be tolerated. In its attempt to prohibit discrimination, the Charter seeks to reinforce the concept that *all* human beings, however different they may appear to the majority, are *all* equally deserving of concern, respect and consideration. (*Egan*, 670.)

What was wrong with the impugned legislation was not merely the denial of monetary benefits to an economically deserving class but also the implied critique of a lifestyle choice. The statute discriminated "by denying [homosexual couples] the right to make a choice in a matter which affects them deeply and personally in a manner that denies their human dignity" (ibid.).

Strong stuff, but not strong enough for Mme. Justice L'Heureux-Dubé. Like the other dissenters, she focused more closely on issues of "human dignity and worth" than on economic justice (ibid., 647); but unlike them, she would have abandoned the analogous grounds standard for an unlimited prohibition of all discrimination that

> is capable of either promoting or perpetuating the view that the individual adversely affected by this distinction is less capable, or less worthy of recognition or value as a human being or as a member of Canadian society. (Ibid., 638.)

The test, moreover, should be a victim-centered one. What matters, she stated, is not whether a "white male" would feel slighted but what a reasonable person in the position of the victim would feel. The more the victim is "socially vulnerable," the more likely it is that a law will be found discriminatory (ibid., 640). Opinions such as this explain why the Supreme Court of Canada, once respected throughout the Commonwealth, is now regarded with a certain derision.

Even Mr. Justice Sopinka suggested that the legislation upheld in *Egan* might need to be revisited before long. While provincial legislatures have begun to extend human rights codes to homosexuals, he noted that this is of recent origin. It might, therefore, be imprudent for the Supreme Court to outrun the legislatures too far. The implication is that the *Egan* case might be reversed in several years, when the novelty of pro-homosexual legislation has worn off.

Economic Rights

At a minimum, homosexual couples now seem entitled to the same economic benefits as unmarried heterosexual couples. Thus, in *M v H*, the Ontario Court of Appeal struck down the restriction to heterosexual couples in the *Family Law Act*'s duties of spousal support.[4]

What is most remarkable about the decision is how far the once-sober Ontario Court of Appeal has bought into the 1970s' clichés of pop sociology. Mr. Justice Charron (with whom Mr. Justice Doherty concurs) accepted the "expert" evidence of a sociologist that "a monolithic definition of the family is no longer adequate to reflect the complex realities of today"and held that the denial of interspousal support duties in a homosexual union violated section 15 of the Charter. Of dissenting voices, he heard only those of the radical "anti-assimilationists" who resist the effort to lower homosexuals to the unenlightened level of a traditional heterosexual marriage. Homosexual unions are happily free of the hierarchical gender roles of heterosexual marriage, and an Ontario court must resist "a stereotypical attribution of roles within a relationship." Thus:

> It is not surprising that many gay men and women would reject any assimilation to such a model since it would in effect require that they abandon the very identity they seek to protect, their sexual orientation towards a person of the same gender. (*M v H*, 37–38.)

4 142 DLR (4th) 1 (1996).

A recent Ontario Law Reform Commission Report (1993) expresses similar fears. It makes no mention of the argument that children are best protected by promoting traditional marriages. Instead, what bothers the commissioners is the possibility that homosexuals who do "not accept sexual monogamy and emotional exclusivity as ideals" might feel left out if homosexual unions were legitimized (ibid.). Because nonmonogamous homosexuals would not marry, homosexual solidarity would be weakened. As well, homosexual unions are more egalitarian and less burdened by relations of dependency than heterosexual marriages, and there is a danger that homosexuals might be corrupted by contact with a hierarchical heterosexual institution. Nevertheless, the commission recommended that homosexual unions be recognized by the state, in the hope that heterosexual marriages would be raised to the level of the egalitarian homosexual union, rather than the reverse.[5]

The Path Ahead

The logic of these cases, read together, suggests that barriers to homosexual marriages will be next to fall. *M v H* found that distinctions between unmarried heterosexual couples and homosexual

---

5 Remarkably, the Supreme Court recently held that the failure of Alberta's human rights legislation to refer to homosexuality is itself an example of unjustified discrimination and that the statute should be deemed to include sexual orientation as a protected classification (*Vriend v. Alberta*, 1998 Can. Sup. Ct. LEXIS 19, April 2, 1998).

The court emphasized the damage to the self-esteem of homosexuals. Writing for the majority, Mr. Justices Cory and Iacobucci stated:

Perhaps most important is the psychological harm which may ensue from this state of affairs. Fear of discrimination will logically lead to concealment of true identity and this must be harmful to personal confidence and self-esteem. Compounding that effect is the implicit message conveyed by the exclusion, that gays and lesbians, unlike other individuals, are not worthy of protection. This is clearly an example of a distinction which demeans the individual and strengthens and perpetrates the view that gays and lesbians are less worthy of protection as individuals in Canada's society. The potential harm to the dignity and perceived worth of gay and lesbian individuals constitutes a particularly cruel form of discrimination.

couples violated equality rights, while *Miron* impeached a distinction between unmarried and married heterosexual couples. If rights are transitive, a distinction between an unmarried homosexual couple and a married heterosexual one is also suspect. Even under *Egan*, any distinction between heterosexual and homosexual couples offends equality norms and is unlikely to survive in the more egalitarian future foreseen by the Supreme Court.

The recognition of homosexual unions might also come through legislative change, such as that proposed in the 1993 report of the Ontario Law Reform Commission. The report does not propose that homosexuals be given the right to marry each other. Instead, it recommends that the Ontario *Family Law Act* be amended to permit homosexuals to enter into cohabitation and domestic partnership agreements. Moreover, in British Columbia, homosexuals are now permitted to sue their partners for maintenance and support under 1997 amendments to that province's *Family Relations Act* and *Family Maintenance Enforcement Act*.

Distributional Theories

What is behind the drive for homosexual marriages? It might first be thought that, as a financial matter, homosexuals deserve to share in the wealth transfers that are an incident of marriage. But this claim is not compelling. The earnings of homosexuals do not appear to differ greatly from those of unmarried heterosexuals. Homosexuals do not seem poorer than the rest of us; if anything, they may be materially richer since they do not bear the burden of raising children. Alternatively, an economic subsidy for homosexuals might commend itself if tax laws placed a disproportionate burden on them. But there is no homosexual penalty tax.[6]

---

6 Indeed, in the United States, there is a *marriage* penalty tax, borne exclusively by heterosexuals. A married couple is required to file a joint income tax return, and when both parties work, they are taxed at a higher marginal rate than an unmarried couple. US tax law thereby subsidizes divorce, not marriage. The disincentive to marry is strongest when there is little likelihood of children and thus little need for one party to specialize in stay-at-home child rearing. As such, the disincentive to marry would be stronger for homosexual than for heterosexual couples.

If homosexuals as a class are not particularly deserving of state subsidies, it might yet be unjust to exclude them from a welfare scheme designed to benefit people whom they closely resemble. This was the rationale for the expansion of homosexual rights in *Egan* and *M* v *H*. The harm seen by the courts was not so much economic as symbolic and political. Excluding a class of people from participation in a state benefit, without valid reason, sends a message that they are second-class citizens.

The question, then, is whether conditioning a benefit on a heterosexual marriage or union may serve a valid state purpose. And indeed it might, as a subsidy for procreation (see Haddock and Polsby 1996). This was how Mr. Justice LaForest regarded the old age pension scheme in *Egan*. Marriage's "ultimate *raison d'être*," he stated,

> is firmly anchored in the biological and social realities that heterosexual couples have the unique ability to procreate, that most children are the product of these relationships, and that they are generally cared for and nurtured by those who live in that relationship. In this sense, marriage is by nature heterosexual. (P. 625.)

Social attitudes to homosexuality may change, as Mr. Justice Sopinka prophesied, without changing these realities, which are the basis for excluding homosexuals from procreation subsidies.

Why should a state not take an interest in who its members will be a generation hence? It gains citizens through immigration and birth, and so long as it is permitted to pick and choose among immigrants, it should also be permitted to promote procreation. To be sure, procreation subsidies may not discriminate on the basis of race or religion. But what of the subsidy that is neutral as to the child's identity and discriminates only between those households that can have children and those that cannot? A state may reasonably condition a subsidy to heterosexual couples and exclude industrial corporations, religious orders, and homosexual couples.

State subsidies for procreation, whether to parents or children, must offer parents an incentive that outweighs the costs they expect to bear in raising a child. These costs are plausibly higher today than in the past, particularly in The United States The decline in the quality of public schools and the dramatic rise in university tuition have increased the cost of raising a child, and this, in part, accounts for a declining middle-class birthrate. Alternatively, the cost of child bearing might be partially offset through direct subsidies to parents, such as the old age pension scheme impugned in *Egan*.

The *Egan* dissenters rejected the possibility that spousal support programs might have something to do with children since the old age pension scheme was not conditioned on whether a couple had had (or could have had) a child. But formalistic *ex post* distinctions of this kind ignore the *ex ante* incentives of the parties at the time of marriage. The prospect of increased financial support for married couples on retirement can be expected to result in higher marriage rates, as the parties react to the subsidy. And this, in turn, might be expected to result in higher birth levels. The subsidy is more direct still since it appeals to stay-at-home spouses who have chosen to forgo a career to look after their children. From an *ex ante* perspective, then, a state may plausibly adopt an old age pension program as a procreation subsidy.

Such policies are underinclusive since some children are raised by homosexual couples; they are also overinclusive since some heterosexual couples are incapable of having children. But this objection is not particularly telling if all but the smallest handful of children are raised by heterosexual couples. How could one legislate if laws might be impeached for underinclusiveness or overinclusiveness? Consider speed limits, which are adopted as a proxy for dangerous driving. They are both underinclusive (some poor drivers cannot drive safely at the legal limit) and underinclusive (some good drivers can drive safely above the legal limit). Should we then ban speed limits and ticket only those whose driving is dangerous from a subjective perspective? That outcome would increase accident rates for it is very difficult to tailor a rule for each individual.

The Private Benefits of Marriage

Thus, the recognition of homosexual marriages cannot be justified on distributional grounds. Might it, however, be defended on efficiency grounds, by affording gains to the couple or to society? In this section, I discuss the private benefits marriage affords a couple; in following sections, I discuss the gains to society at large.

For heterosexual and homosexual couples, marriage offers two possible private benefits: signaling and self-binding gains. *Signaling* refers to the valuable information provided by an offer of marriage or by marriage itself. *Self-binding* gains comes from removing future temptations from one's path.

Signaling Costs

The marriage signal arises because cohabiting couples can leave a relationship at lower cost when they are unmarried. Through an offer of marriage, therefore, they can better persuade each other of their commitment to the union. The marriage bond may thus be seen as a hands-tying device through which parties who want to stay together provide stronger information about their preferences (Bishop 1984). With better information about the probability of the union's survival, spouses can invest in it at less risk. Without the signal provided by marriage, the spouses may hesitate before making major investments in the union, such as children. (The advent of no-fault divorce has regrettably weakened the signal provided by marriage, but it is still a stronger signal than that of mere cohabitation.)

This information is of greatest use to the other spouse. But it may also be of use to third parties if being married correlates with other attributes they value. For example, married men live longer than unmarried men, so insurance companies may wish to separate the two groups into separate pools (unless antidiscrimination norms prevent them from doing so). Employers and clients may also prefer to deal with married people if marriage signals prized qualities, such as stability.

Since homosexuals are not permitted to marry, they are denied these benefits. Yet such costs are much smaller for homosexual than for heterosexual couples. The need to signal information is greatest when the cost of a breakup is highest — when children are born or anticipated. For heterosexuals, therefore, the benefit of the marriage signal vastly exceeds that for homosexuals. Abolish marriage for everyone, and heterosexual couples would still seek to signal through private agreements that imposed costs on the party who caused the breakup. But there is little evidence that homosexuals seek to use private contracts to bargain around the ban on homosexual marriage. This suggests that signaling gains from the recognition of homosexual marriage would be modest.

What of the gains from signaling to third parties, such as employers and clients? For the signal to be effective, the homosexual would likely have to signal his sexual preference as well as his marriage, and he may well hesitate to do so. Even today, relatively few homosexuals would be willing to "out" themselves to third parties, if anti-homosexual sentiments remain as strong as the *Egan* dissenters thought they were. It would be otherwise if anti-homosexual sentiments were weak. In that case, however, there would be little need to adopt largely symbolic legislation whose primary purpose is to raise the status of homosexuals.

Self-Binding Gains

Self-binding gains arise when it is in one's interest to commit to a future choice. Today I may want to choose at a future time to do x, but fear that when that time comes I will lack the strength of will to make the right choice. It may then be rational for me to act today to narrow my range of future choices to x.

Thus, a heterosexual couple may decide to bind themselves against a future divorce through couple-specific investments, such as children. While marriage counselors may criticize such policies, at least when the marriage is on the rocks, they are likely an effective self-binding strategy. In a troubled marriage, the parties may stay together "for the sake of the kids." Or their troubles may seem minor because the children have cemented the union.

Homosexual couples may also employ self-binding strategies. For example, the parties may purchase a house because the need to sell it increases the costs of breaking up the relationship (Buckley 1995). Some couples will stay together "for the sake of the house."

Others will never be tempted to leave the relationship because the house purchase has weakened the temptation to stray.

Andrew Sullivan (1995) advances a conservative case for homosexual marriage that rests on the possibility of self-binding gains. Marriages, he argues, foster more stable and committed relationships for homosexuals as well as heterosexuals, and these are eminently conservative goals.

Religious conservatives will dispute this point. For example, the Catholic Church distinguishes between homosexuals, who are entitled to respect and even compassion, and homosexual activity, which is sinful. On this view, homosexuals should be discouraged from, rather than encouraged toward "marriage." Of course, nonbelievers may feel that religious views on moral issues should not inform the content of our law (with the result that nonreligious beliefs are privileged). But this is not what Sullivan is saying. Instead, he argues that the recognition of homosexual marriages would be consistent with conservative beliefs, and this claim is clearly wrong.

Even if Sullivan fails to persuade conservatives, however, homosexuals may still seek the self-binding gains of marriage. Is there a reason to restrict these gains to heterosexual couples?

One may first suggest that homosexuals do not need to marry since substitute self-binding strategies are available. For example, they can purchase property jointly or enter into a cohabitation agreement. From a financial perspective, a marriage contract might add little by way of an exit penalty in modern no-fault divorce regimes. But this proves too much since the same substitutes are available to heterosexual couples. Moreover, marriage does add something: a solemn sacramental bond, broken at great emotional cost. Why should this be reserved to heterosexuals?

The answer, of course, is children. When a married couple has children, the cost of a breakup is far higher. And couples who have not yet had children are less likely to do so when breakup costs are reduced. Heterosexual couples can thus be expected to adopt stronger self-binding strategies than homosexual couples. Indeed, the presence or possibility of children explains why unmarried heterosexual couples appear more likely to adopt substitute self-binding strategies, such as house purchases, than homosexual couples.

It is no answer that some heterosexual couples are sterile or too old to have children. The self-binding gains are indeed weaker in such cases. However, barring such couples from marriage would amount to imposing a fertiilty test on all heterosexual couples before marriage. This would increase the cost of marriage and reduce marriage levels to little end.

Yet this is not a sufficient answer. Even if heterosexual couples are more likely to adopt self-binding strategies, why deny them to homosexual couples that may want them as well? The answer, which I discuss in the next section, is that recognizing homosexual unions would weaken the signal of heterosexual marriage and reduce the institution's self-binding gains.

Libertarian and Conservative Theories

The Libertarian Argument

The libertarian defense of homosexual marriage is broader in scope than the antidiscrimination theories advanced by the *Egan* dissenters. On antidiscrimination norms, a state may not distinguish among classes of people in conferring benefits on its citizens. In itself, however, this says nothing about what a state must or must not do for them. Thus, a state determined to channel its citizens into or away from marriage might grant all couples the same subsidies or subject them to the same disabilities. But channeling of this kind is anathema for libertarians, who would limit state interference with personal choices. All parties would then be free to marry — without disabilities but without subsides either.

The Harm-to-Others Principle

By banning subsidies, libertarians would avoid most problems of discriminatory state programs. However, they would still have to choose which contracts to enforce (unless they also banned the state machinery of contract enforcement). The most widely accepted libertarian standard for contract enforcement is the harm-to-others principle of John Stuart Mill ([1859] 1985). Under this test, a contract freely agreed to is presumptively enforceable if it does not impose external costs in the form of physical harm on a third party. (Even contracts that impose such harm may be enforced if the contractors take the trouble to include the third party in their agreement, internalizing the externality).

The harm-to-others principle is really two principles in one. First, it is a theory of antipaternalism so far as parties to the contract are concerned. That is, it conclusively presumes that the bargainers are the best judges of their own welfare. The contract may be set aside if tainted by a vice of consent, such as misrepresentation, mistake, or duress, or by a vice of capacity, as when one of the parties is a minor or mentally disabled. But these problems apart, the libertarian would enforce the contract.

Second, the harm-to-others principle is a theory about what counts as a harm. Under the principle, contracts that impose *physical* harm on a third party are banned, while contracts that impose *nonphysical* moral or aesthetic external costs are upheld. Vulgar forms of libertarianism simply deny that the latter kind of costs exist. More sophisticated libertarians admit that private contracts may impose moral and aesthetic costs but nonetheless ignore them because of a fear of excessive interference with personal preferences. As they point out, almost anything may count as a third-party moral or aesthetic cost or benefit. For example, the well-dressed woman who walks down the street confers external benefits on passersby, but this does not argue for subsidizing the well dressed or penalizing the dowdy. To keep paternalism within bounds, therefore, libertarians require a physical harm before they refuse to enforce a contract.

The failure to observe the difference between the two branches of the harm-to-others principle leads to confusion. For example, libertarians would enforce a waiver of divorce rights under the first branch of the principle and homosexual marriages under the second. That is, they would permit the parties to enter into a Louisiana covenant marriage, in which the right to a no-fault divorce is waived, because restrictions on the right to elect the form of marriage are paternalistic. And they would permit homosexual marriages because their moral costs, as perceived by conservatives, are not a physical harm.

The Costs of Homosexual Marriage

The distinction between the two branches of the harm-to-others principle can also be observed from the perspective of those who oppose covenant or homosexual marriages. Many liberals support homosexual marriages but object to covenant marriages because they think that those who are about to marry cannot be trusted to elect marriage options wisely. And most conservatives support covenant marriages while opposing homosexual marriages. They are not paternalists, however, for their opposition to homosexual marriage is based on perceived social costs. They assert that marriage would be less attractive for heterosexuals were homosexuals permitted to marry and that a decline in marriage rates and in the number of children born into married families would be enormously costly to society.

The debate about homosexual marriage is thus a debate about its social or nonphysical costs. Libertarians might first make the empirical claim that homosexual marriages would not impose social costs or that any such costs would be exceeded by social benefits. Second, they might claim that, even if such costs exist, it is wiser to disregard them as a matter of public policy.

Take the second claim first. To do so, one must assume that homosexual marriages would impose social costs, in just the manner that conservatives claim, and that these costs would exceed any possible social benefits. For example, assume that legalizing homosexual marriages would trivialize what had been regarded as a sacrament and that this would contribute to a decline in family ties and general communitarian sentiments. These would be real costs, one assumes, yet still libertarians would ignore them. Economist and ordinary people would find this puzzling. If costs are costs, the difference between physical and social harm should not matter.

Suppose next that the social costs of homosexual marriage lead, in turn, to physical costs — say, more violence in fragmented societies where people do not marry. Libertarians who would still ignore social costs would then be driven to distinguish between direct and indirect physical harm. Contracts that impose direct physical harm would be illegal, but not those where the harm is only indirect. Nor would it matter if the indirect physical harm were far more severe than the direct harm.

Unless one is an absolutist and comfortable with metaphysical distinctions, the libertarians' concession of social costs seems fatal. Their defense of homosexual marriage must, therefore, rest on the first, empirical claim — that social costs would not arise or that if they do they would be exceeded by social gains. Conservatives explicitly deny such claims, for reasons explained below.

The Conservative Argument

The libertarians' empirical claim was more frequently heard 30 years ago, when social experiments seemed costless. No-fault divorce laws would not increase divorce levels, and illegitimacy subsidies would not lead to higher unwed birth rates. Those were the days in which a confident H.L.A. Hart could scoff at Lord Devlin's social conservatism. "No reputable historian has maintained [Devlin's] thesis," which is "absurd" says Hart (1962, 50,51), and for 30 years we thought he was right. But now the evidence is in, and it is less clear that Devlin lost the debate. Stable marriages are better than broken ones, and illegitimate children fare more poorly than those raised in family structures (see generally, Blankenhorn 1995; Popenoe 1996).

Thus, the libertarian's *a priori* assertion that a change in family structures never imposes social costs rings untrue. Still, it does not follow that *every* change in social norms presages the fall of the society and the state. Nor is there much evidence, one way or the other, on the social consequences of legitimizing homosexual unions.

The Liberals' Slippery-Slope Argument

In an empirical vacuum, one falls back on first principles. For liberals, the fundamental principle is one of liberty and free contracting, which amounts to a presumption that bargains do not impose external costs. This is why Mill's distinction between physical and non-physical costs appeals to sophisticated liberals.

The difference is not between real and imagined harm but between readily observable and hard-to-measure harm. Some private choices may impose public costs. But the empirical uncertainties argue for prudence in legislating morality. Since almost anything may count as a social cost and since such costs are so difficult to measure, taking them into account may result in the adoption of illiberal laws. For example, homosexual acts might again be made criminal. Liberals, therefore, assign a value of zero to the social costs of private acts, not because they are costless but because the costs of illiberal laws would exceed their benefits were we to legislate morality so finely.

To conservatives, this assumption of zero social costs looks suspiciously like a preference for round numbers (none being rounder than zero). For if liberals are willing to concede *some* social costs, why assume that they amount to zero, rather than a more plausible higher number? But if the number is higher, then what should it be? The problem is that no higher number readily suggests itself, and for this reason, zero may commend itself as a simple and commonly ascertainable focal point. If we must have a number but cannot agree on its value, then the virtue of zero is that it is clear and easily operationalized; at zero social costs, all contracts are enforced unless they impose physical harm on third parties. By contrast, if we assume that higher but undefined number, then how will we ever have an agreement about what that number is or what contracts will be enforced?

This is an abstract and philosophical argument. Can conservatives rebut it? I believe they can, with an empirical, not a philosophical, answer. Liberals claim that any attempt to legislate general social norms leads down a slippery slope to a moral tyranny. And this claim is asserted so often and so confidently that they are apt to forget that it is really an *empirical* claim. If it is meaningful, it amounts to a prediction that relaxing the assumption of zero social costs will result in a moral tyranny.

Of all people, Canadians should be suspicious of such arguments. If they were correct, then Canadians would be far less free than Americans, with their absolutist constitutional guarantees of free speech and free exercise and free mobility and free elections. And yet, when they think on it, Canadians may reasonably conclude that they have no lessons in liberty to take from Americans. Not every power is taken to the limit. Many states confer a broad authority on lawmakers without thereby losing their liberty.

For this reason, Devlin rejects the slippery slope claim that any effort to enforce morals must lead to tyranny and for his counterexample gives the common law of England. Common law rules, he says, were concerned with the "minimum and not the maximum" (1965, 19). Not every moral rule should be legislated, only those necessary for the preservation of society. Beyond that, "[t]here must be toleration of the maximum individual freedom that is consistent with the integrity of society" (ibid., 16). And this, Devlin thinks, the common law did. Where critics such as Hart have gone wrong is in taking Devlin's concern for the preservation of society as a philosophical definition of his thesis, rather than as a pragmatic restriction on excessive and illiberal laws.

The Conservatives' Slippery-Slope Argument

Suppose, then, that one rejects the liberals' slippery-slope argument and with it the assumption that social costs should be entirely disregarded. But now conservatives may be faulted for relying on their own slippery slope argument. They assume, without evidence, that the recognition of homosexual marriages would result in a general social decline. Yet how is a ban on homosexual marriage necessary for the preservation of society? How is *anything* necessary for the preservation of society save the most basic of physical protections?

Stating the problem in this way may appear to give Devlin's opponents a cheap victory. But the conservative case is not so easily defeated. Between extreme and absolutist positions is a common-sensical *via media*. Moderate conservatives reject both the libertarians' claim that any enforcement of morals must result in a moral tyranny and the extreme conservatives' claim that any relaxation of social norms must destroy society. Homosexual marriage is an example of this: were it permitted, the state would not fall; nor would we lapse into a moral fascism were it banned. The stakes are lower than that, all around.

Let us first recall that the slight to homosexuals is very mild indeed. Of all the ways in which homosexuals may feel injured, barring same-sex marriages is the least intrusive and very mildest. This is not a constable standing before Oscar Wilde at the Cadogan Hotel but a restriction not even recognized as a disability until very recently. And even now, those who regard marriage as a flawed institution do not see this as a disability.

Nor is there anything to stop a homosexual couple from sealing their union with a partnership or joint-ownership agreement. Through such arrangements, two people can bind themselves together almost as closely as a married couple. Of course, neither party can bring an action for breach on nonperformance of sexual favors. But this is also the case for unmarried heterosexuals. Nor are married people likely to sue for breach of a promise for sexual services. Instead, they may simply rely on the unilateral exit option of a no-fault divorce. Thus, a cohabitation agreement, in which either party may leave at will, may give same-sex couples almost as much security as they would have in a marriage contract.

Symbolism: The Real Issue

What a cohabitation agreement does not give a homosexual couple is the status of a marriage certificate. This status, more than anything, is the real issue in the debate. What homosexual advocates want most of all is the recognition that a right to marriage would confer on them. And that recognition is what conservatives are most concerned to resist. The issue is not the economic benefits associated with the symbol so much as the symbol itself and the status it confers on those who marry.

The marriage contract may be thought of as a badge awarded by the state to those who choose to enter into a preferred relationship. It is like an honor or dignity, which is devalued if everyone may share in it. If it were broadened to include homosexual or polygamous marriages, it would become less special and distinct. Its symbolic value would be weakened in the same way that the Victoria Cross would be cheapened if awarded to every member of the Order of Canada. "In asserting that any thing is honourable, we imply some distinction in its favor," noted Edmund Burke ([1790] 1993, 49).

To say that all estates are honorable is to say that none is, for honor exists only in contradistinction to the base. If recognizing same-sex marriages would be of symbolic benefit to homosexuals, it would plausibly impose symbolic costs on heterosexuals that might easily exceed the benefits.

Such costs may arise in one of two ways. First, recognition of homosexual marriage would weaken the sacramental respect accorded marriage by those who think homosexual sex wrongful. *Bien pensant* intellectuals are not apt to hold such people in very high esteem and may be only too happy to suppress their sentiments. However, the cost of weakening the bonds of their marriages must be taken into account on any theory that pretends to be neutral between religion and irreligion.

Second, antidiscrimination norms are distressingly broad in scope. Suppose that homosexual couples were permitted to marry or to share in spousal benefits. What principled basis could be advanced to exclude other "marriages," such as the incestuous couple or the group marriage, from such rights? Such unions violate religious norms, but that cannot be the difference in a religiously neutral state. Incestuous and polygamous unions are subject to greater social sanctions today than homosexual relationships, but if it were simply a matter of social norms, past discrimination against homosexuals would have been justified. Nor can it be a matter of numbers. There are very few incestuous and polygamous couples, but it would be odd if homosexuals argued for the suppression of sexual minorities. Indeed, such groups may be small in size precisely because social sanctions are so severe. The smaller is the size, one might think, the greater the need for remedial antidiscrimination laws.

The broad equality norms enunciated by the *Egan* dissenters are not easy to rein in. "Disagreement, no matter how small, at the foundational level of establishing the right's purpose will only magnify over time in terms of how that right is *applied*" (*Egan*, 629). Is human dignity worth less to the polygamist? Are incestuous couples less deserving of concern, respect, and consideration? "Equality means that our society cannot tolerate legislative distinctions that treat certain people as second-class citizens, that demean them, that treat them as less capable for no good reason, or that otherwise offend fundamental dignity" (ibid., 631). And if a special duty of concern is owed to those who have suffered historic discrimination, as Mme. Justice L'Heureux-Dubé argues, few groups were treated more harshly in North America than the nineteenth-century Mormon pioneers before they banned polygamy.

If marriage would promote monogamy for a homosexual couple, it might do the same for the polygamous couple. Jules, Jim, and Kathe were faithful to each other, in their fashion. But sexual fidelity must be thought a false ideal if the relationship is regarded as wrongful. What matters is whether the relationship is seen as benign or perverse. If it is seen as perverse, then anything that strengthens the bond, such as marriage, seems doubly perverse, for it makes it more likely that a wrongful relationship will persist and weaken the institution of marriage.

Andrew Sullivan seeks to respond to this challenge by arguing that homosexual unions are more fundamental than polygamous and incestuous ones (1997, 278). The distinction is troublesome, however, since it appears to rest on a conception of natural law that offers scant comfort to homosexuals (George 1997; George and Bradley 1995). To say that polygamous unions are not fundamental is much like saying that homosexual unions are unnatural. Neither statement tells one very much, except that the speaker dislikes such unions.

Sullivan might more plausibly argue that the social stigma of homosexuality is weaker than it is for incest or polygamy. If that is so, then homosexual marriages would be less likely to weaken the institution of marriage than incestuous and polygamous marriages. This is not an argument that incest and polygamy are perverse, but only that most people think them so and that majoritarian moral sentiments should shape legal rules because of the possibility of spillover effects on legal institutions. On this theory, the state should follow, not shape, social norms. But if social norms are to be followed, we are unlikely to recognize homosexual marriages if the stigma against them is as great as the *Egan* dissenters supposed. Indeed, one could easily have thought that the whole point was to weaken the stigma of homosexuality.

Respecting Differences

One thing everyone seems to agree on is that homosexual marriages would be quite different from heterosexual ones. Thus, the Ontario Law Reform Commission (1993) reports that homosexuals are less likely to insist on marital fidelity. Nor is this surprising since homosexuals bear no risk of illegitimate children, as heterosexuals do when they stray. Homosexual couples are also likely to have different attitudes to divorce. Since there is no need for one spouse to specialize in child rearing in a homosexual union, both spouses are more likely to be employed and financially independent. The absence of children would also reduce the emotional costs of divorce. Thus, homosexuals, but not heterosexuals, would ordinarily prefer a divorce regime in which either party can leave the marriage without delays or lingering financial responsibilities.

The recognition of homosexual marriages would uneasily yoke two quite different kinds of couples under a common set of rules, and this is unlikely to satisfy either heterosexuals or homosexuals. Heterosexuals would find that the default rules of marriage had changed and no longer suit them so well as formerly. For example, the movement in several US state legislatures to reintroduce fault requirements in divorce might be scotched, even if this change appealed to most heterosexual couples.

To some extent, heterosexual couples might solve this problem through side agreements that ratchet up mutual obligations. However, such agreements would face substantial barriers. Divorce laws cannot be waived (Brinig and Buckley 1998), so heterosexual couples might be forced to live with an excessively lax divorce regime. The parties might also find it difficult to bargain around default marriage rules since doing so might send an unflattering signal about a fiancée's thoughts about the marriage or her own personal qualities. For example, her demand for a tough prenuptual agreement might suggest that she has failed to disclose faults that, when revealed, would lead her husband to seek a divorce. Squabbling over money would also send the wrong signal about the intensity of romantic love.

All this explains why states offer the parties a single marriage regime and why it would be costly to assimilate marriage to a very different kind of union (Allen 1990).

Conclusion

In sum, the case for homosexual marriage is not compelling. To the extent that homosexuals are excluded by policies that seek to promote procreation and child raising, the restrictions are moderate and sensible. The efficiency gains homosexuals might exploit through marriage would be small since they have far less incentive to marry than child-rearing heterosexuals. What remains is the symbol of state approval that the recognition of homosexual marriage would accord them and that homosexuals may desire even if they never expect to marry. I need not comment on whether this goal is desirable. Doubtless, some think that there is no price too high to pay for the single issue they support. I seek only to note the costs of norm manipulation when the engine of change is the recognition of homosexual marriages.

With marriage rates so low today and divorce rates so high, we should be concerned to strengthen, not weaken, marriage. The evidence of its benefits and of the costs of broken homes and divorce is so clear that this can hardly be thought an issue that divides heterosexuals and homosexuals. For while some members of the present generation of homosexuals may seek to marry, future generations of homosexuals have a stake in the heterosexual marriages in which they will be raised. Weakening the institution of marriage would harm them along with everyone else.

References

Allen, Douglas W. 1990. "An Inquiry into the State's Role in Marriage." *Journal of Economic Behavior and Organization* 13: 171–191.

Bishop, William. 1984. "Is He Married? Marriage as Information." *University of Toronto Law Journal* 34: 245.

Blankenhorn, David. 1995. *Fatherless America: Confronting Our Most Urgent Social Problem*. New York: Basic Books.

Brinig, Margaret F., and F.H. Buckley. 1998. "No-Fault Laws and At-Fault People." *International Review of Law and Economics* 18: 325.

———, and F.H. Buckley. Forthcoming. "The Price of Virtue." *Public Choice*.

Buckley, F.H. 1995. "The American Fresh Start." *Southern California Interdisciplinary Law Journal* 4: 67.

Burke, Edmund. [1790] 1993. *Reflections on the Revolution in France*. Oxford: Oxford University Press.

Devlin, Patrick. 1965. *The Enforcement of Morals*. Oxford: Oxford University Press.

George, Robert P. 1997. "Public Reason and Public Conflict: Abortion and Homosexuality." *Yale Law Journal* 106: 2475.

———, and Gerald V. Bradley. 1995. "Marriage and the Liberal Imagination." *Georgetown Law Journal* 84: 301.

Haddock, David D., and Daniel D. Polsby. 1996. "Family as a Rational Classification." *Washington University Law Quarterly* 74: 15.

Hart, H.L.A. 1962. *Law, Liberty and Morality*. Oxford: Oxford University Press.

Lasch, Christopher. 1977. *Haven in a Heartless World: The Family Besieged*. New York: Basic Books.

Mill, John Stuart. [1859] 1985. *On Liberty*. Harmondsworth: Penguin Books.

Ontario Law Reform Commission. 1993. *Report on the Rights and Responsibilities of Cohabitants under the Family Law Act*. Toronto.

Popenoe, David. 1996. *Life without Father*. New York: Free Press.

Posner, Richard A. 1992. *Sex and Reason*. Cambridge, Mass.: Harvard University Press.

Sullivan, Andrew. 1995. *Virtually Normal: An Argument about Homosexuality*. New York: Knopf.

———. 1997. *Same Sex Marriage: Pro and Con*. New York: Vintage.

Truffaut, François. 1971. *Jules et Jim*. Paris: Seuil.

Putting Tax Policy in Its Place:
How Social Policy Took Over the Tax Treatment of the Family

Kenneth J. Boessenkool

Fifty years is an eternity in the evolution of a tax system. For example, not one element in Canada's tax treatment of the family from 1950 survives today. Indeed, hardly an element remains even from as recently as 1985. The need to raise ever-increasing amounts of revenue and satisfy new priorities has increased pressure for change.

Judging by the changes made to Canada's tax laws since 1949, the most pressing of the new priorities have been in the realm of social policy. Particularly with respect to children, the past 25 years have seen a proliferation of social policy mechanisms within the tax system. Between the mid-1980s and the mid-1990s, three different such mechanisms tied to the tax system provided cash payments to parents with children.

In this essay, I argue that social policy has overtaken tax policy as the main objective behind the provisions of Canada's tax system that relate to the family. To make this argument, in the first two sections I distinguish between tax policy and social policy frameworks in the tax treatment of the family, concluding that an equitable and efficient system for raising revenues (tax policy) is quite different from an equitable and efficient system for transferring money to the less well off. In the next section, I look back at the tax policy and social policy treatment of marriage and children in Canada over the past 50 years, and find that Ottawa's social policy tools have edged legitimate tax policy objectives out of the *Income Tax Act*.

The final section begins with a summary of three difficulties that arise from this confusion of social and tax policy objectives. First, the tax system no longer recognizes the cost of raising children in all families. Second, to the extent that the tax system has relieved the burden for middle- and upper-income families with children, it has done so disproportionately for dual-earner families through generous child care exemptions. Finally, the combination of clawed-back social policy transfers plus income and other taxes has created unacceptably high effective marginal tax rates for families earning between $20,000 and $30,000. Any reform must lower these punishing marginal rates, which exceed 60 percent for a significant number of families.

This section then offers several proposals that would make significant progress on all three problems just outlined.

The Principles of Tax Policy

Canada's tax system is about much more than raising the required revenues for government expenditures. It is also an instrument of industrial, cultural, and, of concern here, social policy. This mix of objectives has complicated the tax act, and made it more difficult to analyze the tax system from a tax policy point of view. The objectives of tax policy are, for example, often in conflict with the objectives of social policy. This section and the next discuss the principles underlying, respectively, tax and social policy in Canada, providing a framework from which to evaluate how the tax act has treated families from both of these points of view.[1]

Discretionary Economic Power

It has been more than 30 years since the Carter Commission gave its recommendations on Canada's tax system. The commission put forward the commonly held notion that taxes should be "allocated in proportion to the 'discretionary economic power' of tax units" (Canada 1966, 3:5).

---

1 This discussion borrows liberally from Boessenkool and Davies (1998).

Economic power can be understood either in a utilitarian sense or in terms of the more pragmatic concept of ability to pay. The two are closely related but distinct. Utilitarians suggest that families whose welfare would be equal in the absence of taxation should bear equal burdens (see, for example, Davies 1992, table 5.3 and accompanying text). The ability-to-pay approach admits the possibility that the interpretation of a family's ability to pay will mean something other than its welfare — that is, its annual income. This approach is pragmatic in that it attempts to use more accessible and understandable proxies to measure, and tax, citizens' ability to pay.

The utilitarian approach requires that everything that contributes to welfare must be incorporated into the tax system. Examples of elements to be taken into account include the increase in welfare enjoyed by the family with a stay-at-home spouse ("home production" or the "imputed income of the housewife"); mutual emergency assistance; the imputed rent enjoyed by homeowners; enjoyment of marriage; leisure; and the benefits that stay-at-home spouses contribute to their communities. A utilitarian approach must measure and include all these forms of imputed income if the tax system is truly to reflect individual or family welfare.

The difficulty with the utilitarian approach is that nonmonetary sources of welfare are notoriously difficult to measure. The Carter Commission summarized the difficulties with the utilitarian approach as follows:

> If imputed income cannot be taxed without even a modicum of consistency, we do not think it should be taxed arbitrarily when it is convenient to do so and ignored where there are difficulties. We therefore reject the idea that there should be differences in tax between couples with the same aggregate income as a method of taxing imputed income of husbands and wives who are not working outside the home. (Canada 1966, 118–119).

On the taxation of home production, the Ontario Fair Tax Commission took a similar view, although for different reasons:

> Everyone must keep a house to some extent or pay for the service. As it is an expense that is incurred independently of earning

> income, it is not truly relevant to the determination of an individual's tax liability...Labour necessary for maintaining a household is not relevant to tax at all. (1993, 270.)

While the utilitarian approach may make for good theory, setting it up in practice is difficult. Most analysts, therefore, have accepted the more pragmatic ability-to-pay approach and have gravitated toward accepting money income as the most appropriate, and measurable, proxy for ability to pay.

Choice of Tax Unit

Taxes can be levied on citizens using one of two units: the individual or the family. If ability to pay does not depend on family status, then the appropriate unit of taxation is the individual. A strict interpretation of this view would hold that an individual earning $50,000 should pay the same amount of tax whatever his or her marital status.

If marital status does affect ability to pay, then that information should be reflected in the tax system (Davies 1992, 169). The difficulty comes in determining how. One way to do this is to use adult-equivalent scales, which allow comparisons of the standard of living of families of varying sizes. Such scales are implicit in measures such as Statistics Canada's low-income cutoffs (LICOs), which determine what levels of income provide similar levels of welfare for families of different sizes (Jorgenson 1998; Triest 1998). They are also implicit in the differing welfare rates of various provinces, which provide a minimum (and therefore common) standard of living to different types of families.

For example, the 1995 Ontario basic social assistance level (after the Progressive Conservative government's reforms were in place) for a single, employable individual was $6,240 per year, while a couple with two children received $14,568. These values imply an adult-equivalent scale for the couple with two children of 2.33 ($14,568 divided by $6,240).[2]

---

2 This is the lowest adult-equivalent value for a couple with two children implied by provincial welfare rates. The highest value is New Brunswick's at 4.02. The Canadian average is 2.99.

The case for joint filing would be straightforward in a world that found such an approach morally acceptable and in which the following conditions held:

- there was equal sharing in marriage;
- it was easy to determine who was married and people did not cohabit unless they were married; and
- there existed a broadly accepted procedure for establishing equitable, distinct tax schedules for singles and couples.

To address the first condition, the adult-equivalent approach assumes that all income earned by a family is shared by the members of that family, or at least that the family shares in the consumption benefits the income produces. If this assumption holds true, then it is fair to place the same tax burden on all families with the same income, no matter what the source of that income is (a single earner or two earners).

At the other extreme from equal sharing, we could assume that each spouse's standard of living depends largely on his or her individual earnings.[3] In this view, in single-earner families the primary earner could enjoy a much higher standard of living than the secondary earner. In such a case, giving the high-earning spouse a large tax break compared with a single person earning the same amount, as occurs under a joint filing system, seems inappropriate.

Which view of marriage is correct? Many Canadian families do share income among family members. This must be the case with single-earner families and with nearly all families for certain expenditures, such as housing. The average household expenditure on shelter, household operations, and home furnishings is nearly one-third of after-tax expenditures (Statistics Canada 1998). Thus, al-

---

3 There has been much recent modeling of economic decisionmaking within families, some of which is done in a bargaining context. In some "divorce threat" models, a spouse's bargaining strength increases with the attractiveness of his or her outside option. In other models, a spouse's threat is to retreat to traditional gender roles rather than to seek divorce. See Lundberg and Pollak (1993) and Phipps and Burton (1996).

though the concept of sharing may offend the philosophic tendencies of some, it is clearly a reality for others.

As expressed in the second condition above, joint filing — particularly when it confers benefits or penalties on the taxpayers who make use of it — requires an easy and commonly accepted marker of who is eligible so provisions can be enforced reasonably. But the explosion of common-law relationships and the questions raised by other permanent joint living arrangements,[4] make such a determination increasingly difficult. As the definition of "married" becomes less clear, there are increased opportunities to play the system by revealing relations only when the net tax benefits of doing so outweigh the disadvantages. Joint filing would reduce total taxes for some couples and increase it for others — particularly for couples where both spouses have significant earnings. Common-law couples in the latter situation may, understandably, prefer not to file jointly.

Determining who can, or must, file jointly is an administrative matter that severely complicates a joint-filing tax system. A system of individual filing minimizes complications, although a less severe problem remains as long as the tax code contains some features, such as spousal deductions or spousal Registered Retirement Savings Plans (RRSPs), that recognize family members.

Finally, there is the question of whether broadly acceptable distinct tax schedules can be devised for couples and individuals. This third condition really involves two questions: Can fair distinct tax schedules be devised? Would they be publicly acceptable? The first question boils down to whether a reasonable adult-equivalent scale can be identified. While it would be hard to get all the experts to agree on a single scale, they might be able to agree that an adult equivalent for a married couple of, say, 1.4 makes more sense than an equivalent of 2 or 1. The political feasibility of applying such a scale would depend in large measure on how the changes affected taxpayers and what compromises could be reached between extreme positions.

---

4 The recent federal decision not to appeal the Rosenburg decision suggests that it is contemplating extending "marriage" to same-sex couples.

Where does this leave joint filing? I see no overwhelming reason to reject either joint or individual filing when it comes designing a tax system. While there are conceptual advantages to a joint-filing system,[5] practical considerations favor an individual system. This tension perhaps explains why the Canadian system, while based on the principle of individual filing, includes a number of features that accommodate marriage. This Canadian compromise underpins my analysis in the rest of this essay.

Discretionary and Nondiscretionary Income

Once the unit of taxation has been determined, there are two further considerations in designing a tax code, both of which involve distinguishing between discretionary and nondiscretionary income. The Carter Commission defined discretionary economic power as the proportion of a tax unit's command over goods and services not required to "maintain the members of the unit" (Canada 1966, 3:5).

The first of these other concerns is exempting nondiscretionary income from taxation. The second is progressivity — ensuring that those with greater discretionary income pay a greater proportion of their income in tax.

Exempting Nondiscretionary Income

Exemptions for nondiscretionary income fall into two categories: expenses incurred in earning income and personal nondiscretionary expenditures. In an individual-based tax system, these expenditures are recognized by having a basic personal amount that each taxpayer can use to exclude, for example, health- and disability-related expenditures.

---

5 Davies (1992) and Boessenkool and Davies (1998) go further and argue that the adult-equivalent procedure provides a useful benchmark against which to evaluate any tax system.

There is less agreement as to whether supporting children and nonworking spouses should be considered a nondiscretionary expense. Hedonists reject exclusions for children by arguing that, since parents have children voluntarily and enjoy a higher utility as a result, they should not receive subsidies or tax recognition for these children any more than they would for any other voluntary activity that results in higher utility.

Hedonist arguments ignore, however, the moral and legal obligation parents have to care for their children. From an equity stand-point, therefore, a parent's income should not be taxed on the same basis as it was before a child was present. Parents should be subject to a lower tax rate or to some other recognition of children within the tax system. Dependent spouses have a similar claim on family income.

Efficiency-based arguments are also relevant. Families (including the children themselves) do not capture all of the benefits of the human capital investments represented by raising children.[6] Society overall benefits, if only because of the need to collect future taxes to pay for social policy transfers. From an economic point of view, this argument implies that, without a tax subsidy on child rearing, society would have too little fertility.

These arguments for dependent deductions are not, in the first instance, based on utilitarian concerns. Rather, they are based on the idea that the level of money income available to an individual who has a dependent spouse and/or child is less than the level of money income available to a single individual, and that the tax system should account for this difference in discretionary income by levying different tax burdens.

Progressivity

The most important way of ensuring progressivity in a tax system is to set an appropriate structure. Another progressivity consideration

---

6 This is similar to the arguments for investment in primary and secondary education that compare the public and private return on such expenditures (see Constantatos and West 1991).

is the choice of mechanism for excluding nondiscretionary income — deductions (excluding a determined amount of income from total income before applying the tax rate) or credits (subtracting a determined amount from tax payable after applying the tax rate to taxable income).

In a tax system with a single rate (a flat tax), it would make no difference whether a deduction or a credit were used. In a tax system with a progressive rate structure, however, the choice between deductions and credits affects the level of progressivity.[7] Consider, for example, a tax structure with two rates: 25 percent for taxable income below \$30,000, and 50 percent for taxable income above, that level. Now suppose that Allison earns \$60,000 and has a disability that requires \$10,000 in annual nondiscretionary expenditures; Brent earns \$50,000 but has no disability; and Carol earns \$20,000.

If the tax system contains both a personal and a disability deduction (and the latter is large enough to include all \$10,000 of Allison's disability-related nondiscretionary expenditures), then, since Allison's total income is exactly \$10,000 more than Brent's, they would both pay the same amount of tax (\$12,500) since they have the same amount of discretionary economic power (see Table 1). In tax policy jargon, this is called horizontal equity. Vertical equity also obtains, as Allison and Brent, who have higher incomes, pay a larger proportion of their discretionary income (30 percent) in tax than does Carol (25 percent).

If, instead, the tax system uses credits based on converting deductions at the lower tax rate, two things happen. First, the progressivity of the system increases — that is, as the difference between the amount of tax paid by the high-earning Brent and the amount paid by the low-earning Carol increases. While Carol pays the same amount of tax as before (\$2,500), Brent pays more (\$17,500). Second, horizontal equity is lost — Allison and Brent no longer pay the same amount of tax.[8] A system of credits under a progressive rate

---

7   This example was motivated by discussions with William B.P. Robson.

8   The same thing happens if deductions are converted at higher rates, though in this case the horizontal inequities are transferred to those with taxable incomes below \$30,000.

Table 1:   *Deductions versus Credits under a*
Progressive Tax System: An Example

	Allison	Brent	Carol
	(dollars)		
A. With Deductions			
Total income	60,000	50,000	20,000
Personal deduction	10,000	10,000	10,000
Disability deduction	10,000	0	0
Taxable income	40,000	40,000	10,000
Tax paid[a]	12,500	12,500	2,500
B. With Credits Based on Bottom Rate			
Total income	60,000	50,000	20,000
Tax before credits[a]	22,500	17,500	5,000
Personal credit[b]	2,500	2,500	2,500
Disability credit[b]	2,500	0	0
Tax paid	17,500	15,000	2,500

[a]   25 percent of $30,000 or less and 50 percent of any amount over $30,000.

[b]   25 percent of deduction amount ($10,000).

Source: Boessenkool and Davies 1998.

structure cannot ensure that those with equal ability to pay face the same sized tax bill.[9] But the movement from deductions to credits increases the progressivity of the tax system. On the other hand, changing the rate structure in a system with deductions can increase progressivity without sacrificing horizontal equity.

The Principles of Social Policy

The principles of tax policy as discussed above overlap in certain areas with social policy. However, the goals of the two types of policy are distinctly different. Where tax policy is concerned with how to design an equitable and efficient system of raising the required revenues for governments, the type of social policy that we find in

---

9 Credits could be designed to fluctuate with income levels, but this would completely obscure their rationale.

the Canadian tax system is concerned with providing income transfers to less well-off citizens. Social programs often use the tax system as a convenient source of information on incomes.

Transfer Mechanisms

Social policy goals can be accomplished using either cash or in-kind (subsidized goods or services that taxpayers would otherwise purchase) transfers.[10] An example of the former is the refundable tax credit, which is often confused with the kind of tax credit described above, but which operates more like an expenditure program than tax policy — it is a redistributional tool that provides cash payments to taxpayers. Refundable credits provide payments even when there is no tax liability, using parameters from the tax return to determine benefit payments, which are often phased out at higher income levels (Richards 1998, chap. 11–12). Information from tax returns is also used for seniors' programs. Provincial welfare payments are an example of cash transfers that are not linked to the tax system.

The Choice of Unit

Should social policy cash transfers be paid using the individual or the family as the unit? There are at least two reasons it makes sense to base social policy on the family unit.

First, at lower levels of income, the source of imputed income is largely irrelevant. Most sources of imputed income require a basic level of money income before they can be enjoyed (home production alone cannot pay the rent!). This liquidity constraint means that sharing between spouses is more likely to be the norm, since not to share would deprive a spouse or child of necessities. These liquidity constraints also minimize or eliminate the difficulties posed by sepa-

---

10 Examples of in-kind transfers include subsidized child care and primary, secondary, and postsecondary education. Again, in-kind transfers can be geared to income and can take a variety of forms. For the most part, these programs (unlike refundable tax credits) do not interact with the tax code, though it is possible that they could through, for example, income-contingent loan schemes or education vouchers geared to income. (See Finnie and Schwartz 1996.)

ration or cohabitation that are problematic for the design of a tax system. Thus it is not surprising that examples of adult-equivalent scales exist only at low levels of income, for provincial welfare programs and the LICO.

Second, using the family, rather than the individual, for social policy transfers avoids paying substantial transfers to middle-income single-earner families. It is not surprising, therefore, to find that most social policy transfers geared to low-income individuals are based on family income rather than individual income.

Looking Back

A tax system can contain both tax and social policy (among other elements), but these activities should be kept distinct from one another to ensure that the tax system is defensible on both grounds.

I have argued so far that, in terms of tax policy, taxing discretionary economic power is best done using the individual as the unit of taxation and money income as the measure of ability to pay. The legitimate claim dependants have on the income of the primary earner in a family is best reflected by providing deductions against the earner's money income.

Social policy transfers that use the tax system as their delivery mechanism, on the other hand, should be family based for two reasons. First, liquidity constraints at low income levels reduce the tax-policy-related concerns with family-based taxation; second, a family-based income transfer scheme avoids paying large transfers to middle- and upper-income single-earner households.

With these tax and social policy frameworks in hand, I now look back at how the Canadian tax system has evolved over the past five decades. First, I examine policies relating to marriage, illustrating the impact of applying a progressive rate structure to individual incomes for single- and two-earner families with children, and then I look at the history of personal and spousal deductions. Second, I examine the development of tax and social policies within the *Income Tax Act* directed toward children, again showing the impact of these policies on single- and dual-earner families with children.

Marriage

Despite the Carter Commission's urging to switch to a family basis, the tax policy portion of the Canadian tax system has retained the individual as its basic unit. This decision has had several implications for the treatment of marriage.

Rate Structure

Applying a progressive rate structure to individual incomes means that single-earner families face larger tax burdens than dual earners who take home the same money income. For example, at the median family income in 1965 (just under $30,000 in 1997 dollars), a single-income family would have paid one-sixth of its income in tax and face a marginal tax rate of 25 percent, while a two-earner family (assuming each spouse earned $15,000 in 1997 dollars) would have paid one-eighth of its income in tax, with each earner facing a marginal rate of only 18 percent.

The difference in tax paid by dual-earner and single-earner families earning various levels of total income between 1949 and 1997 is shown in Figure 1. (I have assumed that dual-earner families have two equal incomes.) The thick solid line shows the difference for families earning the median income, giving an estimate of the difference for the "middle class."

Until the late 1960s, the differential was small at most income levels. The gap widened and reached a peak in the mid- to late 1970s, primarily the result of a steepening rate structure. In the late 1980s, the value of this penalty for median-income families fell as both the number of rates and the spread between them shrunk.

These differential tax burdens are the inescapable result of imposing a progressive rate structure on a tax system based on the individual. They are defensible as a way of recognizing the additional costs of earning income faced by dual-earner families. The differential can be narrowed by reducing the number and range of tax rates, which is just what Ottawa did in 1987.

Figure 1:   *Tax Advantage to Dual-Earner Families, 1949–97*

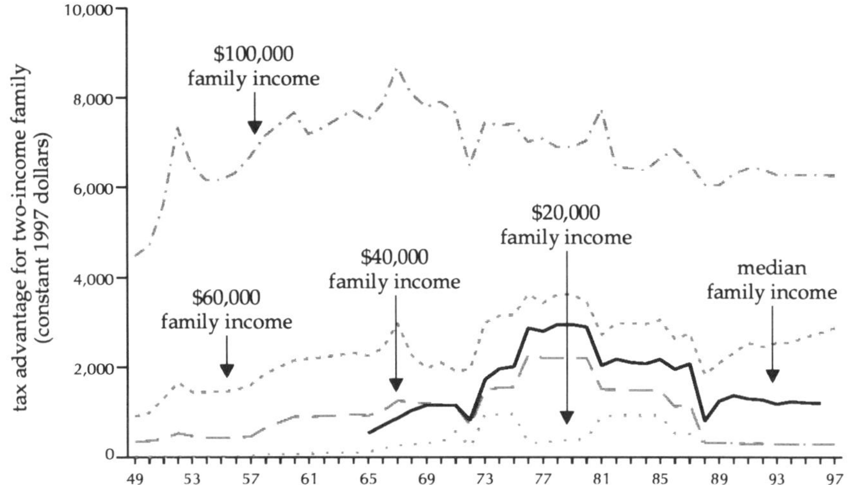

Personal and Spousal Deductions and Credits

Canada's *Income Tax Act* has always contained personal and spousal
allowances; the latter are reduced and eventually eliminated as a
spouse's income rises. Figure 2 shows the total dollar amounts of the
spousal and personal deductions for single- and dual-earner families from 1949 to 1997. A dual-earner family receives a personal deduction against each income, while a single-earner family receives
one personal and one spousal deduction against its single income.

From 1949 to 1971, there were two notable developments in the
dollar value of these deductions. First, inflation eroded their constant dollar value. Second, the value of the spousal deduction
moved in tandem with that of the personal deduction, so neither
kind of family had a financial advantage.

Ottawa increased both deductions in 1972 but raised the personal deduction more than the spousal one. This move could be
rationalized in terms of providing the earner in the family with a
larger deduction than the dependent spouse to reflect the costs of
earning income, although at that time there was a separate deduction for these employment-related expenses. The two deductions
stayed at a relatively constant value over the next 15 years.

Figure 2: **_Personal and Spousal Deductions, 1949–97_**

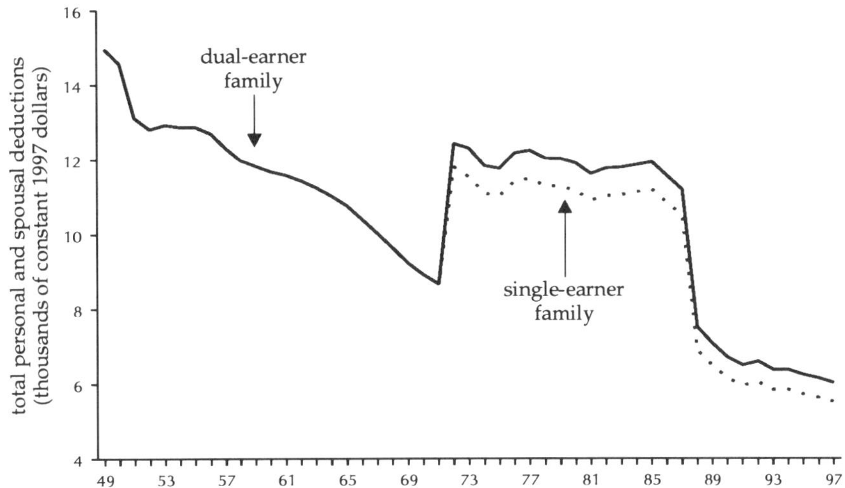

When, in 1987, Ottawa converted the deduction to a credit, a family of either kind paying the average federal-plus-provincial marginal rate of 35 percent[11] (see Box 1 for more details on this calculation) received a credit of much less value than the deduction it had received the year before. (For those paying the lowest rate, the credit represented a slight increase in the amount of exempt income; and for those paying higher than the average rate, the credit represented a much more significant decline than the average shown in Figure 2. This disparity illustrates the problem with using tax credits as opposed to deductions.) Over all, personal and spousal deductions have been consistently and significantly reduced. Today, the value of these deductions for all families is much less than half what they were immediately following World War II.

Child Benefits

The tax and social policy treatment of children in the tax code over the past 50 years is a story of a long-term takeover of tax policy by so-

---

11 Davies' (1998) average marginal tax rate for those who earn income.

Box 1: *Methodology for Calculating Tax-Free Income*

Figures 3 through 9 illustrate the amount of tax-free income available to families due to tax policy plus the cash value of social policy transfers. Following the principles outlined in the text, I treat refundable credits as social policy transfers and nonrefundable credits in a tax policy framework, with the latter converted to deductions at the applicable or average marginal rate.

I assume that family income is all earned income (roughly equivalent to "total income" in the tax system). This income is reduced by personal, spousal, child, and child care deductions to arrive at net income. Net income determines the marginal tax rate, based on schedules of provincial-plus-federal marginal rates found in the Canadian Tax Foundation's *The National Finances* or *Finances of the Nation*. I apply this marginal rate to family allowance payments after 1972 and use it to calculate the deduction-equivalent value of the exemptions converted to a credit in 1987 and later years.

Here is a brief summary of the specific treatment of each program. All amounts were converted to constant 1997 constant dollars:

cial policy. The progress of this takeover was sometimes slow and modest, other times quick and ambitious.

The Early Tax and Social Policy Mix: 1949–72

At its inception, the *Income Tax Act* exempted some income for each dependent child.[12] This exemption was available to all families with children and taxable income. From 1949 to 1972, the nominal value of this exemption doubled, which more than offset the modest levels of inflation experienced over that period.

Federal family allowances, introduced in 1945, topped up this tax-free amount with universal payments, conditional on the number and age of children. Family earnings, and the source of those earnings, made no difference to the amounts paid. This program, which

---

12 Information on changes to the programs in this and the next section was largely drawn from the Canadian Tax Foundation, *The National Finances*, various issues from 1956/57 to 1994, and its successor, *Finances of the Nation*, 1995 and 1996.

Box 1 - continued

- *Family allowances*: The annual dollar value of cheques sent to families is recorded. After 1972, the recorded value of those benefits is reduced at the families' highest marginal rates. The 1987 clawback threshold is based on net income.
- *Child tax credit*: The annual dollar value of cheques sent to families is recorded. The clawback threshold is based on net income.
- *Working income supplement*: The annual dollar value of cheques sent to families is recorded. The phase-in is based on earned income; the phase-out on net income.
- *Sales tax credit; after 1991, the goods and services tax (GST) credit*: The annual dollar value of cheques sent to families is recorded. The clawback threshold is based on net income.
- *Child care expense deduction*: The value of the deduction is recorded. The lower-income spouse is assumed to claim the lesser of the stated maximum or 20 percent of family total income. (The 20 percent limit, which is not part of the legislation, is my attempt to keep the value of the deduction at reasonable limits. Without it, for example, dual-earner families at low income levels could claim half of their family income in child care expenses.)
- *Child tax exemption*: Through 1987, the value of the deduction is recorded. After 1987, the value of the deduction is grossed up by the marginal rate of the higher-income spouse to get a deduction-equivalent value. Note that the analysis in this essay treats two-parent families only. Single parents can claim the child care expense deduction for the cost of out-of-home child supervision.

followed similar initiatives in Europe, was the "second substantial social program to be introduced by the federal government following unemployment insurance." (Perry 1989, 739.)

From 1949 to 1972 Ottawa made only modest changes to the family allowance program. In 1949, benefits had four age categories, with payments ranging from $5 to $8 per month (in 1949 dollars). All families with children in these age groups received these tax-free benefits. In 1957, Ottawa reduced the number of age categories to two. Over the 22-year period, low but persistent inflation chipped away at the real value of benefits.

The value of the child tax exemption in constant dollars, plus the dollar amounts paid in family allowances in 1949 and 1970 for one- and two-earner families at various income levels with two children aged three and five, is shown in Figures 3 and 4. (Dual-earner families were assumed to have two identical earned incomes.) From 1949 to 1970, the real value of family allowance benefits fell, but the total value of family allowance plus child tax exemption benefits increased slightly.

The value of the total package remained nearly constant over this period. But within that constant payment, the tax policy portion (the child tax exemption) crowded out the social policy portion (the family allowance). The total package for single- and dual-income families, as a comparison of panels A and B of Figures 3 and 4 shows, was the same.[13]

Early Triumphs for Social Policy: 1972–84

The early 1970s saw an intense international debate about social policy, motivated in part by the idea of the negative income tax: a government-provided minimum threshold income for all individuals, which would be taxed away as earned income increased. This debate was the beginning of a long struggle to use the income tax system for social policy transfers.

An early, if controversial, product of this debate in Canada was the 1970 Orange Paper that recommended a family income security plan (FISP). The FISP proposed eliminating all family allowance benefits to those with taxable incomes above a fixed threshold (Perry 1989, 741–742.) Money was to be redirected from higher-earning families to those with low or no earnings. The focus of social policy would shift from providing cash benefits to all families with children to targeting those with lower incomes.

The federal government never enacted the FISP, and it took four years before Ottawa even moved in the direction it suggested. In

---

13 The child tax exemption can be applied only against one individual income, so there are slight differences in favor of single-earner families at low income levels.

1974, Ottawa began including family allowance benefits in the taxable income of the spouse claiming the child tax exemption. At the same time, benefits were substantially enriched, bringing the real value of family allowance benefits (before tax) back to their early 1950s' levels.

The taxation of family allowances not only concentrated benefits on those with lower incomes, it also meant that single-earner families received lower benefits after tax than dual-earner families with the same total earnings because of the progressive nature of tax rates. This change is the first explicit interaction of social policy instruments aimed at families (though paid to individuals, usually mothers) interacting with a tax system based on individuals.

Ottawa also made a commitment at this time to index future family allowance payments to inflation. It was a promise that was kept only sporadically, and then often only partially. The result was a further, although slower, erosion in the real value of benefits.

In the midst of the FISP debate, Ottawa also introduced a child care expense deduction, which recognized one of the extra costs of earning income for dual-earner families with children. This deduction allowed a family's second income earner to claim, up to a specified amount, the cost of child care expenses. Between 1972 and 1984 the child care expense deduction doubled in nominal terms, more than offsetting a considerable rise in the cost of living.

Eight years after the introduction of the Orange Paper, advocates for using the tax system for social policy tasted real victory. In 1978, Ottawa introduced, alongside the family allowance program, a refundable child tax credit, which paid full benefits to all families with taxable income below a specified level, after which it was taxed back. Tax parameters determined the level of benefits a family received, reflecting the influence of the negative income tax concept; but it was a spending program rather than a true tax credit. Although Ottawa committed to indexing the value of the child tax credit and its threshold level, in fact the credit has, over time, followed a path identical to that of family allowances.

An important innovation of the child tax credit was that it was to be based on family, rather than individual, earnings. Ottawa's in-

Figure 3:   ***Child-Related Benefits in 1949 for***
Families with Two Children, Ages 3 and 5

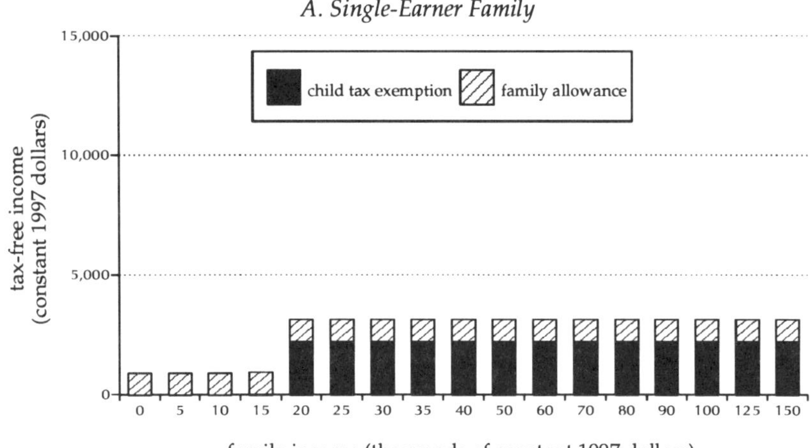

A. Single-Earner Family

family income (thousands of constant 1997 dollars)

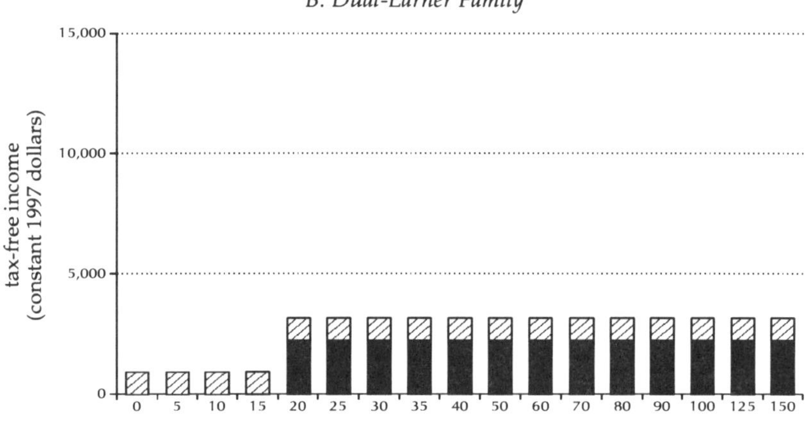

B. Dual-Earner Family

family income (thousands of constant 1997 dollars)

tent was to ensure that equal benefits went to all families. This did
not happen, however, since the amount taxed back was based on net
taxable income (after deductions for pension programs and the
child-care expense deduction) rather than gross taxable income.
Two-earner families who claimed a child care deduction — and
therefore had lower net taxable income than one-earner families —

Figure 4: ***Child-Related Benefits in 1970 for Families with Two Children, Ages 3 and 5***

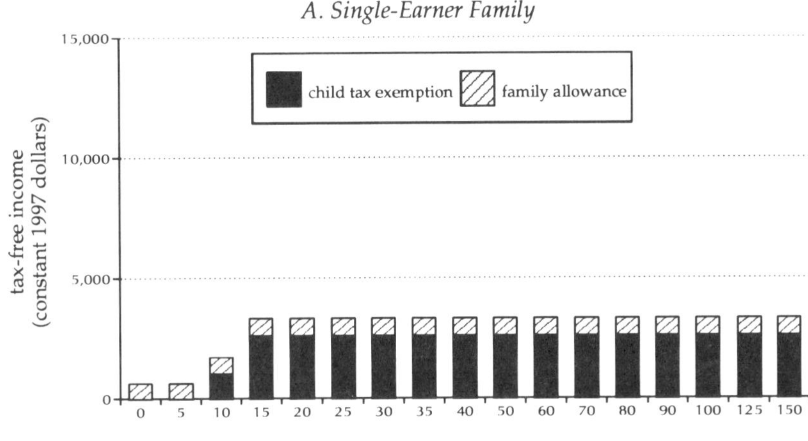

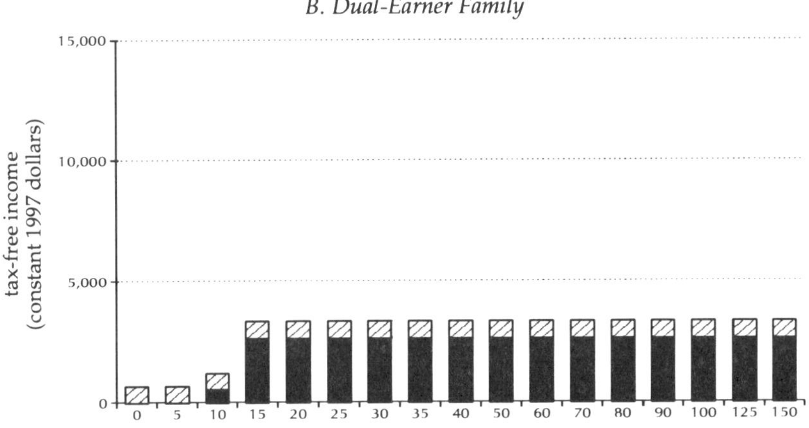

received larger payments even though their gross earnings were the same. The result was higher benefits for dual earners in the range of income in which benefits were taxed back.

Already in 1980, social policy was beginning to grow in importance. For one-earner families (see Figure 5, panel a), the maximum amount of exempt income, plus social policy transfers, occurred at earnings of $15,000 (in 1997 dollars). Above this income level, the value of the total package was reduced because family allowance benefits were taxed back and the child tax credit declined. Two-earner families (see panel B) supplemented this structure with the child care expense deduction (see Box 1 for calculations), which also produced higher family allowances and child tax credit benefits because of the way the taxed-back amount was calculated.

The 1970s and early 1980s thus saw some early steps toward loading social policy onto the tax system. Ottawa augmented its child-related tax policies — an exemption for children plus a deduction for the costs of child care — with family allowances and the child tax credit, both of which were reduced as income rose. Over this period, dual-earner families benefited from a new increasing exemption, while all families experienced reductions in the value of the per child exemption.

The Triumph of Social Policy: 1984–93

The weight of social policy in the tax code increased in the mid-1980s as a result of a flurry of changes to child benefits during the Progressive Conservatives' nine years in office. Nearly every year saw adjustments at the margin that, in total, resulted in substantial changes to the nature of child benefits. One change that persistently ate away at benefits was partial deindexation — benefits, thresholds, and allowances were indexed to inflation only above 3 percent after 1985.[14] However, the broader picture shows that other, larger shifts took place over the course nine years.

Besides partially deindexing benefits, the 1985 Budget reduced the child tax exemption and increased the child tax credit — a direct tradeoff of tax for social policy. The threshold for maximum child tax credit benefits was lowered at the same time. These changes reduced benefits for higher-income families and increased them for lower-income families. Further moves in this direction came when the 1988

---

14 Ken Battle (1993) has described this impact of inflation as "the politics of stealth."

Figure 5: *Child-Related Benefits in 1980 for Families with Two Children, Ages 3 and 5*

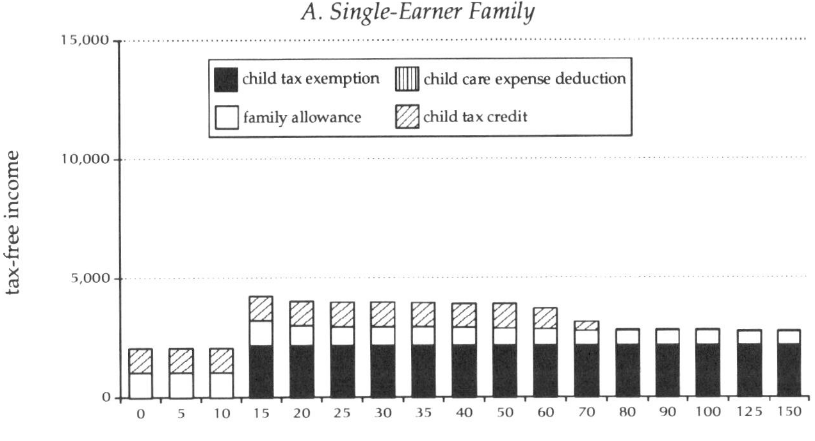

A. Single-Earner Family

family income (thousands of constant 1997 dollars)

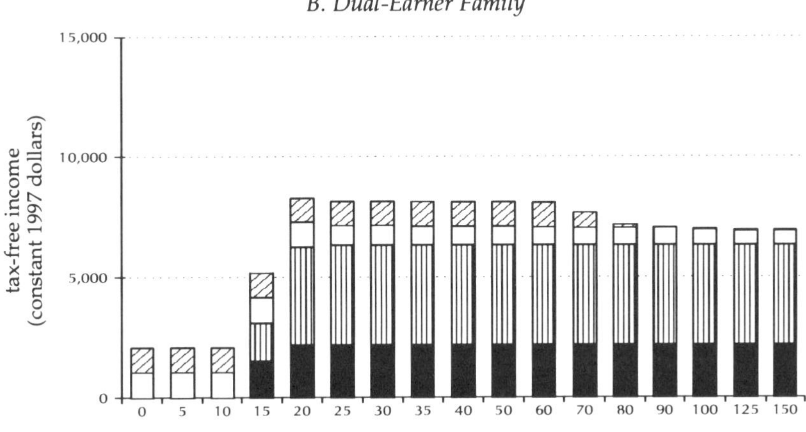

B. Dual-Earner Family

family income (thousands of constant 1997 dollars)

budget converted the child tax exemption to a credit (not, however, a refundable one) and again raised the refundable child tax credit.

In 1986 the federal government introduced a refundable sales tax credit. Ottawa pays the credit based on information from income tax returns, not on the actual amount of sales tax paid. A family's basic benefits are supplemented based on the number of children it contains and, like the child tax credit, the sales tax credit is both re-fundable and taxed back after a specified level of net taxable family income. The threshold for the sales tax credit was initially set well below the child tax credit threshold so that the taxback rates were not "stacked." Ottawa substantially enriched the sales tax credit after the introduction of the GST in 1991, at which time it was renamed the GST credit. GST. Like the child tax credit, the GST credit is a social policy program with parameters for benefit payments based on in-formation from the tax form. In 1992, Ottawa raised the threshold for the GST credit to match the child tax credit threshold, thus stacking the taxback rates for the two programs.

Several changes introduced in 1988 affected the differences in benefits to single- and dual-earner families. A child tax credit sup-plement for children under age seven was added. The supplement disappeared, however, if a family claimed a child care deduction over a certain limit. At the same time, Ottawa converted the child tax exemption to a credit. The credit increased progressivity and pro-vided a bigger "bang" for dual-earner families. Finally, Ottawa again doubled the maximum child care expense deduction for chil-dren under age seven and removed limits on the total amount families could claim.[15]

A large blow to single-earner families came in 1989 when a new clawback was announced on family allowance benefits that were al-ready subject to taxation. This clawback was based on individual, rather than family, net income. A two-earner family could thus earn double what a single-earner family could before facing any reduc-tion in family allowances from the clawback.[16]

These changes meant that, by 1990 for single-earner families, social policy dominated tax policy in the tax system's treatment of children (see Figure 6, panel A). The credit for children provided larger amounts of tax-exempt income at lower levels of income, and

---

15 The latter was a minor change, since the ceiling would previously have been hit only by those claiming the maximum deduction for more than four children.

16 In fact, since the child care expense deduction reduced taxable income, the two-income family might earn more than twice the single-income family before fac-ing clawbacks.

Figure 6: *Child-Related Benefits in 1990 for Families with Two Children, Ages 3 and 5*

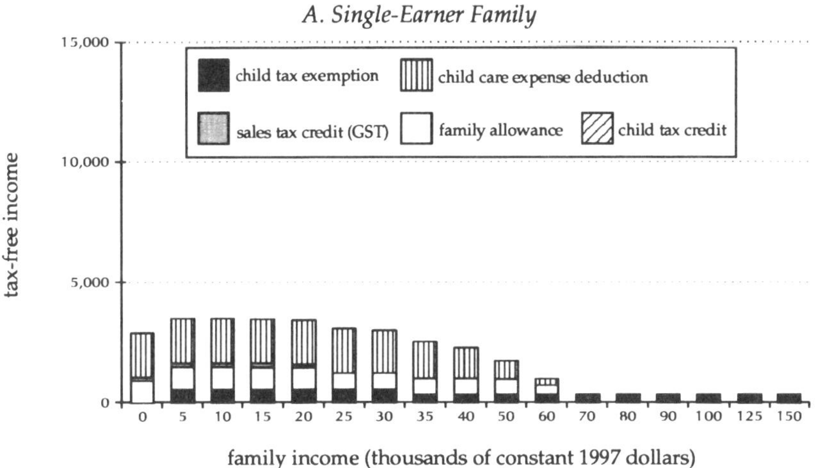

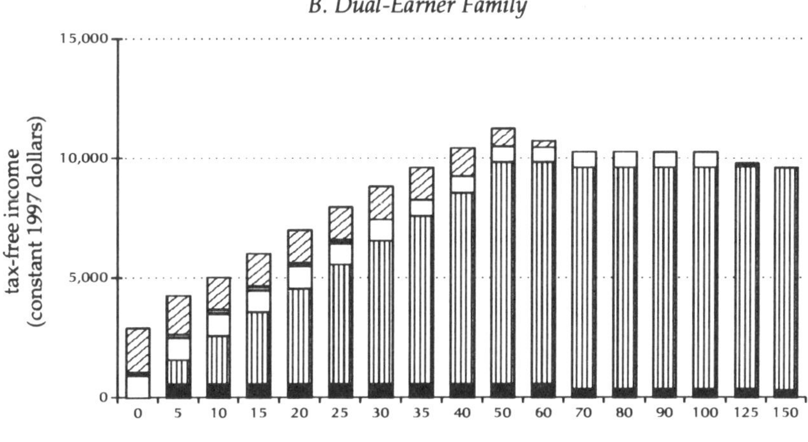

the three social policy programs focused benefits at the bottom of the earnings scale. Dual-earner families, however, continued to enjoy a growing child care expense deduction, which dominated all child-related provisions above very modest levels of income (see Figure 6, panel B).

The 1992 budget saw the final victory of social over tax policy. In a simplification of what had become a complex mess of programs, Ottawa scrapped family allowances and the child tax exemption and expanded the child tax credit, which it renamed the child tax benefit.[17] This eliminated all child-related benefits except the child care expense deduction to families with incomes above $60,000.

Accompanying this consolidation of programs was the creation of an innovative supplement to the child tax benefit named the working income supplement, which was similar to the earned income tax credit in the United States. This supplement was designed to do more than merely provide additional cash to low-income families; it was also meant to encourage people to enter the labor force. It provided no benefits to those with earnings below a specified level, then phased in benefits (at 8 cents per dollar of earned income) up to a specified maximum. Working income supplement benefits were then taxed back when earnings passed a second threshold (for a discussion of this policy, see Richards 1998, chap. 12.) The second threshold and the taxback rates were set so that all of the supplement was taxed back before a family hit the child tax benefit threshold. Reflecting its focus as a labor market program rather than as support for children *per se*, the working income supplement did not vary according to the number of children.

A Period of Calm: 1993–97

Child benefits escaped unscathed the early 1990s' concern over deficits and debts. Since inflation remained below 3 percent in each of these years, the 1997 system was identical to that of 1993 in nominal terms (save for some changes to the working income supplement in the final year). And with low levels of inflation, the real level of benefits declined only marginally.

For single-earner families, the shift to a benefits structure governed by policy was complete. The absence of tax policy measures

---

17 The child tax benefit shared the basic design of the child tax credit and carried forward the same threshold level.

relating to children meant that single-earner families with earnings above $70,000 received no recognition for the costs of raising children. For dual-earner families the continued growth of deductions for child care meant that their child-related benefits peaked at $50,000.

Renewed Expansion: 1998

The 1997 budget proposed a new Canada Child Tax Benefit (CCTB) for 1998 that would combine the existing child tax benefit and the working income supplement (which Ottawa changed to a per child benefit in mid-1997). The biggest change is the end of "ramped-up" benefits — the same amounts are now paid to all families with income below $20,921 and the same number of children.

The new CCTB provides $1,625 for the first child and $1,425 for each additional child to families earning below $20,921. Between $20,921 and the point at which payments reach pre-reform levels (a basic benefit of $1,020 per child plus $213 per child for those who do not claim child care deductions), benefits are taxed back at the following rates: 12.1 percent for families with one child, 20.2 percent for families with two children, and 26.8 percent for families with three or more children (Poschmann 1997, 49–51). Benefits reach pre-reform levels at an income of $25,921 for families with three or fewer children, and at a slightly higher income for those with more than three children because the taxback rate is capped at 26.8 percent. Once benefits hit pre-reform levels, they are taxed back at 2.5 percent for families with one child and at 5 percent for families with more than one child. Figure 7 shows the benefit levels and taxback rates for families who do not claim child care deductions (and therefore get the additional $213).

Besides introducing these changes to the refundable child benefit, the 1998 budget also increased the child care expense deduction from $5,000 to $7,000 per child under age seven, and from $3,000 to $4,000 per child between ages seven and fifteen.

The reign of social policy thus continues for single-earner families which receive only the new CCTB and the GST credit (see Figure 8, panel A). Ottawa concentrates these benefits at the bottom

Figure 7:   *The Canada Child Tax Benefit, 1998*

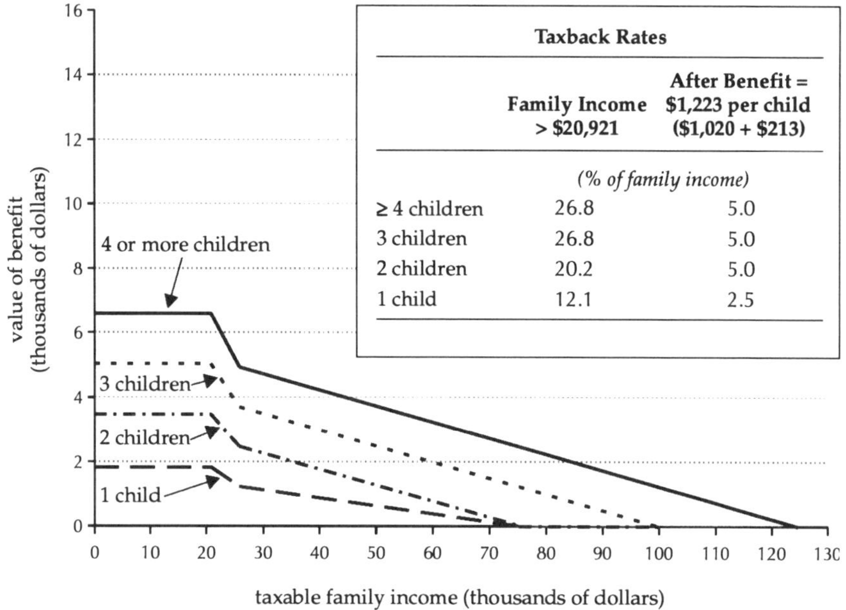

	Taxback Rates	
	Family Income > $20,921	After Benefit = $1,223 per child ($1,020 + $213)
		(% of family income)
≥ 4 children	26.8	5.0
3 children	26.8	5.0
2 children	20.2	5.0
1 child	12.1	2.5

of the income scale. For a family of four, benefits are fully taxed back just above $70,000 in earned income. Dual-earner families supplement these programs with increased child care deductions, which also marginally boosts the role of social-policy programs since the taxback on the latter is based on net taxable income (Figure 8, panel B).

Winners and Losers

So far, I have provided snapshots of the benefits various programs have provided for families of different types and income levels at several points in time. In this section, I focus on the value of total benefits, and show how families at several levels of real income have fared over the past half-century. But first, a couple of conceptual issues need to be addressed.

The first of these issues is how to deal with the child care expense deduction. If this deduction recognizes a legitimate cost of earning income, then it is not a child benefit. A different argument is

Figure 8: ***Child-Related Benefits in 1998 for Families with Two Children, Ages 3 and 5***

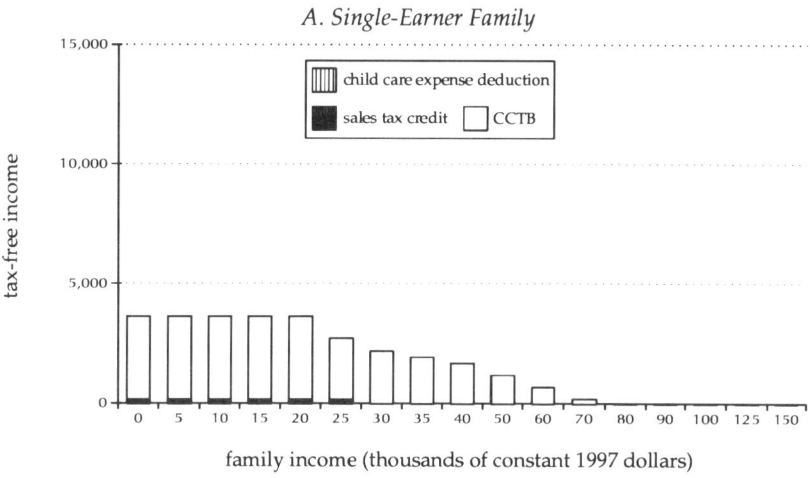

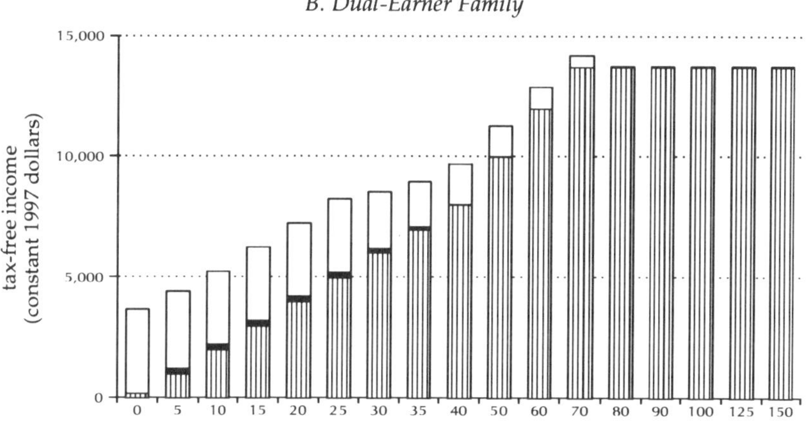

that since the benefits parents receive by raising their children at home (a form of household production) are not taxed, a deduction for parents who pay for child care outside the home should be allowed.

The trouble is, these arguments ignore the context in which the child care expense deduction has evolved. While dual-earner families have seen child care deductions rise, single-earner families have seen the erosion, and eventual elimination, of all exemptions for children. Further, the child care expense deduction is one of only a few deductions for the costs of employment income that have survived the base broadening of the tax system over the past two decades. Finally, those who defend the child care expense deduction as a way of offsetting the nontaxation of household production for single-earner households are being selective about what types of imputed income are relevant to taxation. Together, these arguments make the child care expense deduction look more like a selective exemption for dual-earner families with children than an exemption for the costs of earning income. The argument that the child care expense deduction recognizes a legitimate cost of earning income was defensible when tax policy instruments existed that recognized children in all families, but this argument has lost its force in the current context.

The second relevant issue is whether tax and social policy measures should be looked at independently or in aggregate. The analysis at the beginning of this essay suggests the former — that social policy and tax policy have quite different motivations and rationales within the tax system. However, that discussion ignores the reality that any new tax policy measures must interact with the existing social policy mechanisms within the *Income Tax Act* — even if only for budgetary reasons. It also ignores the fact that social policy instruments, in particular the new CCTB, have been defended as a tax measure for the middle class (who receive some benefits) and a social measure for low-income earners.

Figure 9 traces the development of the total child benefit package, including the child care expense deduction and various social policy measures. It includes the value of personal and spousal deductions (from Figure 2). Adding all these amounts together provides a measure of the amount of tax-free income provided to single- and dual-earner families at various income levels over the past 50 years. In tax policy terms, it is a measure of nondiscretionary income under tax measures plus the cash value of social policy benefits provided through the tax system..

Turning first to single-earner families (panel A), the past 50 years have seen a steady erosion in benefits for those earning above

$20,000 (in 1997 dollars). The rate of reduction has risen with income levels since the early 1980s. For lower-income single-earner families, the level of benefits has been remarkably stable, rising slightly between 1972 and 1988 and falling since then. For those with no earnings, benefits have risen steadily since 1972, although more slowly until the 1998 introduction of the CCTB.

Average real earnings have been rising since 1970. For example, while someone earning $50,000 in 1997 would have been near the median in 1997, an individual earning the equivalent amount (in constant dollars) in 1970 would have been well above the median. To give a perspective, therefore, on how the middle class has fared throughout the decades, the thick line in both panels of Figure 9 shows benefits for a family earning the median family income.[18]

By definition, dual-earner families with no income saw the same increases in benefits as their single-income counterparts (panel B). At all other income levels, however, the story for dual-earner families is different from that of their single-earner counterparts. Dual earners saw a much more substantial rise in tax-free income in 1972. Oddly enough, the families that have faced the least amount of deterioration since then have been those earning between $40,000 and $60,000. This is because these families have received both the growing child care expense deduction and refundable tax credits, since Ottawa calculates the latter on a net taxable income basis. Families earning the median level of family income have consistently outperformed other families in extracting benefits and tax-free income from Ottawa.

At all levels of income, dual-earner families now receive more than they did in the early 1950s. This is due to child care deductions, which provide greater amounts of tax-free income as well as improving the amount of the social policy transfers received by dual-earner families since such transfers are based on net rather than gross income.

---

18 This is the overall median family income, not the median for single-earner families, which is lower.

Figure 9:   *Child-Related Benefits, 1950–98, for Families with Two Children, Ages 3 and 5*

A. Single-Earner Family

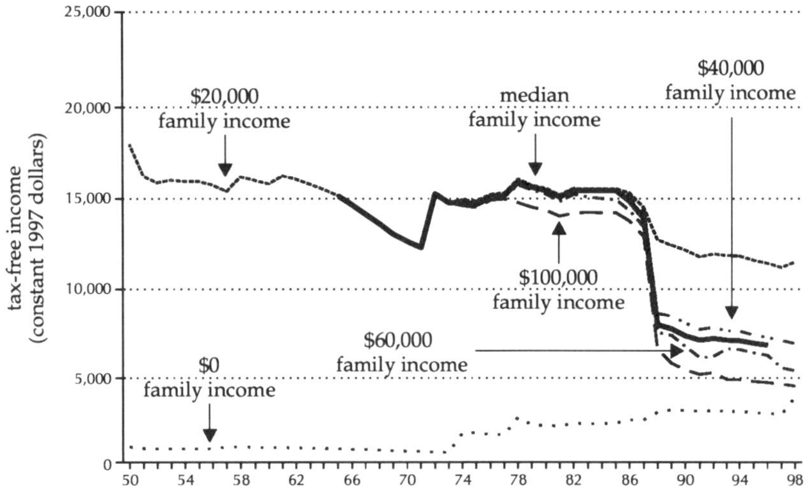

B. Dual-Earner Family

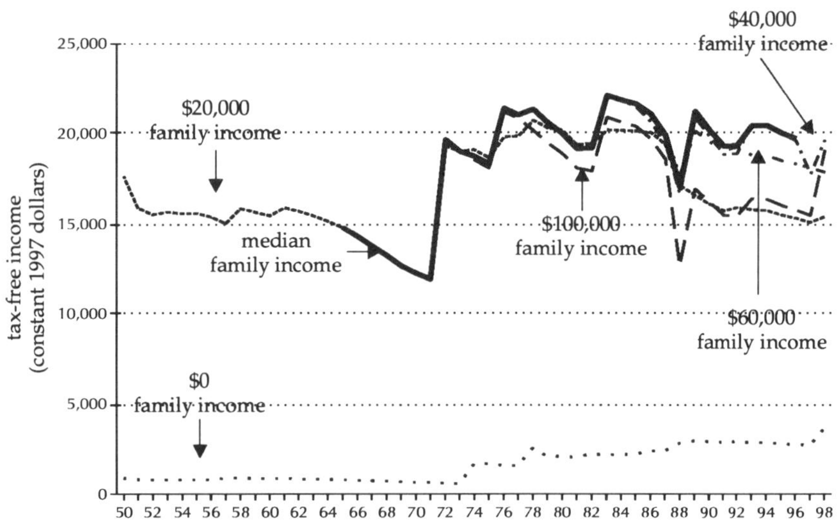

Looking Ahead

This survey of family-related tax policy serves as a jumping-off point for making policy recommendations for the future.

Problems

From a tax policy perspective, the historical development just outlined points to two sources of horizontal inequity. First, the tax system does not recognize that the cost of raising children is a non-discretionary expense that should be exempt from the tax code. The new CCTB provides some benefits to middle-income families, but since those benefits decline with income, the implication is that the cost of raising children also varies with income. Comparing a childless couple with a single-earner family with two children highlights the inequity. If both families earn $70,000, the tax system treats them equally, implying that the two families have the same ability to pay — in effect, that children in the latter family have no claim on the income of the sole earner. In the words of Kesselman, the tax system treats the decision to have children no differently from the decision to purchase a "fancy boat" (1993, 117).

The second inequity is between dual- and single-earner families. The tax system's current treatment of these two types of families suggests that the child care expense deduction is partially a child-related benefit. Ottawa thus indirectly subsidizes the choice of parents who do not raise their children at home.

Another consideration any reform must take account of is the punishing marginal rates of taxation that apply at very modest income levels. These rates result from a failure to distinguish between social and tax policy when designing programs.

The CCTB is a poignant example of this problem. As social policy, the program is designed to provide transfers to low-income individuals. However, presumably due to the absence of tax recognition for families, Ottawa pays the benefit over a broad range of incomes. The result is the stacking of punishing taxback rates. For example, at a family income of between $21,000 and $26,000, child benefit taxback rates are stacked on top of a 26 percent (combined federal and provincial) personal income tax rate and (combined employee/employer) employment insurance and Canada Pension Plan rates of close to 6.5 percent each. Including provincial clawbacks and tax rates, families earning between $21,000 and $26,000 therefore pay higher marginal rates than all families who make more than this amount (Figure 10 shows the situation in Ontario).[19]

Any solution to the problems outlined here should make progress on three fronts. First, it should improve horizontal equity for families with children compared with childless couples. Second, it should reduce or eliminate the implied horizontal inequities between single- and dual-earner families. Finally, it should address the stacking of marginal tax rates at modest levels of income.

Proposals

Solving these three conundrums without making any taxpayers worse off would be prohibitively expensive, not to mention politically difficult. Nevertheless, I think it a worthwhile exercise to lay out a couple of "no-budgetary-or-political-holds-barred" proposals, if only to provide a target that more realistic suggestions can aim for. Even modest changes should, after all, be made with an ultimate target firmly in mind. The first two proposals outlined here are just such no-holds-barred ideas. The next two are less radical attempts at moving the current tax and social policy treatments in the right direction.

Universal Child Benefits

The tax and social policy mechanisms that existed between 1949 and 1972 had neither horizontal equity problems nor punishing marginal rates. The social policy mechanism of family allowances paid universal benefits to all families for each child, and tax policy provided deductions against taxable income for those same children. While the two overlapped, they did so in an innocuous way.

---

19 Welfare clawbacks may be higher for families with very low incomes.

Figure 10: *Marginal and Average Tax Rates, Ontario, 1998, for Single-Earner Family with Two Children)*

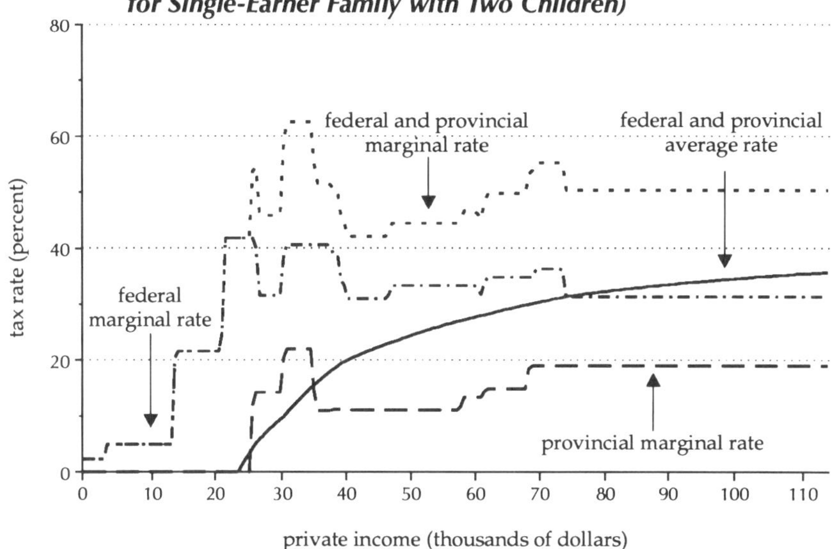

In this vein, Rowe and Woolley (1998) argue for universalizing child benefits. That would eliminate all the taxbacks, making the program a demogrant (refundable credit) for all Canadians with children. It would introduce some horizontal equity between couples with and without children, and weaken the discriminatory nature of the child care expense deduction, since single earners would also receive recognition for their children.

This proposal would cost between $6 and $10 billion to implement, depending on whether the refundable sales tax credit was also made universal. According to the schema laid out in the opening section of this paper, however, universalizing social policy benefits would lead to additional problems. First, demogrants are tools of social policy. Paying them to all families makes it difficult to increase payments to those least well off without entailing enormous budgetary expense. One must ask the question: Do we really want to make cash payments to families making $30,000, $50,000, or more? Doing so appears to be very bad social policy. Second, since these payments are made on a family basis, they do not mix well with a tax system based on individuals. Third, payments made to families are an incomplete way of bringing horizontal equity into the tax system, as they operate like credits for individuals with taxable burdens above the level of the payments (look back at Table 1).

Generous Personal and Spousal Deductions

A better solution than making cash payments to families with incomes above, say, $30,000 would be to provide generous personal, spousal, and child deductions for all taxpayers. If these were generous enough, then federal and provincial social policy would have tax-free "room" in which to operate without interacting with the tax system. This would restore horizontal equity between couples with and without children, and also some balance between single- and dual-earner couples. It would eliminate the stacking of taxback with tax rates. And it would, finally, make a clean break between social and tax policy. Transfers directed to those with low incomes would operate within the range of income created by the deductions.

The difficulty with this system is that the new CCTB payments are larger than combined federal and provincial taxes for single-earner families with two children earning up to $20,000 and dual-earner families earning up to $25,000 (Canadian Tax Foundation 1997, tables 3.19 and 3.20).[20] Thus, to avoid making anyone worse off and to ensure no overlap between social and tax policy, personal and child deductions for a family of four would have to total at least $25,000. Clearly, deductions on this scale would be prohibitively expensive. Alternatively, social transfers could be made less generous at income levels between, say, $15,000 and $25,000. Such a proposal would, however, likely spark significant political resistance.

Both universal child benefits and generous deductions would provide a superior target for the development of tax and social policy than continuing down the historical path that eliminated tax policy in favor of social policy in Canada's tax system. The frame-

---

20 The differences between dual- and single-earners is the result of basing the amount taxed back on net income, i.e., after the Child Care Expense Deduction for dual earners.

works set out in earlier sections of this paper point to the separation of tax and social policy through generous deductions as the better approach. The proposals below are for more modest, and realistic, reforms that would move in this direction.

A $2,000 per Child Deduction

A per child deduction would be an important first step in rationalizing the tax policy side of the tax code. It would introduce a measure of horizontal equity between couples with and without children, ending the tax system's current treatment of children as consumer expenditures. Per child deductions do not come cheap, however. A deduction of $2,000 per child would cost the federal government about $3 billion.

A Three-Pronged Approach

The cost of the per child deduction could be reduced, and equity between dual- and single-earner families enhanced, if the amount of the per child credit was subtracted from the child care expense deduction. This would have no impact on dual-earner families that currently claim the maximum child care expense deduction, as they would receive the per child deduction in its place. Families that do not claim the maximum amounts for the deduction would receive a tax cut.

Introducing a deduction and lowering the child care expense deduction would do nothing, however, to reduce the prohibitive tax rates for families earning between $20,000 and $25,000. But progress on reducing these rates is possible since a per child deduction would deliver a tax cut for all families with earnings above $15,000, creating some room to lower the taxback thresholds, and even rates, without reducing the current level of benefits to families at modest income levels.

A concrete modeling of how changes might work is as follows. First, introduce a deduction of $2,000 per child under 18. Second, reduce the child care expense deduction by $2,000. Third, eliminate the

GST credit and create a unified credit composed of the current CCTB and the child portion of the GST credit. Finally, tax back this unified credit at a rate of 7.5 percent above an income threshold of $15,000.

Without a new child deduction, this new clawback structure would be budget neutral — that is, it would not cost Ottawa anything, although there would be winners and losers among families. When combined with the new deductions, however, this unified credit would increase costs slightly over the existing child and sales tax credits, since the new deduction would lower the net income against which the taxback is applied. This increase in costs would offset most of the savings from lowering the child care deduction.

This combination of proposals would cost just under $3 billion.[21] It would have a negligible impact on families earning less than $25,000 — which receive the maximum amount of benefits under the current system — but it would deliver a modest tax cut for families above that level (see Table 2). The biggest benefit increase would be enjoyed by families earning between $25,000 and $55,000, which would enjoy, on average, a combination of increased benefits and lower taxes amounting to 2 percent of income.

One negative aspect of this proposal is that it would increase (by 2.5 percent) marginal tax rates at income levels between $30,000 and the point at which benefits are phased out. At income levels between $26,000 and about $30,000, it would replace the combined GST (2.5 or 5 percent) and CCTB (5 percent) clawbacks. It would also reduce by 4.6, 12.7, and 19.3 percent the tax rates for families with, respectively, one, two, and three or more children at earning between $21,000 and $26,000. Another negaitive is the loss to low-income families due to the loss of GST credits.

The biggest benefits of this proposal would go to middle-income families. Among two-parent families, those with single earners would receive larger tax savings than those with dual earners. These results are necessary to fix some of the inequities that have crept into the current tax system. The low-income families that do not receive a

---

21 I thank Finn Poschmann for providing the modeling of this and other options from Statistics Canada's Social Policy Simulation Database and Model.

Table 2: ***Average Change in Federal Transfers less Taxes under Proposal***

Family Income Group	Single Parent	Couple with Children	
		Single Earner	Dual Earner
(dollars)		*(percentage of income)*	
0–15,000	0.1	–0.3	0.1
15,000–25,000	0.9	1.0	1.0
25,000–35,000	0.5	2.4	2.0
35,000–45,000	1.5	3.0	1.8
45,000–55,000	1.0	2.4	1.4
55,000–70,000	1.2	2.0	1.1
70,000–100,000	0.9	1.8	1.0
>100,000	0.7	0.8	0.6
All	0.7	1.8	1.0

Source: Statistics Canada, Social Policy Simulation Database and Model, release 6.1; modeling by Finn Poschmann.

tax cut under these changes have, as this essay shows, been seeing regular increases in social policy transfers, culminating in the CCTB.

This three-pronged approach would make progress on the fronts discussed earlier. It would exempt some nondiscretionary income for all families with children — childless couples would pay more tax than couples with children at all income levels. It would reduce the discrepancy in tax savings between single- and dual-earner families with children, but without reducing benefits to any dual-earner family. Finally, it would reduce punishing marginal tax rates at modest levels of incomes.

Conclusion

The proliferation, expansion, and consolidation of social policy mechanisms within Canada's tax system over the past 50 years have created several difficulties. These include the loss of horizontal equity between couples with and without children, a disturbingly high marginal tax rate at low levels of income, and a child care expense deduction that has the effect of a transfer to children in dual-earner families rather than a deduction for the cost of earning income.

Separating tax policy and social policy within the tax system as it relates to the family is long overdue. The obvious solution is to implement generous personal and dependant deductions. This would also render social policy transfers more transparent and targeted, because generous deductions would provide a range of tax-free income within which social policy transfers could operate without interacting with the tax system. Unfortunately, implementing this solution all at once would mean either a massive reduction in Ottawa's revenues or an unacceptable redistribution of benefits.

My more modest proposal for moving the tax system in this direction involves several steps: creating per child deductions, lowering child care deductions, and lowering taxback thresholds, while establishing a single taxback rate for refundable credits. This combination of changes would improve horizontal equity between couples with and without children, as well as between dual- and single-earner families with children. It would also flatten the marginal tax rate schedule for families. The total budgetary cost of these proposals would be modest, and Canadian families would all be as well off, or better off, as a result.

References

Battle, K. 1993. "The Politics of Stealth: Child Benefits under the Tories." In S.D. Phillips, ed., *How Ottawa Spends: A More Democratic Canada ...?*. Ottawa: Carleton University Press.

Boessenkool, K.J., and J.B. Davies. 1998. *Giving Mom and Dad a Break: Returning Fairness to Families in Canada's Tax and Transfer System*. C.D. Howe Institute Commentary 117. Toronto: C.D. Howe Institute. November.

Canada. 1966. Royal Commission on Taxation [Kenneth Carter, chairman]. *Report*. Ottawa: Queen's Printer.

Canadian Tax Foundation. 1997. *Finances of the Nation* (previously titled *The National Finances*). Toronto: Canadian Tax Foundation.

Constantatos, C., and E. West. 1991. "Measuring Returns from Education: Some Neglected Factors." *Canadian Public Policy* 17 (2): 127–138.

Davies, J.B. 1992. "The Tax Treatment of the Family." In R.M. Bird and J.M. Mintz, *Taxation 2000 and Beyond*. Canadian Tax Paper 93. Toronto: Canadian Tax Foundation.

———. 1998. *Marginal Tax Rates in Canada: High and Getting Higher*. C.D. Howe Institute Commentary 103. Toronto: C.D. Howe Institute. March.

Finnie, R., and S. Schwaartz. 1996. *Student Loans in Canada: Past, Present, and Future*. Observation 42. Toronto: C.D. Howe Institute.

Jorgenson, D.W. 1998. "Did We Lose the War on Poverty?" *Journal of Economic Perspectives* 12 (1): 79–96.

Kesselman, J. 1993. "The Child Tax Benefit: Simple, Fair, Responsive?" *Canadian Public Policy* 19 (2): 109–132.

Ontario Fair Tax Commission. 1993. *Fair Taxation in a Changing World: Report of the Ontario Fair Tax Commission*. Toronto: University of Toronto Press.

Perry, J.H. 1989. *A Fiscal History of Canada — The Postwar Years*. Toronto: Canadian Tax Foundation.

Poschmann, F. 1997. "The Child Tax Benefit." In *Issue Highlights for the 36th Parliament*. Ottawa: Library of Parliament, Parliamentary Research Branch.

Richards, J. 1998. *Retooling the Welfare State: What's Right, What's Wrong, What's to Be Done*. Policy Study 31. Toronto: C.D. Howe Institute.

Rowe, N., and F. Woolley. 1998, forthcoming. "The Efficiency Case for Universality." *Canadian Journal of Economics*.

Sayeed, A. 1985. "Choosing Between Tax Credits and Exemptions for Dependent Children." *Canadian Tax Journal* 33(5): 975-982.

Statistics Canada. 1998. The Daily. February 12.

———. Cat. 13-215-XPB. *Characteristics of Dual Earner Families*. Ottawa, 1995.

Triest, R.K. 1998. "Has Poverty Gotten Worse?" *Journal of Economic Perspectives* 12 (1): 97–114.

The Case for
Earnings Supplements:
The Devil's in the Detail

John Richards

This paper is concerned with the potential of social policy to help low-income families with children. It offers two recommendations. The first is that provinces experiment with programs to subsidize earnings among such families. What may appear incongruous, the second recommendation calls for a major tax cut for middle- and upper-income families with children.

A brute fact to keep in mind is that families with children comprise slightly over half of all Canadians deemed poor by conventional poverty measures (Statistics Canada 1997, 41). This provided the rationale for policy initiatives by Ottawa earlier in the 1990s to increase benefits targeted to families with children and, in both the 1997 and 1998 budgets, to enrich them further (Canada 1998, 109–112). Since 1992, a major element among these transfers has been the Canada Child Tax Benefit (CCTB), which functions as a modest negative income tax. Since 1997, the provinces have collectively undertaken to build new provincial programs on the federal CCTB platform.[1] Some

Several friends and colleagues have contributed specific information, and commented on earlier drafts. Without attributing any remaining inadequacies to them, I thank my co-editor Doug Allen and the following: Rick August, Jean Bernier, Ken Boessenkool, Keith Horner, Jon Kesselman, and Finn Poschmann.

1 The negative income tax concept is discussed in more detail later in the essay. The CCTB provides a maximum transfer to families with no earnings and, beyond an annual family income threshold of approximately \$21,000, claws it back as earnings rise. The CCTB clawback rate depends on the number of children and level of earnings.

provinces — notably British Columbia — have opted to expand the CCTB into a more generous negative income tax. However, negative income taxes pose serious incentive problems. Preferable alternatives, I shall argue, are programs to supplement employment earnings among low-income families.

The final section raises a second matter: the case for restoring universality to child benefits, by extending the CCTB "up the income level." To transform the CCTB from its present status as a negative income tax into a universal tax credit — costing the federal treasury about $6 billion annually — can be portrayed both as a tax cut appropriate to an era in which Ottawa has finally balanced its budget and as a social policy initiative intended to recognize more adequately the costs incurred by parents in raising children well. The link between these two recommendations is that universalizing the CCTB would lower the excessively high marginal effective tax rates of those modest-income families that face the combined disincentives of income tax plus clawback on the CCTB and other targeted benefits.

Earnings Supplements: What Is at Stake Here?

At first reading, a policy discussion about earnings supplements, negative income taxes, and tax credits may seem arid. The underlying issues at stake are anything but that — they concern passionate debates about core social values.

The CCTB supplements provincial social assistance programs, which are by far the more important source of income for very poor families with no earnings. Families with children can avail themselves of social assistance in all provinces, and no major political party suggests otherwise. Hence, it is fair to conclude that the majority of Canadians are prepared to tax themselves to provide a tolerable standard of living to such families. *Tolerable standard* is, however, an imprecise term. What should it be for families with no earnings? Answering this question goes to the core of divergent beliefs about the extent and nature of Canadians' mutual responsibilities to one another as citizens of a community. In answering this question, one inevitably finds oneself posing others: Why are poor families without work? To what extent do income transfers to families reduce employment? To what extent does unemployment itself — independent of income levels — exacerbate family problems?

My own answer to these questions is that, for parents with limited skills living in countries with reasonably generous social programs (here I include Canada), government transfer payments do act as a significant disincentive to work. Furthermore, long-term reliance on transfer income, as opposed to income from work, exacerbates destructive family dynamics that are conducive to family breakup, single parenthood, and lowered prospects for children. Longitudinal studies that attempt to assess intergenerational effects of parental choices seem to confirm the commonsense wisdom of our grandparents: the role-model effects from one or more working parent significantly and positively affect many basic choices children make in matters such as completing high school, avoiding pregnancy, and avoiding welfare as adults. And living in neighborhoods with high concentrations of "ghetto" characteristics — such as high rates of single-parent families, high-school dropouts, low-wage jobs, and dependence on transfer programs — negatively affects children's outcomes. This ghetto effect operates in addition to the consequences of these characteristics among members of individual families.[2]

The modern welfare state has created "poverty traps": if parents with limited market skills forgo government transfers for full-time work, they may do little to increase family income and may well lower it. The "trap" cannot be defined solely in terms of financial incentives; it has a long-term psychological component. Long-term dependence on transfer income leads to erosion of market skills, which lowers the probability of ever re-establishing stable employment and financial independence. By definition, transfer in-

---

2 This paragraph contains undocumented conclusions based on my interpretation of admittedly contestable evidence. For an excellent introduction to the empirical literature on determinants of children's outcomes, I refer readers to two surveys by Haveman and Wolfe (1994; 1995).

come substitutes for the parents' income-earning role. This leads to feelings of worthlessness and depression among parents — among fathers in particular — and to self-destructive behavior. In sum, these poverty traps tend to weaken individual families and the communities in which ghettos form.

The welfare-to-wage ratio is certainly not the only factor determining whether parents work; many families find themselves without earnings for reasons beyond their control. These reasons range from the intensely personal (such as the death of the income-earning parent) to the social (such as technological change, which creates widespread unemployment among those with obsolete skills). Also, many parents consciously reject the possibility of welfare income, even though they are eligible and it would increase family income. An honest discussion of all this requires, however, that we admit to a painful tradeoff between two goals: relieving poverty by income redistribution and, on the other hand, assuring that families rely essentially on income from employment among their members — not on transfers from government.

Subsidizing Work

Given the complexity of the reasons underlying family poverty, it is foolish to present any one policy option as a panacea. With that caveat, I think the time has come for Canadian governments to experiment more ambitiously with programs that subsidize work among low-income families with children, by supplementing family earnings. I label such programs as generic earnings supplement programs, and I offer two introductory comments:

- These programs are intended to be ongoing subsidies to any and all earnings by family members and to be accessible by all low-income families with children — as opposed to a host of discretionary programs that subsidize employment income among designated groups of people for a limited period.
- Since current welfare benefits are much more generous for parents with children than for single individuals, the poverty trap

is of more concern among the former. Earnings supplement programs are intended to shift the welfare-to-wage ratio low-income parents face; they are not intended for single individuals or families without children.

In several countries, these programs have become a significant social policy instrument. The United States' Earned Income Tax Credit is one example; expenditures on the program in 1994 were C$40 billion (OECD 1997, 52). In Britain, the Labour government of Tony Blair gave a high priority in its first budget to enhancing an equivalent, the Working Families Tax Credit (WFTC), with an estimated annual cost of C$12 billion when fully phased in by 2000 (United Kingdom 1998, para. 2.08).[3]

Canadian examples of earnings supplement programs also exist. Quebec's APPORT[4] is important as the pioneer. The federal government included a small program in its 1992 reform of child benefit programs, but subsequently terminated it.[5] In the 1990s, Ottawa has also undertaken the Self-Sufficiency Project (SSP), a pilot earnings supplement project in regions of New Brunswick and British Columbia. Saskatchewan introduced a province-wide earnings supplement program in 1998.

---

3 To provide a reference point, the federal government is currently spending approximately $6 billion on the CCTB. Hence, by 2000, Britain's expenditures per resident on the WFTC will be similar to current expenditures per Canadian resident on the CCTB. Analogously defined, the United States' per capita 1994 spending on the Earned Income Tax Credit is about four-fifths of Canada's current per capita spending on the CCTB.

4 An irresistible urge among politicians is to give new names and acronyms to social programs. In this case, the name of the program in English is Parental Wage Assistance (PWA). But the program is usually designated in both languages by its French acronym, APPORT, derived from *Programme d'aide aux parents pour leurs revenus de travail.*

5 This program, labeled the Working Income Supplement (WIS), supplemented annual earnings at a rate of 8 percent over the range of $3,750 to $10,000 for all families with at least one child. The maximum supplement payable was $500. This remained in place over the earnings range of $10,000 to approximately $21,000; thereafter, it was clawed back at a rate of 10 percent, and disappeared for earnings above approximately $26,000. The program was conceived behind closed doors, with little public debate. In 1997, representatives of the 11 senior governments agreed to let it die and to transfer the funds to the expanded CCTB.

Despite these examples, earnings supplement programs remain to date a marginal and experimental component of Canadian social policy — and are subject to considerable controversy. Their opponents include conservatives who fear distortions to labor markets, antipoverty advocates who want generous unconditional income transfers, and union leaders who do not want an increase in the number of low-skilled workers in the labor market.[6]

In understanding the controversy, the first point to appreciate is that, by construction, programs that supplement earnings link benefits to earnings from work and are less redistributive than programs of equal budgetary cost that deliver maximum benefits to those without earnings. The second point is that beneficiaries are poor and usually lack high-level skills; hence, the work subsidized usually pays low wages. These programs increase the supply of low-skilled workers in the labor force and — subject to minimum-wage provisions — lower the cost to employers of hiring them. Low-wage jobs are often menial jobs, involving repetitive tasks and hard physical labor. Why should public policy encourage such jobs? Although their rationales diverge, conservative supporters of free markets, antipoverty activists, and left-wing union leaders answer in unison: do not!

Admittedly, many self-described conservatives are prepared to intervene aggressively in the work choices the poor make.[7] Typically, however, conservatives want less government intervention in the labor market, and view earnings supplement programs as yet more exercises in social engineering that distort market signals. True enough, all transfers blunt market incentives to work. But in no

---

6 Michael Mendelson, of the Caledon Institute of Social Policy, offers a left-wing critique of earnings supplements. Written to warn a British audience against such programs, Mendelson's monograph criticizes the modest Canada-wide WIS, arguing that it "diminished social cohesion and promoted the politics of division" (Mendelson 1998, 26).

7 Prominent examples are Walter Mead, a US social policy analyst who has written extensively on workfare and is quoted below, and the Republican administration in Wisconsin, which has aggressively implemented workfare programs during the 1990s.

wealthy industrial society has the majority been prepared to accept the prospects for children that arise when parents with low or narrow skills are required to depend solely on what they can command in the labor market. The majority has been prepared to tax itself to bring all families above some "tolerable standard of living." Even in jurisdictions with low benefit levels (such as conservative-led US states), families with several children are often eligible to receive more via transfers than low-skilled workers can earn from full-time employment. The combination of the *laissez-faire* conservatives' policy bias plus majority preferences leads to large numbers of low-skilled parents opting for more-or-less permanent cycling between bouts of social assistance and low-wage employment.

Quite legitimately, union leaders seek to increase members' wages. An increased supply of low-skilled, usually nonunion, workers in the labor market does not help: part of any earnings supplement benefit goes to employers in the form of a lower net cost of labor.[8] Instead of employment supplements targeted on low-skilled workers, argue union leaders, *à voix haute*, increase the income for such families by increasing the minimum wage. They add, *à voix basse*, that a high minimum wage will reduce employer demand for such labor and redirect demand toward higher-skilled union workers. Therein lies the contradiction of this position. A major disadvantage of a high minimum wage as social policy is that employers avoid those who, for multiple reasons, have low productivity and low attachment to the labor force. In the past, traditional left-wing governments have accompanied a higher minimum wage with higher welfare benefits. Thus, leaving aside the labor demand side and looking at labor supply, the ranking remains the same as under con-

---

8 The net effect of an earnings supplement on wages and employment levels depends on the elasticity of supply of affected workers and on the elasticity of demand among potential employers. If, as is likely, the supply elasticity is high, the net effect may be a sizable increase in employment but little increase in wages. Minimum-wage regulations serve as a constraint in this market dynamic. See Burtless (1998) for a discussion of recent employment experience among US welfare recipients.

servative governments: reliance on social assistance transfers is financially more rewarding than reliance on paid work.[9]

The case for earnings supplement programs rests on two empirical propositions. The first is that financial incentives matter and that employment subsidies can (in combination with other programs) significantly increase employment. The second is that the role-model effects from working parents matter a great deal in explaining the prospects for children — whether from poor or nonpoor families. On this second proposition, I quote Walter Mead,[10] writing about inner-city poverty in the United States:

> Today's seriously poor people typically do not believe that they will ever have a chance to make it, although black success is now commonplace and discrimination in the old sense is rare. And because their problems are perpetuated by weak families, no further reforms by government are likely to convince them otherwise. They project their hopelessness onto the environment, but the feeling really arises in the first instance from weak or abusive parenting....
>
> The solution lies in rebuilding the family, not society. Most children acquire a sense of possibility not because society is fair to them but because adults near to them are. By identifying with parents and teachers, they internalize values. By meeting their expectations, they also derive a sense of mastery that makes them approach life hopefully, without defeating themselves. The wider world has no comparable influence. If parents are effective, children will be well formed even if the surrounding society is unfair....The main task of social policy is no longer to reform society but to restore the authority of parents and other mentors who shape citizens.
>
> Government has no easy way to do that, but the best single thing it can do is to restore order in the inner city. Above all, it

---

9 For an up-to-date discussion of the relative advantage of minimum-wage and earnings supplement programs in increasing employment income, see *Employment Outlook*, published by the Organisation for Economic Co-operation and Development (OECD 1998, 31–79).

10 In this instance, Mead was writing for the Institute of Economic Affairs (IEA), a conservative British policy institute. The intent of the IEA was to influence the newly elected Labour government.

can require that poor parents work, because employment failures are the greatest cause of family failures. If parents do not
work, no program to help the children is likely to achieve much.
(1997, 14–15.)

Some will disagree with Mead's emphasis on "rebuilding the
family, not society." Almost inevitably, policy discussions bearing
on families pinch moral nerves among those who disagree. Maybe
I am wrong, but as a working hypothesis I suggest that large changes
in financial incentives do matter and that work is sufficiently important that it is worthwhile for government to subsidize it — thereby
incurring the political cost of frustrating those conservatives who
want wages to reflect relative productivity, those antipoverty activists who prefer more generous untied transfers, and those union
leaders who want to restrict employer access to low-skilled labor.

In the guise of a conclusion to this section, let me state what I
take to be the three pertinent values or goals that should be implicit
in any discussion of social policy for low-income families:

- *Redistribute: Government social programs should redistribute to poor
  families with children in a manner more generous than to families (or
  individuals) without children.* We are discussing programs explicitly designed for families with dependent children. Whatever
  we collectively decide about redistribution toward nonhandi-
  capped, able-bodied adults without dependent children, we
  collectively want to be more generous to adults who are caring
  for children.

- *Make work pay: Government social programs should provide a significant fiscal incentive to undertake paid employment among poor
  parents, even when their children are young.* Redistribution is not
  the only relevant goal. A concern for children's outcomes suggests that source of family income matters. Hence, social policy
  intended to redistribute toward low-income families must also
  contain incentives to undertake employment.

- *Reciprocal obligations: Government social programs should discourage
  long-term reliance on transfer programs by requiring a "copayment"*

from the able-bodied poor in exchange for receipt of benefits. Traditional social assistance is a kind of insurance against dire poverty. As with other forms of insurance, people can abuse social assistance programs. Earnings supplement programs can be considered an element in a social contract of reciprocal obligations that requires the nonpoor to undertake redistributive taxation and the poor to engage in employment and/or training.

Social Trends: Effects on Families

Over the course of this century, men and women in industrial countries have profoundly changed family life and their expectations about it. Until this century — in both agricultural and industrial societies — the norm was that mothers worked in and around the home and so be available to undertake child rearing; fathers had an emotional and financial responsibility to support their wives and children in this lifestyle. Throughout western industrial society, those expectations have changed.

An important catalyst for change was the disruption of family life engendered by two world wars. Husbands and wives were separated as men went off to fight, and the economic demands of the war economy induced women into the paid labor force. When the wars ended, women were reluctant to return to the prewar status quo.

Declining family size, combined with rising life expectancy, means that child rearing now occupies a smaller share of adult time than in earlier decades of the century. As late as the 1970s, only one in three married women with young children (under age six) was in the paid labor force; by the 1990s, this ratio had become two in three (Canada 1994, 4). By the 1990s, the female labor force participation rate in Canada had become four-fifths that for men. One consequence of all this has been the massive growth of care for young children by adults other than their parents.

Another dimension of changed expectations has been a decline in commitment to the traditional two-parent family. This decline is manifest in higher divorce rates and in the prevalence of non-conventional arrangements (such as common-law and single-parent families). It is also manifest in changes to family law — such as "no-fault" divorce laws — that have accommodated changing values by relaxing the conditions required of a dissatisfied spouse who wants to terminate a marriage.

Before proceeding further, it is worth sketching more precisely several social trends that bear on the case for pursuing earnings supplement programs.

1. Since the 1970s, the proportion of single-parent families, and of children living in such families, has doubled in Canada, and the majority of these families are poor. In urban centers, the poor are becoming more geographically concentrated in ghetto-like neighborhoods.

The proportion of single mothers in Canada increased from 8 percent in the early 1970s to 14 percent by the early 1990s. The proportion of children living in single-parent families increased from 9 percent in 1975 to 16 percent in 1996. Of the remaining children, in 1996, 11 percent lived in common-law families and 73 percent with married couples. This trend to single parenthood has arisen in most industrial countries; it is certainly not unique to Canada.

The distribution of children by family type is far from uniform among Canadians. Among aboriginal children in 1996, for example, 32 percent lived in single-parent families, 25 percent in common-law families, and 43 percent with married couples. Among aboriginals living in cities, the proportion of single parenthood is higher yet: about one-half of aboriginal children in Winnipeg, Regina, and Saskatoon lived in such families (Dooley 1995, 43–45; Statistics Canada 1998, 5).

As the introduction mentions, slightly over half of all Canadians deemed poor are members of families with children (see Table 1). Due to the increasing prevalence of single parenthood, the proportion of the poor living in single-parent families has been on the rise. In 1980, the members of such families constituted 16 percent of all those deemed poor. By 1996, they were 22 percent of the poor. Among these poor, single-parent families in 1996, 93 percent were headed by a mother.

Table 1:		***Incidence and Share of Poverty by Family Structure, Canada, 1996***

	Incidence[a]	Share[b]
	(percent)	
Economic families	14.5	70.0
Elderly, over age 65	8.7	4.4
Childless couples	10.0	7.3
Two-parent families with children under 18	11.8	29.4
Two-parent families with other relatives	5.3	3.0
Single-parent families with children under 18	56.8	21.7
Male head	31.3	1.5
Female head	60.8	20.2
Other	17.8	4.3
Unattached individuals	40.2	30.0
All categories	17.9	100.0

[a]	"Incidence" refers to the proportion of persons in a particular category whose incomes fell below the relevant measure as defined by Statistics Canada's Low-Income Cut-Off (LICO), 1992 base. The LICO methodology designates families or individuals to be poor if they spend significantly more of their income (above 60 percent) on necessities than do typical Canadian families or individuals in the relevant category (who are assumed to spend 40 percent of their income on necessities).

[b]	"Share" refers to the proportion of persons deemed poor according to the LICO, by family structure.

Source:	Derived from Statistics Canada 1997, 29–41.

The overall incidence of poverty among elderly families has been declining (from 19 percent in 1980 to 9 percent in 1996). Among non-elderly families, however, the incidence has been rising (from 12 percent in 1980 to 16 percent in 1996). Several factors explain these trends. More generous government transfers have aided the elderly. Among the non-elderly, the state of the business cycle matters: between 1980 and 1996, the lowest incidence of poverty was in 1989, a boom year. Another important reason for the increase has been the rising number of families headed by a single parent. Throughout the 1980–96 period, the incidence of poverty among families with children was roughly five times higher among single-parent families than among two-parent families.

Another dimension of family poverty is its increasing geographic concentration. In the United States, ghetto neighborhoods have become a prominent and intractable feature of urban poverty over the past half-century. Cities in Canada are also generating ghetto-like neighborhoods — areas with high concentrations of negative characteristics. And more of the Canadian poor are living in such neighborhoods.

In an attempt to describe this dynamic more rigorously, Hatfield (1997) identifies "distressed neighborhoods" by an abnormal incidence of five social indicators. To qualify as distressed, the neighborhood has to be more than one standard deviation away from the mean on each of the following dimensions:

- a high individual poverty rate (above 28 percent);
- a high proportion of total household income coming from government transfer payments (above 17 percent);
- a low proportion of the 15–24 age cohort attending school full time (below 43 percent);
- a low proportion of adult males employed full time (below 36 percent); and
- a high incidence of families with children headed by a single parent (above 31 percent).

Between 1980 and 1990 (two years for which income was measured in national censuses), the proportion of poor families changed little. However, the proportion of poor Canadian families living in distressed neighborhoods rose from 12 percent in 1980 to 17 percent in 1990. Large increases took place over the decade in the share of the urban poor living in such neighborhoods. For example, 30 percent of Montreal's poor lived in those areas in 1980; 40 percent did so in 1990. Other cities with significant increases were Winnipeg (24 percent to 39 percent), Edmonton (4 percent to 28 percent), Calgary (6 percent to 20 percent), Vancouver (7 percent to 16 percent), and Toronto (15 percent to 21 percent).

Aboriginals are greatly overrepresented in such very poor neighborhoods, particularly in western Canadian cities. This is a politically sensitive fact to emphasize. While ghetto effects are important in understanding aboriginal poverty, this is not a critique of aboriginals relative to nonaboriginals. The effects operate equally in very poor neighborhoods everywhere — from east-end Montreal to east-end Vancouver.

2. Male earnings from low- or narrow-skilled employment have declined, and median income among young families has declined relative to that among older families.

In most industrial countries, including Canada, earnings from low- or narrow-skilled work have declined in the past generation. A typical result appears in a recent study by researchers at Statistics Canada: between 1973 and 1989, real annual earnings among men in the bottom fifth of wage earners declined by 16 percent; roughly half of this decline occurred because of a reduction in the number of hours worked, but even among men who worked full time full year, real annual earnings of the bottom fifth fell by 7 percent over the period (Morissette, Myles, and Picot 1995, 28).

The explanation for this decline is far from settled. The single most important factor probably has been a technology-induced increase in employer demand for skilled labor. Technological change has simultaneously created a demand for highly skilled workers (such as computer technicians and programmers) and destroyed many moderately skilled jobs (such as manual letter sorters). It has also created a demand for many low-skilled jobs (such as telephone operators) that require less physical strength than such jobs did in previous decades, and have thus diminished employment prospects more for low-skilled men than for women. This may be the major reason increased wage polarization has affected men, not women (see Beach and Slotsve 1996).[11]

---

11 "Polarization" refers to the number of individuals in the tails of a distribution relative to the number who are reasonably close to the middle. By definition, polarization increases over time when the proportion in the tails rises.

Technological change is not the only relevant factor. Trade liberalization has permitted greater exploitation of international comparative advantage, one aspect of which is the Third World advantage in low-skilled, labor-intensive manufacturing activities such as textiles. The result is a decline in demand for low-skilled labor in the Canadian manufacturing sector.

In addition, prolonged lax fiscal policy combined with bouts of monetary restriction generated recessions in the 1980s and 1990s that were more serious than any since the Great Depression of the 1930s. Recessions are particularly bad for wage and employment trends among the low skilled.

Finally, over time, unions and other occupational organizations have probably become more entrenched. The result has been to increase the wage premiums and employment security they can provide to *inside* workers relative to the wages and working conditions enjoyed by *outsiders*. In many cases, these benefits go well beyond what is warranted by relative productivity. Young workers tend to be outsiders; older workers are far more likely to be insiders. This final factor helps to explain the declining ratio since the 1960s of earnings among young families relative to earnings among older families (Picot and Myles 1995).

3. From the 1970s through the 1990s, transfer programs to low-income families became more generous and more targeted on the truly poor, and marginal effective tax rates rose over a broad range of low- and modest-income levels.

These transfer programs include provincial social assistance programs, federal unemployment insurance, and a variety of benefits in the income tax system (for example, the child tax benefit, the goods and services tax (GST) credit, and provincial benefits for low-income families). As Canadian senior governments addressed their respective deficits in the 1990s, the social assistance regimes of most provinces and the federal unemployment insurance program have become less generous. That does not gainsay the generalization: relative to the 1970s, Canadian programs that transfer income to low-income families have either remained constant in real terms or have become more generous.

As an example, between 1975 and 1995, the real value of benefits for single parents increased by 8 percent in British Columbia and by 20 percent in Ontario. Following the election of a Progressive Conservative government in Ontario in June 1995, provincial welfare benefits were cut to levels that were 2 percent lower than in 1975. A comprehensive nationwide survey reported an 18 percent increase in the real value of single-parent benefits between 1981 and 1993.[12]

Between the mid-1970s and the mid-1990s, the proportion of Canadians receiving social assistance rose from roughly 5 percent to 10 percent; since 1994, the proportion has declined by one percentage point.[13] Single-parent families remained a fairly constant quarter of this much-enlarged group of Canadians. As of the early 1990s, 44 percent of single mothers received some welfare income. Receipt of welfare is much more pronounced among single mothers under age 35 (58 percent received welfare) than among older single mothers (only 31 percent of whom received welfare) (see Barrett and Cragg 1998; Dooley 1995, 52).

Increased transfers targeted to low-income families have offset the effect of the polarization of male earnings. This can be seen in the fact that there has been little change in polarization of incomes among Canadian families over the past two decades. However, among poor families with children (defined as those with income less than half the median amount), the relative importance of earnings to transfers has shifted substantially (see Figure 1). In the early 1970s, two-thirds of income in such families derived from earnings

---

12 The statistics for Ontario and British Columbia refer to a single parent with one or two children (Brown 1995, table 3; Canada 1997a, table 5). The nationwide study is by Lefebvre, Merrigan, and Dooley (1998, table 5), which uses data from Statistics Canada's Survey of Consumer Finances.

13 From a peak of 3.1 million Canadians in receipt of social assistance in March 1994, the number had declined to 2.8 million by March 1997. These numbers were prepared by the Social Program Information and Analysis within the federal Department of Human Resources Development.

Figure 1:   *Sources of Disposable Family Income,*
                  Families (with Children Aged 0–14) Earning
                  Less than Half the Median Income, Canada, 1973–91

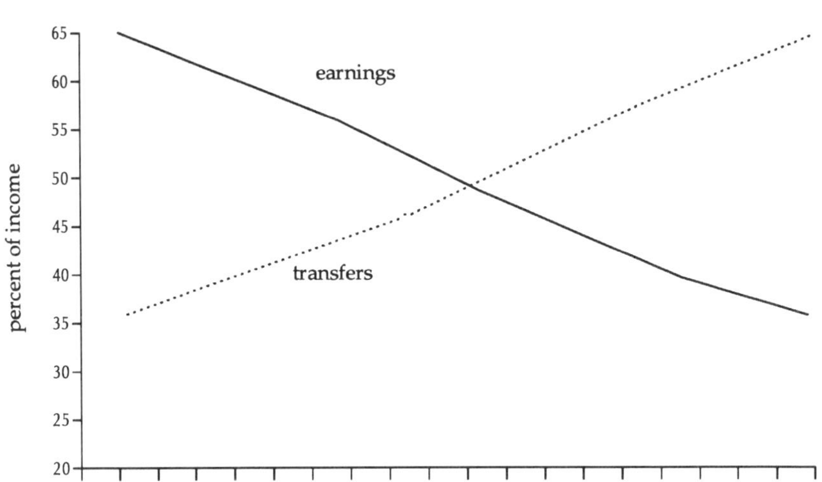

Source: Picot and Myles 1995, 14.

and one-third from transfers; two decades later, the ratio was reversed
and two-thirds of such families' income derived from transfers. In
1991, provincial social assistance provided half of this transfer income; Ottawa provided the other half via unemployment insurance,
the family allowance, and a child tax credit (Beach and Slotsve 1996;
Picot and Myles 1995, 14).[14]

An important social policy trend in the past generation has
been the abandoning of universal transfers to families in favor of
transfers targeted on the poor. By design, targeted programs provide
less generous benefits to those with positive earnings. In other
words, they claw back benefits as earnings rise, thereby generating
similar work disincentives as do explicit income taxes. The most dramatic example of a targeted program is social assistance: in the
typical province, a single parent with two children will be eligible for

---

14 The family allowance and child tax credit were subsequently combined into the
   CCTB.

Figure 2: ***Marginal Effective Tax Rates, Actual and with Proposed Universal Child Tax Benefit***

(single earner with two children, Ontario, 1998)

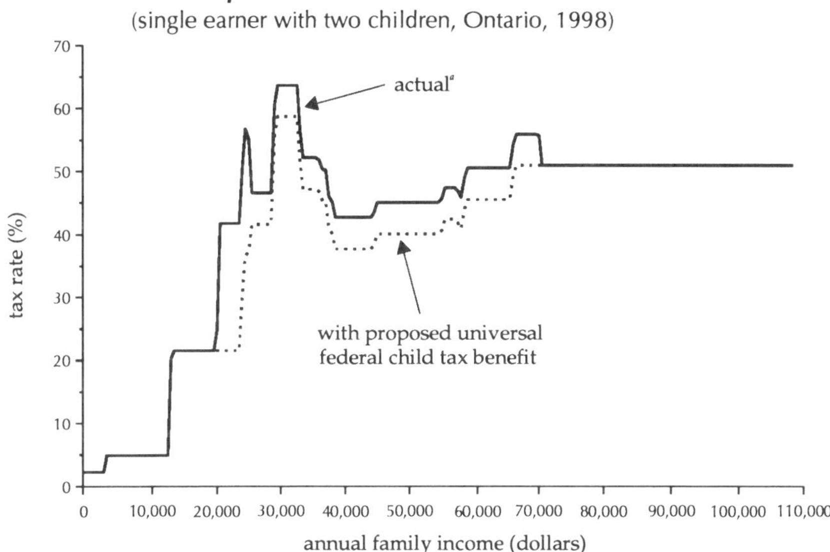

[a] Includes CPP and EI premiums and allows for GST and other refundable credits, plus the Ontario tax reduction and sales tax credit. Excludes the clawback on social assistance and the Ontario Child Care Supplement for Working Families, an earnings supplement for families with children under age seven.

Source: Calculations by Finn Poschmann.

roughly $12,000 in welfare. For welfare recipients, provinces allow a small earnings exemption, beyond which the clawback rate on incremental earnings is close to 100 percent.

An inevitable consequence of public sector expansion since the 1970s has been increased taxes. Currently, most families with children start paying personal income tax (PIT), employment insurance (EI) premiums, and Canada Pension Plan (CPP) premiums when income exceeds $15,000. Provinces attempt to avoid overlap between social assistance and these taxes, but the transition is messy. Some families in this range wind up with marginal effective tax rates in excess of 100 percent — especially if account is taken of the phase-out of in-kind benefits that are available to social assistance recipients. At approximately $20,000, Ottawa and the provinces start clawing back targeted benefits other than social assistance, such as the CCTB and GST tax credit.

The typical family may well receive more from senior governments in the form of targeted benefits than it pays in PIT until annual family income exceeds $25,000. But the combined effect of all this — social assistance clawback, PIT, income-based levies, and the clawback of other targeted benefits — has resulted in poor families' facing marginal effective tax rates on incremental earnings in excess of 50 percent over most income ranges below $35,000. (The solid line in Figure 2 illustrates 1998 marginal effective tax rates in Ontario. Note that this figure excludes the clawback of social assistance.)

How important are high marginal effective tax rates in discouraging work effort among low-income families? I do not have a good enough answer to this key question but I can offer a few comments.

The most severe clawback occurs among recipients of social assistance, who, not surprisingly, report low employment earnings.[15] In the late 1990s, in the context of the federal budgetary surplus, much attention is being devoted to tax reduction among upper-income taxfilers subject to the highest marginal income tax rates. One of the rationales is the damaging incentive among professionals either to relocate to lower-tax regimes or to work less. Often ignored in this discussion is the fact that even higher marginal effective tax rates occur among families with several children in low income ranges (refer to Figure 2).

I add the "tentative conclusions" from the white paper accompanying the 1998 British budget:

> Modelling labour supply responses to tax and benefit changes is notoriously difficult. It is necessary to overcome a series of problems, including the estimation of potential "entry wages" for those out of work, work related costs and stigma and awareness effects. In addition, it is necessary to take into account the possi-

---

15 In Saskatchewan, for example, 17 percent of family caseloads have some reported earnings. (The sources for this statistic are unpublished analyses of the provincial social assistance caseload.) Social assistance recipients earn, however, an impossible-to-quantify level of unreported income.

bility of involuntary unemployment, and the interaction between family members. All too often, studies focus on one group of people and assume the employment status of their partners remains constant: however, the polarisation of working and workless households suggests this assumption can lack plausibility. The ideal study would cover a panel of individuals over a long period of time, covering the period before and after a major policy change. The use of a control group of individuals who are unaffected by the policy change and can be used as a benchmark against which to draw comparisons, greatly increases the accuracy of the results, making it possible to net out time variations, such as the state of the labour market. But control groups are impossible to define where the policy is a tax or benefit change affecting everyone....

Subject to these caveats, it is possible to draw some tentative conclusions from academic studies of work incentives in the USA and UK

- in-work credits, such as the [US] EITC and Family Credit [the UK program now renamed WFTC], have the potential to raise substantially labour market participation for poorer families, particularly lone parents, both in respect of part-time and full-time work;
- a fall in [clawback] rates can help more people move up the earnings ladder. But the withdrawal of in-work support as income rises can also reduce modestly the hours worked of those already employed (United Kingdom 1998, paras. 4.12–4.13.)

This passage stresses the analytic difficulties in answering questions about work effort. In attempting to determine the work effects of alternate social policies, Canada enjoys a great advantage over Britain. Thanks to Canada's decentralization of social policy jurisdiction, individual provinces can experiment while the remaining provinces serve as a control group.

What Do These Trends Mean?

"All happy families resemble one another, but each unhappy family is unhappy in its own way." The famous opening sentence to Tolstoy's *Anna Karenina* is a reminder that unique reasons lie behind individual cases and that a novelist's skill may be necessary to explain what goes on in a particular family. To the extent that one can generalize about something as complex as families, it is foolish to insist on only one relevant variable. There are multiple reasons for the above trends.

Tolstoy was not just a novelist but also a fervent advocate of communal pacifism and, arguably, a feminist. A century later, few subscribe to Tolstoy's communal pacifism but, in discussions of family policy, feminism has become an important integrating ideology. Feminists believe society is finally bringing to light what, in Tolstoy's time, was kept behind closed doors and discussed by women among themselves. Typically, feminists interpret the trend toward increased single parenthood as positive, inasmuch as more women are now free from the strictures of traditional family values and are able to leave abusive partners. If this is the relevant way to view the above social trends, the appropriate policy response is to provide generous income support in order that these women and their children not be condemned to live in poverty.

In part, feminists are right. Some hard-to-determine fraction of the increase in the number of single parents is to be welcomed, reflecting as it does the avoidance by some women (and a few men) of exploitative partners. But feminists frequently insist that the sole relevant cause for family breakup is women fleeing "bad" men. This is a serious oversimplification. To take a limiting case, nearly half of all aboriginal families in prairie cities are headed by a single parent — a rate three times the national average. Surely it is wrong to conclude therefrom that one aboriginal man in two is inherently a bad spouse or that three times as many aboriginal men as nonaboriginal men are "bad" fathers. There must be other relevant variables to explain the growth of single-parent families.

One such variable, discussed in this volume, is changes in divorce law. Feminists have defended relaxed divorce law because it allows wives to escape at lower cost from emotionally hollow or physically abusive relationships. Men, too, have valued this enhanced liberty. On the other hand, no social policy should be judged solely in terms of benefits. By rendering marriage termination easy, "no-fault" divorce regimes have lowered the cost to parents —

usually fathers — who wish to avoid the investment required for successful child rearing. Most noncustodial parents are little involved in the lives of the children from their terminated marriages and contribute little to the financial support of these children, many of whom fall into poverty.

Another relevant variable is the *price effect* implicit in the changing ratio of welfare benefits available to single parents compared with the likely earnings of their partners. On the numerator are more generous but more highly targeted government benefits for low-income families; on the denominator are declining wages among men who are low skilled and young. There are alternate measures for the magnitude of this shift, and it has differed across provinces and over time. But it is undeniably substantial — perhaps in the order of 40 percent since the 1970s.[16]

Do such price effects matter? It is an understatement to observe that this question is subject to ideological debate. Those on the right typically stress perverse effects from increased welfare benefits, while those on the left discuss perverse effects from a decline in earnings. The appropriate consideration is that both trends matter in explaining reliance on social assistance and increased single-parenthood.

Ken Boessenkool and I (see Boessenkool 1997; Richards 1997) have attempted to explain trends in welfare use in three provinces from the early 1980s to the mid-1990s via three variables: the state of the economy (measured by the provincial unemployment rate), the ratio of welfare benefits to a reference male earnings level available from low-wage employment, and shifts in administrative culture. Examples of such shifts arise with changes of governing party and major policy initiatives such as the "Cardinal reforms" in Alberta in 1993 (named after Mike Cardinal, the provincial minister responsible for a reduction in benefit levels and administrative measures to render access to social assistance more difficult).

---

16 This 40 percent estimate simply combines two of the above-cited changes: the 18 percent increase between 1981 and 1993 in the real value of single-parent benefits and the 16 percent decline between 1973 and 1989 in earnings among the bottom fifth of Canadian male wage earners.

We obtained the following results. In Ontario, the caseload (cases per 1,000 population) roughly doubled between 1989 and 1993. During this period, welfare benefits, unemployment, and the reference earnings level all moved in directions that increased welfare use. Rising unemployment and welfare benefits each accounted for about 40 percent of the explained increase; a decline in the reference wage accounted for the rest. In Alberta, the caseload was halved between 1993 and 1996. Nearly 90 percent of the explained decline was due to the Cardinal reforms. A falling unemployment rate explained about 35 percent of the decline. A fall in the reference wage offset these effects, bringing the total for the explained decline to 100 percent. In British Columbia, the caseload increased by 30 percent between 1991 and 1995. The most important variable was again a shift in administrative culture, here operating in the opposite direction to Alberta. Replacement of a right-of-center Social Credit government by a left-wing New Democratic Party government in 1991 led to a relaxation in access to welfare, accounting for about 80 percent of the explained caseload increase. A rising provincial unemployment rate explained most of the rest. A minor increase in welfare benefit levels and in the reference earnings level roughly offset one another.[17]

Lefebvre, Merrigan, and Dooley (1998) recently completed a far more rigorous analysis of a related question: what variables affect the probability that a woman will become a single-parent mother? They use a large sample of nationwide data from 1981 through 1993,

---

17 In Ontario, welfare cases per 1,000 population rose by 29.7 from 31.0 in 1989 to 60.7 in 1993. The caseload change explained by the regression was 34.7: 13.6 due to higher unemployment, 15.9 due to higher welfare benefits, and 5.1 due to a decline in the reference male earnings level. The unexplained change was –5.0 (29.7 minus 34.7). In Alberta, welfare cases per 1,000 population declined by 17 from 35 in 1993 to 18 in 1996. The caseload change explained by the regression was –11.6: –10.2 due to the Cardinal reforms, –4.1 due to lower unemployment, and +2.7 due to a lower reference earnings level . The unexplained change was –5.4 (–17.0 minus –11.6). In British Columbia, welfare cases per 1,000 population increased by 11.2 from 37.2 in 1991 to 48.3 in 1995. The caseload change explained by the regression was 13.1: 10.8 due to the change in government from Social Credit to New Democrat, and 2.3 due to higher unemployment. The unexplained change was –2.0 (11.2 minus 13.1). See Boessenkool (1997); Richards (1997, 154–161).

and their results can be summarized as follows. Age matters: the probability that a woman below age 25 will become a single mother is significantly higher than it is for an older women. Both what they earn and the expected earnings of their male partners matter: the higher a woman's earnings, the lower the probability of her becoming a single mother, while the lower her partner's expected earnings, the higher the probability. Welfare benefits may or may not matter independently of other variables. In specifications that introduce both provincial welfare benefit levels and a "dummy" variable to capture other province-specific characteristics, welfare benefits do not matter. In specifications that include provincial welfare benefits but exclude the provincial "dummy," higher provincial welfare benefits increase the probability of single parenthood in that province.

Low-income parents have always faced two options:

- *Option A*: The parents live together and jointly raise their children. While the children are young, the primary source of income will probably be the father's earnings, which, given his limited training, are likely to be low. Unless the extended family provides child care, the cost of paid child care — even in the informal sector — is likely to mean that the mother works, at most, part time.

- *Option B*: The parents separate or, if living apart at the time of their child's birth, decide not to live together. In the overwhelming majority of cases, the mother becomes the sole custodial parent. As family head, she becomes eligible for a range of transfer programs, while the father earns what he can. If there are two or more children present, the mother will receive as transfer income more than her partner could earn from full-time work at minimum wage. As the noncustodial parent, the father faces some obligation to support his children, but the probability of the mother's realizing consistent long-term financial support from him is much reduced when the two do not live together. One obvious reason for this is that the father has a reduced psychological link to his children and may start a new family. And if the mother receives social assistance, the financial incentive to seek such support is absent. Under most provincial programs, any income from the father reduces, dollar for dollar, the mother's social assistance benefits.

To summarize the discussion so far, over the past generation more poor families are choosing option B and fewer option A. Almost certainly, the change in relative financial rewards between the two options is a major component of the explanation.

Policy Options:
Negative Income Taxes
versus Earnings Supplements

The goal of earnings supplement programs is to increase participation in the paid labor force by "making work pay." Over some range of low earnings, program benefits increase as earnings increase, thereby augmenting what would otherwise be the income derived from employment. Earnings supplement programs are intended to assist low-income families: what goes up for the poor, however, comes down for the middle class. Over some range of higher earnings, the earnings supplement benefit is clawed back as earnings rise.

Overall, these programs can be expected to have a positive effect on labor supply, increasing it for the poor more than they reduce it for those with higher earnings. Earnings supplement programs draw nonparticipants into the labor force and increase the labor supply over the phase-in range. It is important to recognize, however, that such programs adversely affect the labor supply over the phase-out range because here they increase the marginal effective tax rate on earnings (Dickert, Houser, and Scholz 1994).

As mentioned, the federal child tax benefit operates as a modest negative income tax (NIT), and several provinces have introduced top-up programs that operate in a similar manner. NIT programs are a close relative to earnings supplement programs (see Figure 3). Unlike an earnings supplement program, a NIT program does not seek to supplement the reward from incremental employment earnings: maximum benefits accrue at zero earnings. The choice between the two rests on the relative priority given to enhancing paid employment versus redistribution. By design, a NIT is more redistributive than an earnings supplement program of equal budgetary cost. On the other hand, a NIT can be expected to have a negative overall impact on the labor supply because it lacks the earnings supplement program's positive labor supply effect over the phase-in range. As with earnings supplement programs, the NIT is clawed back at earnings above some threshold. Both programs adversely affect the labor supply over the phase-out range.

Two generic versions of earnings supplement programs can be usefully distinguished, "discontinuous" and "continuous" (see Figures 4 and 5.) Canada has experimented with both. Under the former, the potential beneficiary must demonstrate a major commitment to undertake paid work. If earnings fall below the designated threshold, the would-be beneficiary receives nothing. If earnings exceed the threshold, he or she receives a lump sum. Over a defined range above the threshold, the supplement may stay in place, but for earnings beyond a second threshold, the supplement is clawed back as a percentage of incremental earnings. Under the latter, the program designates a phase-in range of earnings over which the supplement operates as a percentage bonus on incremental earnings. Beyond the phase-in earnings range, the design of the continuous program is similar to that of the discontinuous program.

Earnings Supplement Programs: "The Devil's in the Detail"

Although, as we have seen, there are some conceptual difficulties in the design of earnings supplement programs, equally important are a number of administrative conundrums. As noted, three Canadian jurisdictions — the federal government, Quebec, and Saskatchewan — have undertaken major, administratively well defined earnings supplement programs (Table 2 summarizes the key program parameters for each). Other provinces have undertaken more *ad hoc* programs.

Figure 3:   ***A Negative Income Tax***

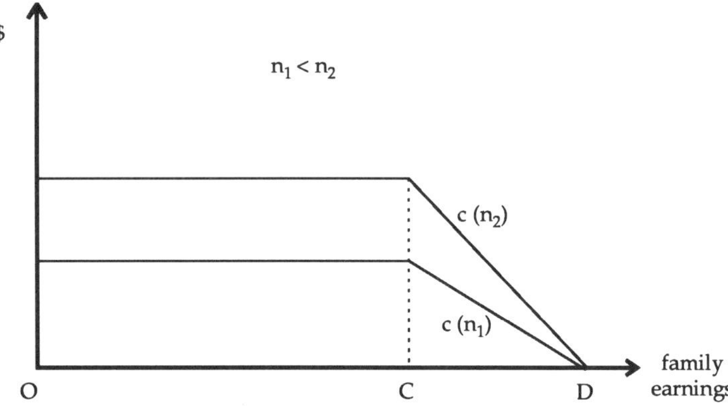

Figure 4:   ***A Discontinuous Earnings Supplement***

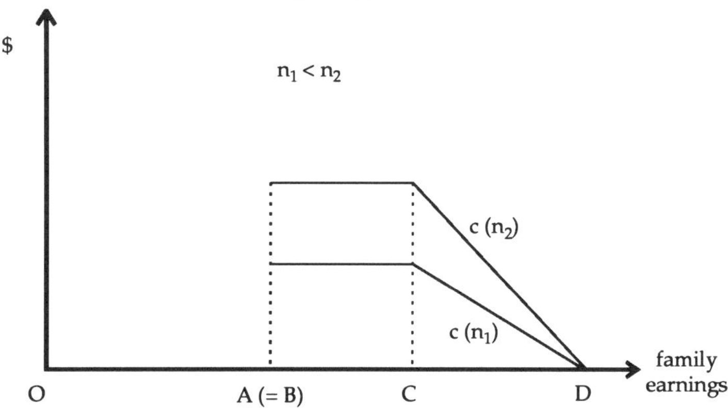

Figure 5:   ***A Continuous Earnings Supplement***

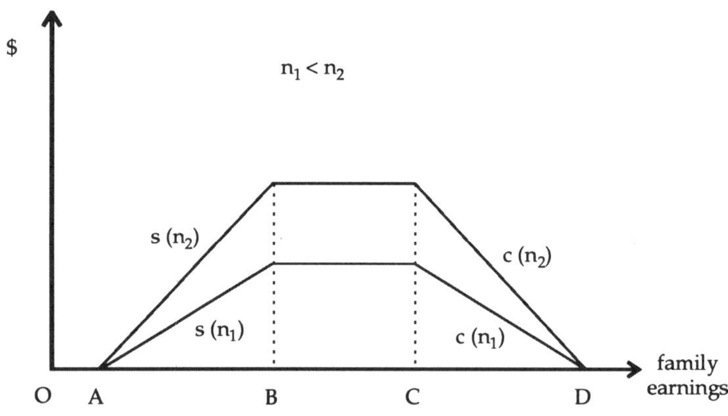

Parameters for Figures 3–5

A Minimum required earnings or eligibility threshold. Earnings must exceed OA before a beneficiary becomes eligible for any supplement payment. (A may be set at zero earnings.)

B Plateau threshold. For earnings above OB, no further supplement is paid. The maximum supplement, payable at OB, remains available however.

C Clawback threshold. Earnings above OC are subject to clawback. (C may coincide with B, in which case there is no plateau range.)

D Breakeven threshold. At earnings above OD, the supplement is entirely clawed back.

AB Phase-in range of earnings. Over this range, earnings are supplemented.

BC Plateau range of earnings. Over this range, the beneficiary receives the maximum value of the supplement.

CD Phase-out range of earnings. Over this range, the supplement is clawed back.

s(n) Earnings supplement rate. This is the rate at which earnings are augmented over the phase-in range. The parameters need not be constant over the phase-in range, and the rate may vary with the level of earnings. The supplement rate may also vary according to characteristics of the beneficiary's family. In many programs, the rate is set higher, the larger the number of children (designated n) in the family.

c(n) Earnings supplement clawback rate. This is the rate at which earnings are clawed back over the phase-out range. As with the employment supplement rate, this parameter need not be constant over the phase-out range, and may vary according to family characteristics.

Which is preferable, discontinuous or continuous programs? The US Earned Income Tax Credit is a continuous program; the UK Working Families Tax Credit is discontinuous. Ottawa's Self-Sufficiency Project is discontinuous, whereas Quebec's APPORT and Saskatchewan's SES programs are continuous. Why one or the other?

A rationale for discontinuous programs is to provide a dramatic fiscal incentive to people to undertake full-time work, thereby breaking the cycle of part-time work and part-time dependence on transfer programs. Under discontinuous programs, eligible workers usually work full time and receive the full benefit (less any clawback); there is no phase-in range. This eliminates administrative difficulties arising from beneficiaries' adjusting hours of part-time work over the phase-in range of earnings.

My preference, nonetheless, is for continuous programs. They accommodate more adequately the increasingly important phenomenon of part-time work. For single parents, for those with partial disabilities, and the like, part-time work is more attractive than full-time work. Even though they are administratively more complex, continuous programs can almost certainly achieve much higher labor force participation rates.

How can earnings supplements be made to "feel" like wages? A central feature of the standard employment contract is that the lag between work and remuneration be minimal. In stressing the need "to reinforce the link between receipt of the [earnings supplement] credit and rewards of work" (United Kingdom 1998, para. 2.15), the UK budget highlights a short lag as crucial to the success of any supplement program. Otherwise, the earnings supplement will "feel" to recipients like an untied transfer from government.

When earnings supplement programs are organized via the income tax system, the time lag is unacceptably long. The potential for excessive delay in payment was a fatal flaw of the small program (the Working Income Supplement) introduced as part of the federal child benefit reforms in 1992. To give a simple example, consider someone who took a temporary job during the holiday rush in December 1996 and was paid in January 1997. The wages became part of the individual's 1997 earnings and entered the calculation of the earnings supplement paid in 1998. Quite reasonably, the federal government abolished this program in 1998, leaving this policy option to interested provinces.

One administrative option is that the supplement become part of the regular paycheque, as in Britain and in the United States' advance EITC payment option. Here, the disadvantage is to add to employers' administrative costs and potentially discourage their support. Another option is to set up a "quick-response" payment system, as Quebec and Saskatchewan have done.

What is the optimal tradeoff between realizing contractual simplicity and providing checks against strategic behavior and outright fraud? For those who simultaneously receive welfare and an earnings supplement, the same fiscal incentives could be generated by lowering the clawback rate on social assistance (to a rate equal to the welfare clawback rate less the earnings supplement rate). Why not do the latter? One answer is that earnings supplement programs benefit many low-income families where parents have chosen not to participate in welfare, even though eligible. A second answer is that these programs are intended to avoid the adversarial culture characteristic of social assistance.

A universal feature of social assistance programs is pervasive government intrusion in the lives of beneficiaries. The poor frequently feel this to be demeaning, but citizens who are not poor will never endorse social policy that provides large per capita income transfers without significant monitoring. Almost inevitably, the relationship between most welfare recipients and the system has an adversarial dimension, often manifest in public social policy debates. Interest groups representing welfare recipients typically advocate generous, rules-based redistributive programs (such as the NIT) that minimize government monitoring. Conversely, provincial politicians are conscious that social assistance is a major budgetary expenditure about which the nonpoor are leery. Accordingly, governments continue to provide social assistance based on complex *ex ante* eligibility rules and *ex post* monitoring for fraud. By way of contrast, the contractual relationship between employer and employee also has an adversarial dimension, but the monitoring problems are less complex and mutual mistrust usually less pervasive. It is important that earnings supplement programs strive to adopt employer/employee monitoring techniques rather than replicate social-worker/welfare-recipient monitoring.

To illustrate the tradeoff entailed, contrast Quebec's APPORT and Saskatchewan's SES, launched in 1998. APPORT administrators have developed a complex set of regulations derived simultaneously from precedents in administration of social assistance and the income tax. The underlying principle of APPORT is to augment earnings if, on an annual basis, they are low. Since APPORT beneficiaries have a tenuous link to the job market, their monthly earnings fluctuate. This renders calculation of eligible benefits complex. Also, both supplementation and clawback rates are high, giving an incentive to beneficiaries to cheat in reporting incomes. A recent provincial evaluation estimates that overpayments occur among roughly a quarter of beneficiaries (Quebec 1996, ch. 5.3).

The underlying principle of the SES is that the supplement rewards work performed if, at the time, the worker's earnings are low; there is no attempt to reconcile on an annual basis. Based on earnings for a given month, the supplement is electronically deposited into the beneficiary's bank account before the end of the subsequent month. Hence, the lag is no more than one month. Once every three months, a beneficiary must provide relevant financial information. The beneficiary is supposed to report changes in financial status when they occur. But, within a three-month period, receipt of the supplement is not conditional on reporting financial status. Payments continue, based on the last reported financial status. To simplify the contract and maximize take-up of the program, the SES contains no provisions to recapture overpayment within a quarter.

Both APPORT and SES are subject to strategic behavior — and to outright fraud — by recipients. As with any earnings supplement program, beneficiaries may adjust work effort to maximize the supplement. To the extent that this happens, beneficiaries remain at a low level of earnings and frustrate the intent of the program, which is to encourage a transition to higher earnings and no reliance on the program. The simplicity of the SES program design may abet such strategic behavior. The quarterly reporting design enables a beneficiary potentially to receive two months' unwarranted supplements simply by failing to inform the government of a change in financial circumstances.[18]

---

18 Suppose that, at the end of December, a mother with two children reports her monthly earnings for that month. She then does not work during January, February and March or report this fact to the government. In January, she receives a supplement equal to roughly 30 percent of her December earnings, and identical supplements in February and March. At the end of March, she again reports her financial status, as required. Declaring no earnings for March, she receives no further supplement, but she has already received two unwarranted supplements amounting to roughly 60 percent of her December earnings. The use of standard auditing techniques should limit this kind of abuse.

The potential exists for more ambitious fraud. For example, supplement rates may be sufficiently high to induce unscrupulous "entrepreneurs" to establish phantom firms that issue earnings records to enable phantom workers to claim a supplement. By a side contract, the supplement is shared between the phantom worker and phantom employer.

In summary, the success of earnings supplement programs depends on whether most recipients treat the income they receive as they would wages or as another form of welfare payment, and whether fraud can be contained to tolerable levels.

Should earnings supplement programs vary the generosity of the supplement according to family characteristics or provide a standard supplement to all eligible families? The primary goal of earnings supplement programs is, as the name suggests, to "make work pay" by supplementing earnings. They also act as a child care subsidy for working parents and, to the extent that this is the goal, it makes sense to vary the generosity of the supplement by the number of children. This presents program designers with yet another tradeoff. With a given budget, they can increase the ability of the program to act as a child care subsidy by accommodating family size and age of children, but at the cost of reducing the work incentive for recipients with few children.

Saskatchewan and Quebec illustrate divergent approaches to this tradeoff. Saskatchewan has designed a program that differentiates ambitiously according to family size. The tradeoff comes in the form of a lower supplementation rate for families with few children (see Table 2). However, given that earnings supplement programs are primarily intended to subsidize work, my preference is to adopt Quebec's strategy of using two supplement rates, one for one-child families and a higher rate for families with two or more children; by 1999, it intends to use one supplement rate for all families.[19]

---

19 Quebec will still accommodate family size to some extent because the taxback threshold remains higher for families with two or more children than for families with only one child.

Table 2: ***Major Earnings Supplement Programs in Canada — Summary of Parameters***

	Self-Sufficiency Project (SSP)[a]	Programme d'aide aux parents pour leurs revenus de travail (APPORT)[b]	Saskatchewan Employment Supplement (SES)[c]
Sponsoring agency	Human Resources Development Canada	Quebec, Ministère de l'Emploi	Saskatchewan, Social Services
Generic type	discontinuous	continuous	continuous
Thresholds			
Minimum required earnings	30 hours per week (equivalent to 125 hours/month, or $875/month at $7/hour)	$100/month	$125/month
Plateau	none	none	$825/month
Clawback	$875/month (if beneficiary works fewer than 125 hours/month, no supplement is paid; threshold calculation assumes beneficiary works the minimum required hours, 125/month, at $7/hour)	parameters vary by number of parents (p), but not by number of children provided family is caring for at least one dependent child: $649/month if p = 1; $948/month if p = 2 (phase-out range abuts phase-in range; hence, no plateau range)	$1,075/month
Breakeven	$2,500/month in New Brunswick; $3,083/month in British Columbia	$1,178/month if p = 1; $1,279/month if p = 2	threshold varies by number of children (n): $1,775/month if n = 1 $1,915/month if n = 2 $2,055/month if n = 3 $2,195/month if n = 4 $2,335/month if n ≥ 5

Table 2 - continued

	Self-Sufficiency Project (SSP)[a]	Programme d'aide aux parents pour leurs revenus de travail (APPORT)[b]	Saskatchewan Employment Supplement (SES)[c]
Maximum supplement	$813/month in New Brunswick; $1,104/month in British Columbia (supplement in each province equals half the relevant break-even earnings threshold less half of all earnings; for each province, calculation assumes that beneficiary works for 125 hours at $7/hour and earns $875/month; recipients must be parents, but supplement does not vary by number of children)	$227/month if p = 1; $332/month if p = 2	Varies by number of children (n): $175/month if n = 1; $210/month if n = 2; $245/month if n = 3; $280/month if n = 4; $315/month if n ≥ 5
Supplement and clawback rates			
Supplement	none	35% (average rate over entire earnings range from $0 to taxback threshold; $100/ month minimum earnings threshold creates small discontinuity)	25% if n = 1; 30% if n = 2; 35% if n = 3; 40% if n = 4; 45% if n ≥ 5
Clawback	50%	43%	25%

[a] Parameters for the SSP are derived from Lui-Gerr et al. (1994). Annual values have been transformed into monthly equivalents.

[b] Parameters for APPORT are derived from Quebec (1997, 5B). Quebec parameters in this table are scheduled to be in effect in 1999. Annual values have been transformed into monthly equivalents.

[c] Parameters for the SES are derived from Saskatchewan (1998).

What is the best way to integrate an earnings supplement with other social policies? There are many aspects to the question of integrating earnings supplement programs with other social policies.

A sizable minority of earnings supplement beneficiaries also receive social assistance income. Among this group, earnings supplement programs encourage employment by lowering the taxback rate from the prohibitive to the high. In designing an earnings supplement program to run in parallel with social assistance, the clawback threshold should not be set below the breakeven threshold for most welfare recipients. If the clawback threshold for the supplement is below the welfare breakeven threshold, the marginal effective tax rate on incremental earnings (in the range between the two thresholds) will equal that for welfare plus that for the earnings supplement, a figure well in excess of 100 percent (see Figures 3, 4, and 5).

Poverty among single-parent families is aggravated by noncustodial parents (overwhelmingly this means fathers) who do not contribute financially to their children after separation. Social assistance programs encourage this behavior because they usually lower welfare benefits dollar for dollar as child support increases from a noncustodial parent. Understandably, mothers are reluctant to pursue estranged spouses for support if it contributes nothing to their family income. In a modest way, earnings supplement programs would provide an incentive to mothers to pursue child support if such income is counted as earnings subject to supplementation.

Difficult tradeoffs exist in designing the clawback features of an earnings supplement program. Over the phase-out range, these programs add to the already unduly high marginal effective tax rates faced by modest-income families. If the clawback rate is reduced, however, the increase extends into higher earnings ranges where personal income tax rates are higher. Program costs also rise dramatically as the clawback rate is lowered and large numbers become eligible for the benefit. In sum, lowering the clawback rate raises the benefit for a family of any given earnings level over the phase-out range, extends eligibility to families with higher earnings, raises marginal tax rates for higher-income families, and increases program costs.

As already noted, it is hard to determine the effect of high marginal effective tax rates on work effort. I suspect, however, that this is the Achilles' heel of all targeted programs. Unless this problem is addressed, the beneficial employment effect on the phase-in range will nearly all be lost on the phase-out range.

What is required is for enterprising politicians to transform this problem into an opportunity. This brings me to the subject of universalizing the existing CCTB as a complementary reform to earnings supplement programs.

Universalizing Child Tax Benefits

Elsewhere in this volume, Boessenkool argues that the personal income tax should be levied on a measure of taxable income that nets out more adequately the costs of child rearing — among single-earner as well as dual-earner families, among higher-income as well as lower-income families. It is an important argument, and one with which I agree. His policy recommendation is for more generous personal, spousal, and child deductions; my preferred policy is simpler: leave intact the existing federal CCTB as a universally accessible tax credit. (The dotted line in Figure 2 illustrates the effect, for a single-earner Ontario family with two children, of thus universalizing the federal CCTB.)

Boessenkool illustrates that the clawback rates for the CCTB vary by both income and the number of children. The CCTB remains in place until taxable family income reaches roughly $21,000. Over the next $5,000 range, the clawback rate adds a minimum of 12.1 percentage points and a maximum of 26.8 points to the total marginal effective tax rate a family pays. Beyond $26,000, the clawback adds either 2.5 or 5 percentage points to the marginal effective tax rate until the CCTB is exhausted.

The impact on marginal tax rates would be most dramatic among families in the maximum clawback rate income range. Since most families with incomes above $70,000 are currently not eligible for any CCTB payment, this reform would bring about no reduction in their marginal tax rates. On the other hand, such a policy change would, in terms of tax reduction, benefit middle- and upper-income Canadian families with children. By construction, it would provide no additional benefit for single individuals, for families without children or for the 17 percent of families with children who already receive the maximum CCTB. Families earning between $21,000 and $50,000 comprise 38 percent of families with children; they would receive roughly 30 percent of the benefit. Families earning between $50,000 and $70,000 comprise 23 percent of such families and would receive another 30 percent of the benefit. Finally, families earning more than $70,000 comprise 22 percent of the total and would receive nearly 40 percent of the benefit (see Table 3).

Some will find it contradictory that a paper devoted to improving the incomes of the poor concludes with a call for a tax change in which fully 70 percent of benefits are expected to accrue to families earning above $50,000 annually. I have already provided one rationale: the need to lower the marginal effective tax rate over the phase-out range of targeted benefits. Another is to point out that middle- and upper-income Canadians also have children — and to repeat Boessenkool's argument, the Canadian tax regime should use a measure of taxable income to take this into account.

In introducing the third rationale, I stress that the welfare state is far more than an exercise in income redistribution. Rather, one of its basic goals is to provide services that markets offer poorly (such as health insurance) and to realize values that are broadly shared in society (such as majority agreement to tax a measure of income net of the costs of child rearing). The majority must feel that, under appropriate circumstances, they too become beneficiaries of social programs. Universal health insurance programs satisfy that criterion. Highly targeted welfare programs fail that test. Most people are skeptical of social assistance spending, but agree to pay provided they are persuaded the expenditures produce the intended outcome of relieving poverty without inducing undue dependency. In terms of public support, existing child tax benefits lie somewhere between health insurance and social assistance. Universalizing them would secure their hold on political legitimacy.

Table 3:   ***Estimated Decrease in Federal Personal Income Tax (PIT) on "Universalizing" the CCTB[a]***

Annual Income Range of Family	Families with Children	Decrease in Federal PIT	Cumulative Percentage of Families with Children	Cumulative Percentage of PIT Decrease
(dollars)	*(thousands)*	*($ millions)*	*(percent)*	*(percent)*
0–20,921	659.3	0	17.1	0
20,922–25,921[a]	232.9	91.4	23.1	1.6
25,922–30,000	205.7	183.5	28.4	4.7
30,001–40,000	513.0	616.9	41.7	15.2
40,001–50,000	511.9	811.0	55.0	29.1
50,001–60,000	504.4	993.0	68.0	46.0
60,001–70,000	370.5	834.6	77.6	60.3
70,001–100,000	552.7	1,433.4	91.9	84.7
> 100,000	311.6	895.9	100.0	100.0
Total	3,862.2	5,859.5		

Note: The figures in this table are projections for 2001, using Statistics Canada's Social Policy Simulation Database and Model Release 6.1. The assumptions and calculations underlying the simulation results were prepared by Finn Poschmann, and the responsibility for the use and interpretation of these data is entirely his.

[a]   Clawback of the federal CCTB begins at a family income level of $20,922. The most aggressive clawback occurs over the range $20,922–$25,921. The clawback rate declines thereafter. See text for further elaboration.

Finally, what is the opportunity cost of spending $6 billion on universalizing the CCTB? Compared with *ad hoc* social policy proposals (such as the Millennium Scholarship Fund), the opportunity cost of this proposal is low!

Conclusion

Earnings supplement programs are not a panacea. They are, however, an attractive policy innovation that addresses many of the basic poverty trends as well as evidence on the undesirable consequences of existing social programs. They redistribute income to families with children in a manner that simultaneously subsidizes income from work. With supplementation rates that vary with the number of children, they are a means to offset child care costs. And they can be designed so that recipient families would find them only minimally intrusive.

As with all targeted programs, the Achilles' heel of earnings supplement programs is what to do about high marginal effective tax rates over the phase-out range. Herein lies the policy link to Boessenkool's argument in favor of more generous tax treatment of families with children.

Appendix:
Generic Policy Options

Given high rates of poverty among families with children, a debate is now under way in Canada and many other countries on new social policies. Not surprisingly, different countries are pursuing different strategies, just as are Canada's provinces. Unfortunately, if our understanding of the nature of families is decidedly imperfect, so too is our understanding of the outcomes from alternate policies. To date, Ottawa has wisely limited most of its initiatives to what it can do well, which is to use the income tax system to provide a "platform" of modestly enriched child tax benefits. The provinces have a comparative advantage in administratively complex social programming, and are undertaking the most ambitious policy experiments.

Earnings supplement programs are not a panacea, and in seeking to tackle the problems of families and poverty, no wise government will put all its eggs in this one basket. Among the generic options under active policy debate and experimentation are the following.

Programs of early childhood intervention: These include a vast range of cognitively oriented preschool programs, family support programs, child care programs, and others. Quebec, for example, is phasing in a heavily subsidized early child care program available for all parents. One comprehensive recent review of early childhood programs in the United States concludes:

> The hundreds of demonstration and large-scale programs that now exist provide very strong evidence that most programs of relatively good quality have meaningful short-term effects on cognitive ability, early school achievement, and social adjustment. There is also increasing evidence that interventions can produce middle- to longer-run effects on school achievement, special education placement, grade retention, disruptive behavior and delinquency, and high school graduation. (Reynolds et al. 1997, 6.)

The authors insist, however, that most such programs have received no long-term evaluation, and there is much uncertainty about the extent to which short- and medium-term benefits can persist if other negative factors remain a part of children's lives.

Stricter regulation of access to social assistance and employment insurance: While it is difficult to document, it appears that in the 1990s most senior social program administrators and the Canadian public in general have come to feel that access to social programs was relaxed too much over the past generation. Although the catalyst for this 1990s' re-evaluation was the severity of public sector deficits, many people have come to this conclusion independent of fiscal constraints. In response, the majority have wanted to reduce the use of welfare and employment insurance, particularly among the young, and to provide more robust incentives to undertake training or work. Two obvious manifestations of this strategy have been the post-1993 welfare reforms in Alberta and major post-1995 reforms that transformed "unemployment insurance" into "employment insurance" (Boessenkool 1997; Nakamura 1996).

Both reforms have been controversial. The Alberta welfare reforms more than halved the provincial social assistance caseload, primarily by rendering access by able-bodied young adults more difficult. The one study that tracked former recipients to determine where they went is reasonably optimistic, inasmuch as two-thirds of former recipients had found full- or part-time employment (Elton et al. 1997).

Provision of more and better coordinated training programs, particularly among young people who are making the transition from school to work: A consensus also exists among senior social program administrators on training programs. All provinces are improving programs for teenagers and those in danger of developing long-term welfare dependency.[20]

---

20 For a useful survey of a number of these provincial initiatives, see Canada (1997b).

Providing work-related benefits to part-time workers: Historically, part-time work has been treated as a form of "nonstandard employment" to be curtailed, not accommodated. But for many low-income parents — single parents, in particular — part-time work is preferable to full-time work. Part-time work's share of total employment is growing, and social policy is slowly making it more attractive by extending work-related benefits to permanent part-time workers — for example, the major 1995 reforms of unemployment insurance increased access to the program by part-time workers. Some provinces, such as Saskatchewan, now require employers to pro-rate fringe benefits for permanent part-time employees.

References

Barrett, G., and M. Cragg. 1998. "An Untold Story: The Characteristics of Welfare Use in British Columbia." *Canadian Journal of Economics* 31 (1):165–188.

Beach, C.M, and G.A. Slotsve. 1996. *Are We Becoming Two Societies? Income Polarization and the Myth of the Disappearing Middle Class in Canada*. The Social Policy Challenge12. Toronto: C.D. Howe Institute.

Boessenkool, K.J. 1997. *Back to Work: Learning from the Alberta Welfare Experiment*. C.D. Howe Institute Commentary 90. Toronto: C.D. Howe Institute. April.

Brown, D.M 1995. "Welfare Caseload Trends in Canada." In J. Richards et al., *Helping the Poor: A Qualified Case for "Workfare"*. The Social Policy Challenge 5. Toronto: C.D. Howe Institute.

Burtless, G. 1998. "Can the Labor Market Absorb Three Million Welfare Recipients?" *Focus* (University of Wisconsin-Madison, Institute for Research on Poverty) 19 (3): 1–6.

Canada. 1994. Department of Human Resources Development. *Child Care and Development: A Supplementary Paper*. Ottawa.

———. 1997a. National Council of Welfare. *Welfare Incomes 1996*. Ottawa.

———. 1997b. National Council of Welfare. *Another Look at Welfare Reform*. Ottawa.

———. 1998. Department of Finance. *The Budget Plan 1998*. Ottawa. February 24.

Dickert, S., S. Houser, and J. Scholz. 1994. "The Earned Income Tax Credit and Transfer Programs: A Study of Labor Market and Program Participation." Paper delivered at a National Bureau of Economic Research conference on tax policy and the economy, Cambridge, Mass.

Dooley, M.D. 1995. "Lone-Mother Families and Social Assistance Policy in Canada." In M.D. Dooley et al., *Family Matters: New Policies for Divorce, Lone*

Mothers, and Child Poverty. The Social Policy Challenge 8. Toronto: C.D. Howe Institute.

Elton, D., et al. 1997. *Where Are They Now? Assessing the Impact of Welfare Reform on Former Recipients, 1993–1996*. Calgary: Canada West Foundation for the Alberta Department of Family and Social Services.

Hatfield, M. 1997. "Concentrations of Poverty and Distressed Neighbourhoods in Canada." Ottawa: Department of Human Resources Development.

Haveman, R., and B. Wolfe. 1994. *Succeeding Generations: On the Effects of Investments in Children*. New York: Russell Sage Foundation.

———, and B. Wolfe. 1995. "The Determinants of Children's Attainments: A Review of Methods and Findings." *Journal of Economic Literature* 33 (December): 1829–1878.

Lefebvre P., P. Merrigan, and M. Dooley. 1998. "Lone Female Headship and Welfare Policy in Canada." Department of Economics working paper 98-02. Hamilton, Ont.: McMaster University.

Lui-Gurr S., S. Vernon, and T. Mijanovich. 1994. *Making Work Pay Better than Welfare: An Early Look at the Self-Sufficiency Project*. Vancouver: Social Research and Demonstration Corporation.

Mead, L., et al. 1997. *From Welfare to Work: Lessons from America*. Choice in Welfare 39. London: Institute of Economic Affairs.

Mendelson, M. 1998. *The WIS that Was: Replacing the Canadian Working Income Supplement*. Layerthorpe, York, UK: Joseph Rowntree Foundation.

Milne, W.J. 1995. "Revising Income Assistance Programs in New Brunswick: A Look at the Demonstration Projects." In J. Richards et al., *Helping the Poor: A Qualified Case for "Workfare"*. The Social Policy Challenge 5. Toronto: C.D. Howe Institute.

Morissette, R., J. Myles, and G. Picot. 1995. "Earnings Polarization in Canada, 1969–1991." In K. Banting and C. Beach, eds., *Labour Market Polarization and Social Policy Reform*. Kingston, Ont.: Queen's University, School of Policy Studies.

Nakamura, A. 1996. *Employment Insurance: A Framework for Real Reform*. C.D. Howe Institute Commentary 85. Toronto: C.D. Howe Institute. October.

Organisation for Economic Co-operation and Development (OECD). 1997. *Making Work Pay: Taxation, Benefits, Employment and Unemployment. The OECD Jobs Strategy*. Paris: OECD.

———. 1998. *Employment Outlook*. Paris: OECD.

Picot, G., and J. Myles. 1995. *Social Transfers, Changing Family Structure, and Low Income among Children*. Research Paper Series 82. Ottawa: Statistics Canada, Analytical Studies Branch.

Quebec. 1996. *Monitoring d'évaluation du programme APPORT*. Quebec: Ministère de la Sécurité.

————. 1997. *Manuel d'interprétation APPORT.* Quebec: Ministère de l'Emploi et de la Solidarité. Date of revision, September 25.

Reynolds, A., et al. 1997. "The State of Early Childhood Intervention: Effectiveness, Myths and Realities, New Directions." *Focus* (University of Wisconsin-Madison, Institute for Research on Poverty) 19 (1): 3–11.

Richards, J. 1997. *Retooling the Welfare State: What's Right, What's Wrong, What's to Be Done.* Policy Study 31. Toronto: C.D. Howe Institute.

Saskatchewan. 1998. *Building Independence: Investing in Families.* Regina: Department of Social Services.

Statistics Canada. 1997. *Income Distribution by Size in Canada, 1996.* Cat. 13-207. Ottawa.

————. 1998. "1996 Census: Aboriginal Data." *The Daily.* Cat. 11-001E. January 13.

United Kingdom. 1998. *The Modernisation of Britain's Tax and Benefit System: The Working Families Tax Credit and Work Incentives.* Supplementary document to 1998 budget. London: HM Treasury.

The Contributors

Douglas W. Allen is Associate Professor of Economics at Simon Fraser University in Burnaby, British Columbia. He received his PhD from the University of Washington in 1988, and taught at Carleton University in Ottawa before moving to Simon Fraser. His field of study is the economics of property rights, and he has applied this to marriage, divorce, welfare, agriculture, and economic history. He has published in the *American Economic Review*, the *Journal of Law and Economics*, and the *RAND Journal of Economics*.

Kenneth J. Boessenkool was, until recently, a policy analyst with the C.D. Howe Institute, where he specialized in social and monetary policy. He has written or co-authored numerous Institute publications on Bank of Canada policy as well as on welfare, training, and family issues. He has since accepted a position with Alberta Treasury, providing policy advice to the minister.

Margaret F. Brinig is Professor of Law at George Mason University, Arlington, Virginia. She teaches courses in family law and alternative dispute resolution. She has taught family-law-related courses for more than 20 years, although her primary research focus, the law and economics of the family, has developed more recently. She is the co-author (with Carl E. Schneider) of *An Invitation to Family Law* (West Publishing); and *The Contract and the Covenant: Beyond Law and Economics* (to be published in 2000 by Harvard University Press).

F. H. Buckley is Professor of Law at George Mason University, Arlington, Virginia, and holds degrees from McGill University and Harvard University. He is the co-author (with Robert Yalden and Mark Gillen) of *Corporations: Principles and Policies*, 3rd ed. (Emond-Montgomery, 1995); and editor of *The Fall and Rise of Freedom of Contract* (Duke University Press, 1999).

Donald S. Moir is Associate Counsel, Moir & Moir, Vancouver, and former Associate Counsel with Alexander, Holburn, Beaudin & Lang. He has been a member of the British Columbia Bar since 1952. He is Past President of the Association of Family and Conciliation Courts, Founding Director and now Honourary Director of Family Mediation Canada, and a member of the Canadian Bar Association. He is the author of a number of papers on family law, including "Putting Children First: A Reconsideration of Family Law" (1997); and "No Fault Divorce and the Best Interests of Children" (1992).

John Richards grew up in Saskatchewan and served as a member of that province's legislature during the first term of the Blakeney government from 1971 to 1975. For the first two years of his term, he was legislative secretary to the minister of health. In mid-term, he crossed the floor and sat as an "independent socialist." In his words, he has "since mellowed and rejoined the NDP." Trained as an economist, he currently teaches in the business faculty at Simon Fraser University, Burnaby, British Columbia. He has written on resource policy, labor relations, and public policy. He is an Adjunct Scholar of the C.D. Howe Institute, and co-edited (with William Watson) the Institute's "The Social Policy Challenge" series.

Members of the
C.D. Howe Institute[*]

---

[*] The views expressed in this publication are those of the authors and do not necessarily reflect the opinions of the Institute's members.

Consoltex Group Inc.

E. Kendall Cork

Co-Steel Inc.

Marcel Côté

John Crispo

Glen E. Cronkwright

Crown Life Insurance Company Limited

Paul R. Curley

Thomas P. d'Aquino

Peter Davies, C.M.G.

Leo de Bever

W. Ross DeGeer

Catherine Delaney

Deloitte & Touche LLP

Desjardins Ducharme Stein Monast

Robert Després

Dr. Wendy Dobson

The Dominion of Canada General
    Insurance Company

Donner Canadian Foundation

DuPont Canada Inc.

EdperBrascan Corporation

The Empire Life Insurance Company

Enbridge Consumers' Gas

ENSIS Growth Fund Inc.

Ernst & Young

Export Development Corporation

Ronald J. Farano, Q.C.

Fidelity Investments

First Marathon Securities Limited

Aaron M. Fish

Fishery Products International Limited

Dr. James D. Fleck

Formula Growth Limited

L. Yves Fortier, C.C., Q.C.

Four Seasons Hotels Limited

GSW Inc.

Paul E. Gagné

Jim Garrow

General Electric Canada Inc.

General Motors of Canada Limited

Joseph F. Gill

Gluskin Sheff + Associates Inc.

Goldman Sachs Canada

Goodman Phillips & Vineberg

Peter Goring

Dr. John A.G. Grant

The Great-West Life Assurance Company

Le Groupe Canam Manac

Dr. Geoffrey E. Hale

Larry M. Hall

Stephen J. Harper

Harvard Developments Limited, A Hill
    Company

Cliff Hatch

G.R. Heffernan

Lawrence L. Herman

Hewlett-Packard (Canada) Ltd.

Hollinger Inc.

Honeywell Limited

Hongkong Bank of Canada

David Hughes Inc.

H. Douglas Hunter

Lou Hyndman, Q.C.

IBM Canada Ltd.

Imasco Limited

Imperial Oil Limited

Inco Limited

Inland Group

The Insurance Council of Canada

Investment Dealers Association of
    Canada

The Investment Funds Institute of Canada

Investors Group Inc.

IPSCO Inc.

J & H Marsh & McLennan Limited

The Jackman Foundation

The Jarislowsky Foundation

KPMG

Mark D. Kassirer

Koch Oil Co. Ltd.

Robert M. Kozminski

Joseph Kruger II

Claude Lamoureux

Lantic Sugar Limited

R. John Lawrence

Jacques A. Lefebvre

Gérard Limoges

David Lindsay

Loewen, Ondaatje, McCutcheon Limited

J.W. (Wes) MacAleer

McCarthy Tétrault

W.A. Macdonald

McIlroy Inc.

Bruce M. McKay

Maclab Enterprises

Jack M. MacLeod

McMillan Binch

Manulife Financial

Dr. Georg Marais

Michael Marzolini

William M. Mercer Limited

Merck Frosst Canada Inc.

Merrill Lynch Canada Inc.

Methanex Corporation

Metropolitan Life Insurance Company

Robert Mitchell Inc.

The Molson Companies Limited

Monitor Company

The Montreal Exchange

Moore Corporation Limited

Morgan Stanley Canada Inc.

Hugh C. Morris, Q.C.

Dr. F.W. Orde Morton

A. Warren Moysey

John P. Mulvihill, CFA

The Mutual Life Assurance Company of
     Canada

National Trust

Nesbitt Burns

Dr. Edward P. Neufeld

Newcourt Credit Group Inc.

Eric Noitakis

Noranda Inc.

North Limited

NOVA Corporation

Novartis Pharmaceuticals Canada Inc.

Onex Corporation

Ontario Hydro

The Oshawa Group Limited

Osler, Hoskin & Harcourt

Katsuhiko Otaki

James S. Palmer

PanCanadian Petroleum Limited

Louis W. Pauly

Andy Perry

Petro-Canada

Philips, Hager & North Investment
     Management Ltd.

Pioneer Natural Resources Canada Inc.

Pirie Foundation

Les Placements T.A.L. Ltée.

Placer Dome Inc.

Dr. John T. Por

Power Corporation of Canada

Pratt & Whitney Canada Inc.

PricewaterhouseCoopers LLP

J. Robert S. Prichard

Procor Limited

ProGas Limited

RBC Dominion Securities Inc.

Redpath Sugars — Division of Tate & Lyle
     North American Sugars Ltd.

Retail Council of Canada

William E. Rogan

Rogers Communications Inc.

J. Nicholas Ross, C.A.

Royal Bank of Canada

Royal & SunAlliance Insurance Company
     of Canada

SNC Lavalin Group Inc.

St. Lawrence Cement Inc.

Samuel, Son & Co., Limited

SaskEnergy

Guylaine Saucier

Sceptre Investment Counsel

Schaefer & Associates Ltd.

Dick Schmeelk

The S. Schulich Foundation

ScotiaMcLeod Inc.

Shirley B. Seward

Gordon Sharwood

Shell Canada Limited

Sherritt International Corporation

Murray Sigler

Helen Sinclair

Southam Inc.

Spar Aerospace Limited

Speirs Consultants Inc.

Philip Spencer, Q.C.

Stelco Inc.

Sun Life Assurance Company of Canada

Suncor Inc.

Swiss Re Life Canada

Syncrude Canada Ltd.
TELUS Corporation
Laurent Thibault
3M Canada
The Toronto Dominion Bank
The Toronto Stock Exchange
Torstar Corporation
Tory Tory DesLauriers & Binnington
TransCanada PipeLines Limited
Tribal Resources Investment Corporation
TrizecHahn Corp.
Robert J. Turner

Unilever Canada Limited
Vancouver International Airport
    Authority
VIA Rail Canada Inc.
Voxcom Inc.
J.H. Warren
Weston Forest Corporation
D.G. Whitcomb
Alfred G. Wirth
M.K. Wong & Associates Ltd.
Fred R. Wright
Xerox Canada Inc.
Adam H. Zimmerman

Honorary Members

G. Arnold Hart
David Kirk

Paul H. Leman
J. Ross Tolmie, Q.C.